PHONICS ACTIVITIES IN STORY & RHYME

276 Ready-to-Use Activities
for Grades K-3

HELENE D. HUTCHINSON

Illustrated by Etsuko Yamane

THE CENTER FOR APPLIED
RESEARCH IN EDUCATION
Paramus, New Jersey 07652

Library of Congress Cataloging-in-Publication Data

Hutchinson, Helene D.
Phonics activities in story and rhyme : 276 ready-to-use activities for grades K-3 / Helene D. Hutchinson ; illustrations by Etsuko Yamane
p. cm.
Includes bibliographical references.
ISBN 0-87628-492-6
1. Reading—Phonetic method. 2. English language—Phonetics—Study and teaching (Primary)—Activity programs. 3. Children—Books and reading. I. Title.
LB1525.3 .H88 2001
372.46′5—dc21 2001028099

Resource Consultant: Ronald Banion
Curricular Consultant and Public School Administrator
Principal and Director of Special Education
Sandridge School
Lynwood, Illinois

Mr. Banion, who has over twenty years' experience in teaching and administration, has been acknowledged in *Who's Who in American Education*.

Printed in the United States of America

10 9 8 7 6 5 4 3 2 1

ISBN 087628-492-6

THE CENTER FOR APPLIED RESEARCH IN EDUCATION
Paramus, NJ 07652

On the World Wide Web at http://www.phdirect.com

Dedication

To my daughter, Laura Hutchinson, Attorney-at-Law, who has loved poetry since childhood and has taken time from her busy schedule to listen to these verses.

Acknowledgments

I would like to thank my editor, Connie Kallback, for her enthusiasm, encouragement, and ready accessibility. She has not only melted away redundancies but found fresh childlike words and images for this resource. She has even written some verses herself when I deadended. She has really been more than an editor—she's been more nearly a co-author and friend.

About the Author

Helene Hutchinson was plunged into teaching first-grade reading when the war babies hit the elementary schools. Though she had initially planned to teach high school or college English when she completed her master's degree at the State University of Iowa, the demand was for teachers at the primary level. The schools were in crisis. Innumerable first-grade classrooms had no teachers and others were being babysat by volunteer moms or eighth graders. The need was so urgent that colleges and universities generated accelerated summer programs to qualify college graduates for primary school teaching credentials. Ms. Hutchinson had the good fortune to take a twelve-hour seminar in teaching reading in the primary grades with Frances Horwich at Roosevelt University. Dr. Horwich's popular *Ding Dong School* was the precursor of *Sesame Street*.

When Ms. Hutchinson moved from elementary to high school and ultimately to college teaching, she always taught English as a second language on school faculties and privately. In conjunction with private tutoring, she taught reading to the children of the foreign born and was able to stay abreast of innovative methods.

Ms. Hutchinson is the author of Scott Foresman's 1970's English textbook best-seller, *Mixed Bag,* which won state and national awards, went around the world on a tour of American graphics, and sold in 51 countries. Subsequent publications include Holt Rinehart and Winston's *Black Culture: Reading and Writing Black,* Glencoe Press's *The Hutchinson Guide to Research* and *Horizons: Activities for the Vocational Technical School English Class,* as well as Prentice Hall's *ESL Teacher's Book of Instant Word Games for Grades 7-12,* published under The Center for Applied Research in Education imprint in 1997.

Ms. Hutchinson, now retired from Kendall College in Evanston, Illinois, currently teaches English as a second language to Japanese business people and their families who are in the United States as temporary residents, staffing and managing American subsidiaries of Japanese companies. As before, kindergarten and primary children come for reading assistance. The phonics methods are much the same though special pronunciation assistance is needed—and there is an important intervening step: Children must learn that the picture of a cat isn't only the Japanese *neko* but the English c-a-t.

About the Illustrator

Etsuko Yamane was born in Tokyo, Japan in 1960. She graduated from Kawamura College in Japan in 1980 with a major in Early Childhood Education. In 1986 she completed graduate work in oil painting at Musashino University. In 1988 she participated in an exhibition of modern naive art, a genre that reflects the purity, innocence, and directness of the childhood consciousness. In 1988 Yamane was co-illustrator of *Book of Illustrations for Teachers*, published by Hikarinokomi Press in Japan. The book consisted of charming border designs and figures for notes regularly sent to parents by Japanese kindergarten teachers. Yamane and her husband lived in the United States in Wilmette, Illinois between 1988 and 1995. In 1990 Yamane won a prize from the North Shore Art League for an oil painting. After a four-year interval in Japan, the Yamane family moved to Jakarta, Indonesia. While Yamane's husband pursues his career in banking, Yamane cares for their daughter, Hiroko, and studies Indonesian language and culture.

About This Resource

The method used in *Phonics Activities in Story & Rhyme* is based on studies of what children do naturally in decoding words—what they do, that is, when they're left to their own devices. Even though children are often taught to use context clues, studies indicate they never do. Even though they're often taught to use phonic rules, they don't use them. Even though they're taught to sound out words letter by letter, they don't. Instead, they sound out words in terms of initial consonants or consonant blends followed by an easily pronouncable word part. For example, they will not sound out h-a-t, but h-at. They will not sound out d-r-o-p, but dr-op.

Additionally, learning takes place through making analogies. Witness the young child's use of "foots" instead of feet or "I hurted myself." Word groups presented in a rhymed family fill the mind's need for predictable patterns.

Though *a* can have many pronunciations, *a* followed by a consonant or consonant blend usually signals a short vowel.* Section 1 in this resource presents initial consonants which, of course, also occur in final positions as highlighted in Section 2. The second section offers the whole spectrum of short vowels and single final consonants. Children can move effortlessly from *ad*, for example, to *bad, dad,* then perhaps to the unfamiliar *fad* or *lad,* and on to *glad, mad, pad,* and *sad.* The rhymes, bringing an endless variety of new words, come as easily and effortlessly as a song. This resource has verses or rhymed stories for every phonic element included in the book.

The resource progresses from short vowel–final consonant combinations to long vowel sounds in Section 3 with easily pronouncable syllables like *ace, base, case, face,* and *ice, dice, mice, nice.* Section 4 moves to final long vowel sounds, including the predictable *be, he, me, we.* Section 5 presents more easily pronouncable word parts involving regular vowel teams like the *eat, beat, heat* group and *boat, coat, goat* family. Although Section 6 brings the somewhat more variable diphthongs, there is still pattern and regularity in groups like *jaw, law,* and *paw* or the *oil* family. The *r*-controlled vowels in Section 7 bring some variety that can more readily be assimilated through rhyme families like *car, far, tar.* Even the erratic /ûr/ group can be systematized through rhyme, although here it's useful for children to learn that sometimes different letters stand for the same sound. The most formidable "monsters" of irregularity are tamed in Section 8 when children meet them in rhymed groups: Billy Big Bat went to the mall/To buy himself another ball.

---

*Thomas G. Gunning, "Word Building: A Strategic Approach to Teaching Phonics," *The Reading Teacher: A Journal of the International Reading Association,* Volume 48, Number 6, March 1995, pp. 484–488.

Sections 9 and 10 end the resource with initial and final consonant blends that teachers can introduce whenever they wish in the reading process.

In addition to phonic verses and stories, the book features Student Reading Selections or Student Reading Activities. These use only previously taught phonograms. Children can read them independently after learning or reviewing sight words listed in the page directions. The verses, on the other hand, do not contain restricted vocabulary and are designed for teacher reading and student listening and participation.

Nearly all pages contain activities planned to reinforce learning of phonograms being studied. These activities vary in kind to prevent boredom and are embellished with engaging pictures drawn by an experienced illustrator of children's books in Japan, Etsuko Yamane.

How to Use Verses

First teach the phonogram at the top of the page. For example, in teaching initial consonants, give the name of the letter and then its sound. Show children the letter at the top of the page in the resource. Write the letter on the chalkboard. Point to the picture and ask children to tell you what it is. Then ask them to name other objects beginning with the same sound. Encourage the children to draw pictures (in their notebooks or journals) of objects whose names begin with the letter being studied. Suggest making a picture dictionary of drawings and pictures cut out of magazines and newspapers. Pass out manuscript journal pages with shadow letters to trace and later print.

In moving to vowel–consonant combinations, sound out the letters separately, then slowly blend the sounds, gradually blending them more rapidly and smoothly until children hear a familiar word. Print the nucleus vowel–consonant on the board along with a list of single consonants. Ask children to make as many words as they can. Encourage children to use the words in the phonic group in sentences and guessing games. *Examples:* "I'm thinking of someone who's bigger than you are and sometimes says, 'No.' " "I'm thinking of how my mother feels if I don't clean my room." (These are possibilities with study of the *ad* group.) Have children develop a notebook-dictionary with pictures of their words. Have children trace and write words in their notebooks or manuscript journals.

Next read the verse aloud, discussing unfamiliar words and ideas if there are any. Ask children to do the movements suggested in the page directions each time they hear the nucleus sound. Kinesthetic activity will strengthen children's association of sound and symbol. Children learn best by doing, John Dewey argued.

Next read the verse a second time and ask children to circle letters that stand for the targeted sound. The first time you read the verse, children are making an association between sound and symbol—the letter at the top of the page. Children are going a step further the second time you read the verse. They are engaging in a process of selection and differentiation—picking out correct symbols from a collection of squiggles on a printed page. If they can do this, the reading process has begun.

"What matters is to surround children with happy opportunities to learn language—both through the ear and eye—during the years when brain development is optimal for this learning."*

Last, have children do the follow-up activity on the page. Sound and symbol association will be strengthened by kinesthetic learning, symbol differentiation, and written reinforcement.

Sight Words

Sight words included in Student Reading Selections are always listed in the teacher's directions for the page. Words identified as sight words sometimes include words that haven't yet been introduced in the phonic sequence. Later they will no longer be included as sight words. What follows is a list of sight words used in Student Reading Selections and the number of times they occur throughout the book. It's probably best to teach or review them as you go along.

Sight Words	Number of Occurrences	Sight Words	Number of Occurrences
a	3	my	1
are	3	of	4
but	1	on	1
come	1	said	12
comes	1	say	2
for	1	says	4
has	2	the	13
have	2	to	4
he	3	want	1
her	1	was	7
his	1	who	1
I	2	with	4
in	1	you	44
is	11		

*Joan Beck, "Can We Start the Pointing of Fingers on Why Johnny Can't Read?" *Chicago Tribune*, September 12, 1996, Section IV, p. 21.

Methods for Teaching Sight Words

1. Print the sight word on the chalkboard and make observations about its shape. Perhaps draw a shape outline on the board.

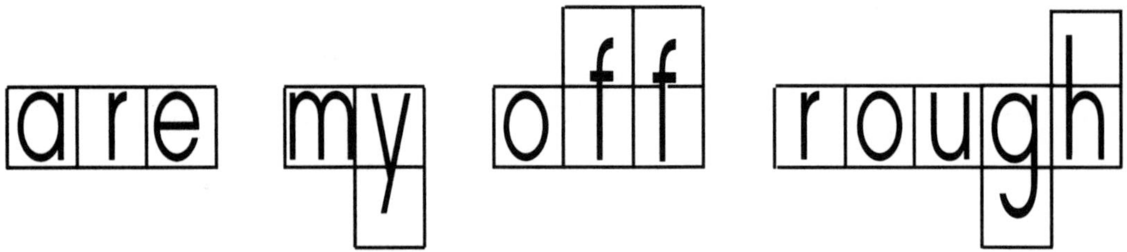

2. Give children dotted-line flashcards of the word. Have them trace the word.
3. Have children print sight words in their journals.
4. Show flashcards and ask children to read the sight words, maybe in groups of three for purposes of differentiation.
5. Have children use the sight words in sentences.
6. Print a sentence on the board with a missing sight word. Have children give you the word and spell it.
7. Last, have children read the Student Reading Selection.

Cross References for Teacher Planning

Student Reading Selections

Differentiation Activities

Phonogram Reviews

Spelling Variations

6-165.	/ô/ Words
8-211.	/ī/ Words
8-212.	Assorted Long Vowels
8-219.	/o͞o/ Words
8-220.	More /o͞o/ Words

Pronunciation of Final *s* in Plurals, Possessives, and Third-Person Singulars of the Present Tense

Final *s*'s occasionally occur in Student Reading Selections. Teach pronunciations as you go along. A general principle is that *s*'s following voiceless consonants are pronounced /s/. *S*'s following voiced consonants are pronounced /z/.

Examples

ck	ducks	/s/	p	bats	/s/
d	pads	/z/	r	cars	/z/
f	laughs	/s/	t	pets	/s/
g	bags	/z/	v	drives	/z/
l	pals	/z/	w	cows	/z/
m	hams	/z/	y	days	/z/
n	pins	/z/			

Pronunciation of Final s *After Sibilants*

ch	churches	/ĕz/
sh	bushes	/ĕz/
s	bosses	/ĕz/
x	boxes	/ĕz/
z	topazes	/ĕz/

Pronunciation of Final *ed* in Past Tense of Regular Verbs

Past-tense verbs occasionally occur in Student Reading Selections. Teach students how to read past-tense verbs as you go along.

Final ed *Pronounced as /t/ After Voiceless Consonants*

k	cooked	cook/t/
	looked	look/t/
	walked	walk/t/
	asked	ask/t/
ch	punched	punch/t/
	touched	touch/t/
sh	pushed	push/t/
	washed	wash/t/
ss	missed	miss/t/
	erased	eras/t/
p	helped	help/t/
	dropped	drop/t/
f	coughed	cough/t/
	laughed	laugh/t/

Final ed *Pronounced as /d/ After Voiced Consonants*

n	rained	rain/d/
	dined	dine/d/
v	raved	rave/d/
	dived	dive/d/
l	filled	fill/d/
	failed	fail/d/
z	pleased	please/d/
	sneezed	sneeze/d/
r	barred	barr/d/
	remembered	remember/d
y	stayed	stay/d/
	enjoyed	enjoy/d/
w	rowed	row/d/
	glowed	glow/d/

Final ed *Pronounced as /əd/ After* <u>d</u> *and* <u>t</u>

d	molded	moldəd
	needed	needəd

t	dated	datəd
	shouted	shoutəd

Pronunciation Key

Spellings	AHD*	Spellings	AHD*
pad	ă	pot	ŏ
date, pay, fail	ā	note, toe, grow	ō
care	âr	paw	ô
father	ä	boy, boil	oi
boy	b	book	o͝o
chair	ch	cool	o͞o
dad, filled	d	shout	ou
pet, head	ĕ	pig	p
he, see, bead	ē	rat	r
fat, laugh, phrase	f	sit	s
gas	g	shell, fish	sh
ham	h	Tom, tot	t
white	hw	think, both	th
him	ĭ	that	*th*
bite, by, tie	ī	but	ŭ
ear	îr	turn, sir, term	ûr
join, George	j	vest, live	v
kiss, cat	k	win	w
lip	l	yet	y
man	m	zoo	z
no	n		zh
sing	ng	above	ə

American Heritage Dictionary

CONTENTS

Section 3: Long Vowels and Final Silent e

Section 4: Final Long Vowels

Section 5: Long Vowel Teams

Section 6: Diphthongs

Section 7: r̲-Controlled Vowels

Section 8: Irregular Vowel and Vowel Consonant Combinations

Section 9: Initial Consonant Blends

Section 10: Final Consonant Blends

Section 1
Initial Consonants

Candy lost a curly cat.
Carrie Carson found it.

Name: ______________________ Date: ____________ 1-1

Bb 

Read the verse aloud and tell children to pretend they're bowling a big ball when they hear the /b/ sound as in ball. Read the verse again and tell children to circle all the letter b's in the story.

Billy Big Bat

Bowls a ball

Right into

The bedroom wall.

Ask children to add another line to the verse. What else does Billy Big Bat do that gets him in trouble?

Next read the sentences under the pictures and ask children to circle pictures that illustrate /b/ words and also bad things Billy Big Bat does.

Billy bites into birthday cake.

Billy cuts cake.

Billy blows beans.

Billy bangs bed.

Billy feeds Fido.

Billy breaks balloon.

Name: ______________________________ Date: ______________

Cc

Read the verse aloud and tell children to draw circles around all letter c's in the story.

Candy lost a curly cat.
Carrie Carson found it.
It had a can tied to its tail
And a cape around it.

Tell children you are going to read them some words and they should listen to the beginning sound of each word. If the word begins with the sound of /k/ as in cat, they should color the circle beside the number. Now read the following numbered words: 1. cat, 2. bad, 3. big, 4. candy, 5. cap, 6. can, 7. boy, 8. box, 9. cab, 10. car, 11. bat, 12. ball, 13. coat, 14. cold, 15. Ben.

1. ◯ 6. ◯ 11. ◯

2. ◯ 7. ◯ 12. ◯

3. ◯ 8. ◯ 13. ◯

4. ◯ 9. ◯ 14. ◯

5. ◯ 10. ◯ 15. ◯

Name: ______________________ Date: ______________ 1-3

Cc

Tell children that in this story, c has the sound of /s/ as in city, not the sound of /k/ as in cat. Read the story aloud and tell children to circle all the c's that have the sound of /s/ as in city.

Celia Centerfield went to the circus when it came to Cedar City. The circus cost seventy cents. The ceiling of the circus was the tent top. The floor was cement. Celia sat on a seat. She drank cider in a cup and ate celery curls. The circus was fun.

Tell children to put an X through those pictures whose names begin with the sound of /s/ as in city.

Name: ______________________ Date: ____________ 1-4

Dd 

Read the verse aloud and tell children to pretend they are driving a car when they hear the /d/ sound as in duck. Read the verse again and tell children to circle the letter d's in the story.

Davy Dale drove to Denver
On a dark December day.
But why he went,
He didn't remember
And so he drove away.

Tell children to print a d in the box next to each picture that begins with d.

Name: ______________________________ Date: ______________ 1-5

Ff

Read the verse aloud and tell children to circle all the letter f's.

Fergie and Felix
And Fanny and Fay
Followed a fiddler
From far away.
They followed him far
For many a day
So they could hear
The fiddler play,
"Fiddle de, fiddle de,
Fiddle de fay."

Tell children to circle letters that are like the circled letters under the picture.

f T F s
x I f p
j J b B
f F j k
h H l
f F t
(f)unny (f)ox
d f F b
F j l

Name: ______________________ Date: ____________ 1-6

Gg 

Read the story aloud and tell children to circle all the letter g's.

Gary Gates met Goofy Goose.

Goofy Goose gave Gary a goofy gift. What was the goofy gift Gary got? Gary got a gold garbage can from Goofy Goose. Why is a gold garbage can a goofy gift? Because Gary can't give garbage to the garbage man in a gold garbage can.

Tell children to print lowercase and uppercase g's under pictures if their names begin with the sound of /g/ as in goat.

Name: ______________________ Date: ____________ 1-7

Gg

Tell children that in this story, all the g's have the sound of /j/ as in George, not the sound of /g/ as in goose. Read the story aloud and tell children to circle all the g's.

General George Gerald met
a gentle and generous German giant.
The gentle giant handed General
Gerald a shining gem from Germany.
General Gerald loved the gem
and thanked the gentle giant.

Read the numbered words in the list to children and ask them to color the circle beside each number for words that begin with the sound of g as in George: 1. giant, 2. girl, 3. go, 4. gate, 5. George, 6. general, 7. give, 8. Georgia, 9. ginger, 10. get, 11. gelatin, 12. goose, 13. gum, 14. gift, 15. giraffe.

1. ○ 6. ○ 11. ○

2. ○ 7. ○ 12. ○

3. ○ 8. ○ 13. ○

4. ○ 9. ○ 14. ○

5. ○ 10. ○ 15. ○

Name: ______________________ Date: ____________ 1-8

Read the story aloud and tell children to circle all the h's in the story.

Harry Hopper had a hundred hats. Hannah Haynes hid half of Harry's hats. How many of Harry's hats did Hannah Haynes hide? (*Answer*: Hannah Haynes hid fifty of Harry Hopper's hats.)

Tell children to color the drawings if their names begin with the sound of /h/ as in home.

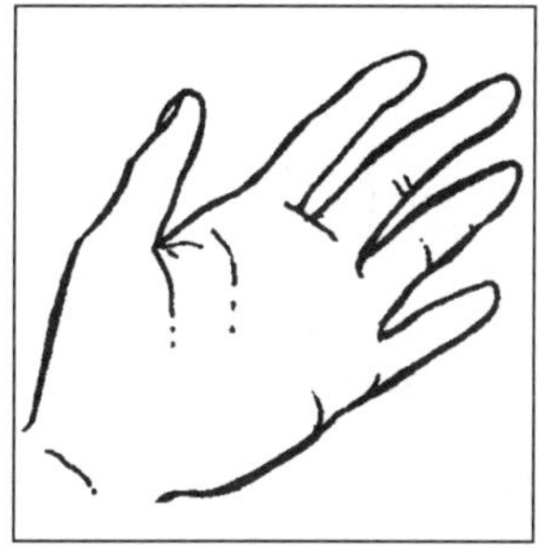

Name: ______________________ Date: ______________ 1-9

Jj

Read the verse aloud and tell children to circle all words that begin with j.

Jerry Jones and Jenny Black
Jogged to Jersey
And journeyed back
Just to visit
Brother Jack.

Tell children to circle the letter that begins the name of each picture.

j k l

h i j

h i l

b c d

h i j

b l j

Name: ______________________ Date: ____________ 1-10

Kk

Read the story aloud. Tell children to circle all the letter k's. Tell them k has the sound /k/ as in kitten. Explain that sometimes the sound /k/ is written with a c, but on this page the sound /k/ is written with a k.

Kim Kent was a little girl from Kansas City, Kansas. One day, she brought her kitten to kindergarten. The kids were excited about Kim's kitten, but Kim's teacher, Mrs. Kantor, was not happy. Mrs. Kantor was kind, but she said, "Kim, you may not keep your kitten in this room. Here is a key. Please put your kitten in the empty room next door." Kim kissed her kitten and took it next door. She said, "Mrs. Kantor, I won't bring my kitten to kindergarten again."

Tell children to color all the pictures whose names begin with the sound /k/ as in kitten.

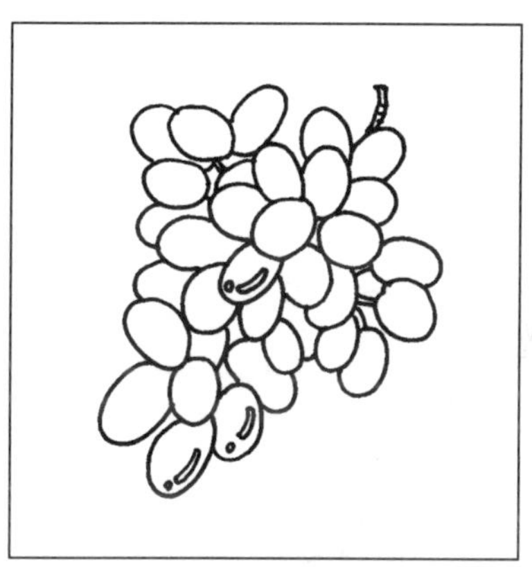

Name: ______________________ Date: ______________

Read the story aloud. Tell children to circle all the letter l's. Tell them this letter has the sound of /l/ as in lamp.

Larry and Laura were very lucky. Their teacher, Mrs. Lawson, let them play a lovely game. First, they sang the line, "London Bridge is falling down, my fair lady." Then everybody laughed and fell down any way they liked. They then could be anything they liked. Larry was a lion. Laura was a lamp post. Lonnie was a lamb. Leslie was a head of lettuce. Lenni Lopez was a letter from his uncle in Mexico. Mrs. Lawson was a grown-up lady, which she is. Then Mrs. Lawson had to guess what everybody was. She missed the lion, the lamb, the lamp post, and the head of lettuce. But she guessed that Lenni Lopez was a letter, because he had licked a stamp and put it on his nose!

Tell children to circle those in the pictures which they think are the lion, the lamb, the lamp post, the head of lettuce, and the letter.

Name: ______________________ Date: ______________ 1-12

Read the verse aloud and tell children to circle all the letter m's.

Mary Mullins
Met Monster Mouse
In the middle
Of her house.
Who else might
Mary Mullins meet?

First ask children if they can add another line to the verse. Who else might Mary Mullins meet whose name begins with m? Next, read to children the sentences under the picture. Ask them to circle pictures that illustrate the /m/ sound.

Mary Mullins meets a man from Mars.

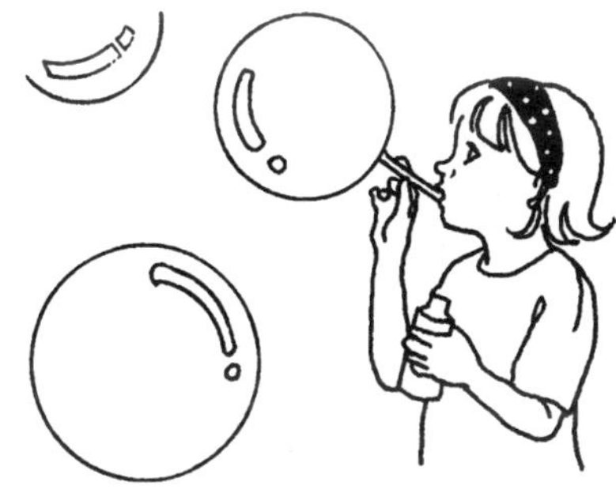

Mary blows bubbles.

Mary finds a funny friend.

Mary meets a monkey in a mask.

Name: ______________________ Date: ____________

Nn

Read the verse aloud and tell children to pretend they are nibbling nuts when they hear the /n/ sound as in nuts. Read the verse again and tell children to circle all the letter n's.

Nancy Nichols
Shuts the door
And nibbles nuts
On the floor.
What else might
Nancy Nichols nibble?

Tell children to circle pictures that begin with n.

Name: ______________________________ Date: ______________ 1-14

m,n

This is an initial m/n differentiation activity. Tell children to circle the letter that **begins** *the name of each picture.*

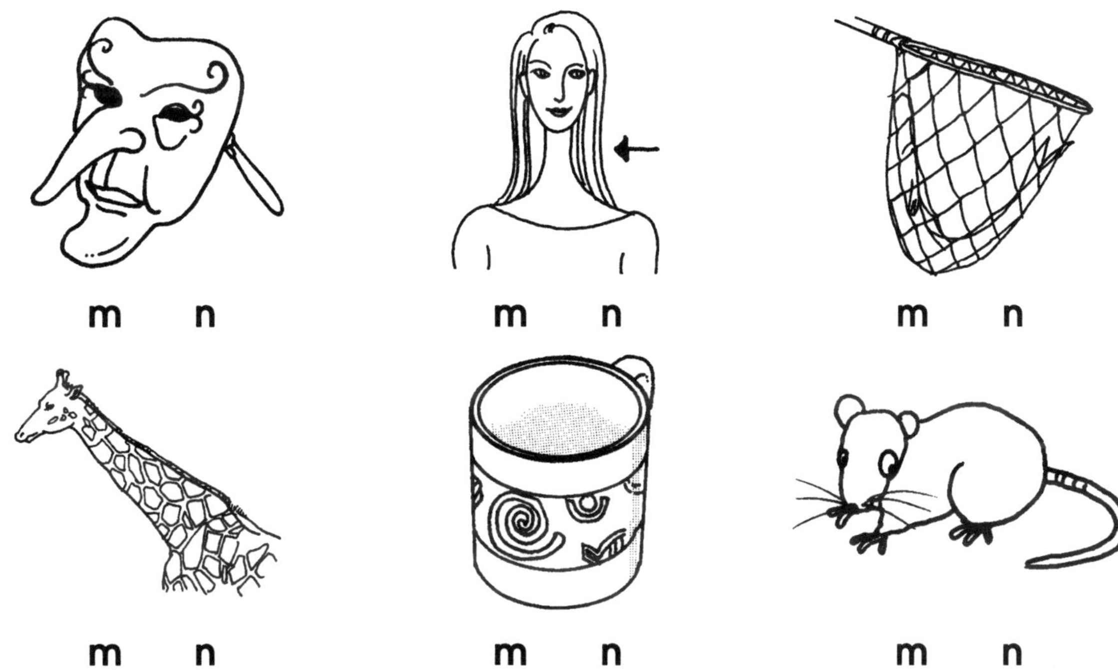

Tell children to circle the letter that **ends** *the name of each picture.*

Name: ______________________ Date: ____________

m,n

This is a final m/n differentiation activity. Dictate the numbered words and ask children to circle the letter that **ends** *each word: 1. dim, 2. him, 3. in, 4. Jim, 5. bin, 6. chin, 7. Kim, 8. din, 9. fin, 10. pin, 11. rim, 12. skim, 13. thin, 14. skin, 15. Tim, 16. tin, 17. slim, 18. swim, 19. win.*

1. m n
2. m n
3. m n
4. m n
5. m n
6. m n
7. m n
8. m n
9. m n
10. m n
11. m n
12. m n
13. m n
14. m n
15. m n
16. m n
17. m n
18. m n
19. m n

Tell children to circle the ending letter of the word that names the picture.

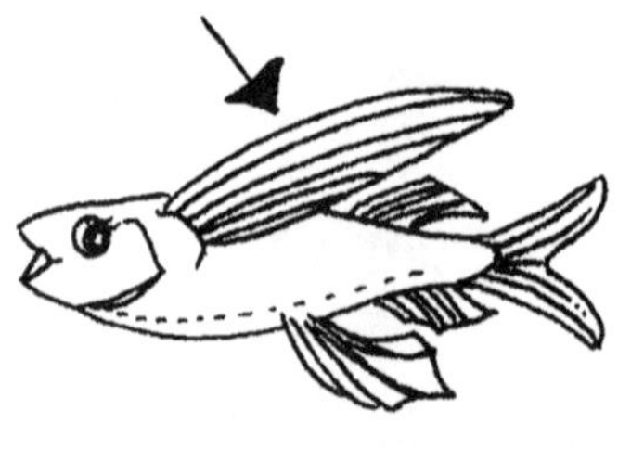

m

n

m

n

m

n

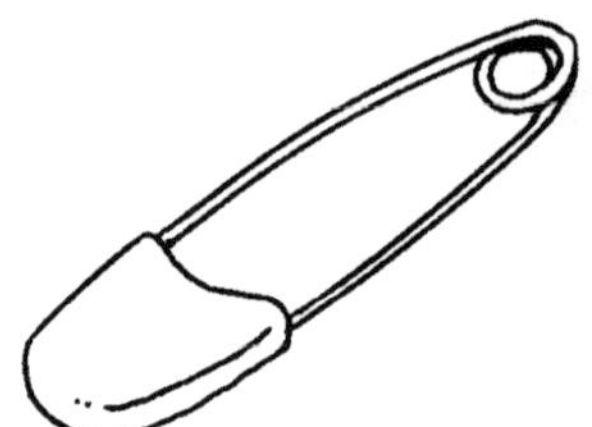

m

n

Pp

Read the verse aloud and tell children to bark when they hear the /p/ sound as in puppy. Read the verse again and tell children to circle all the letter p's.

Peter and Patty,
Perry and Pam
Ate a peanut butter sandwich
With Grandma's purple jam.
Then Patty's puppy, Penny,
Woke up from a nap
And plunked herself with a thump
Into Patty's lap.
It was very funny.
I'll tell you what I saw,
Patty's pretty puppy
With a peanut butter paw.

Tell children to circle the pictures whose names begin or end with the /p/ sound as in puppy.

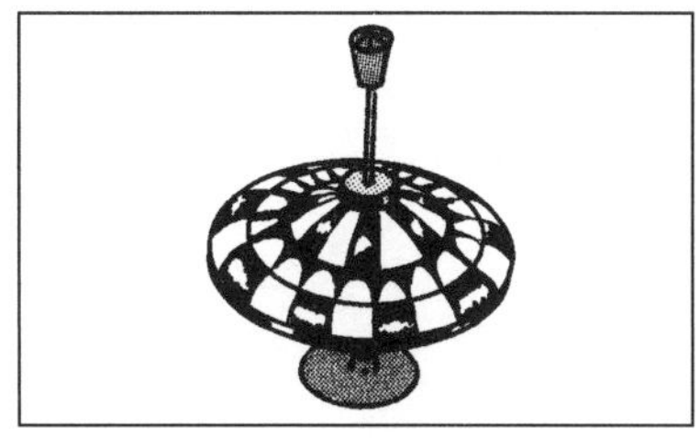

cab
mop
pan
pig
top

Name: ______________________ Date: ____________ 1-17

Qu, qu 

Read the verse aloud and tell children to say "quack, quack" when they hear the /kwa/ sound as in quack. Read the verse again and tell children to circle all the qu combinations.

Queenie was a duck
Swimming in the lake.
When the water quivered,
She began to quake.
When the water hit her back,
Queenie cried out,
"Quack, quack, quack."

First ask children to brainstorm and call out as many qu words as they can. Next, tell children to draw lines between qu words in the diagram below. If they draw lines correctly, they will form a quadrangle. Draw a quadrangle or a rectangle on the board.

• quiet • quick

• gum • guide

• gate

• guitar

• gray

• guess

• grade

• gulp

• queen • quack

Name: ______________________ Date: ____________ 1-18

Rr 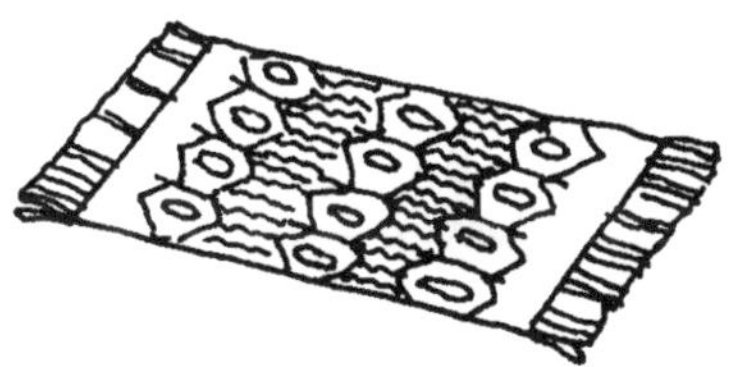

Read the verse aloud and tell children to pretend they are riding a race horse when they hear the /r/ sound as in rug. Read the verse again and tell children to circle all the letter r's.

Randy rode a race horse
Down a road so wide,
And all the people watching
Shouted, "Ride, Randy, ride."

Tell children to print an r under all pictures whose names begin with the sound of /r/ as in rug.

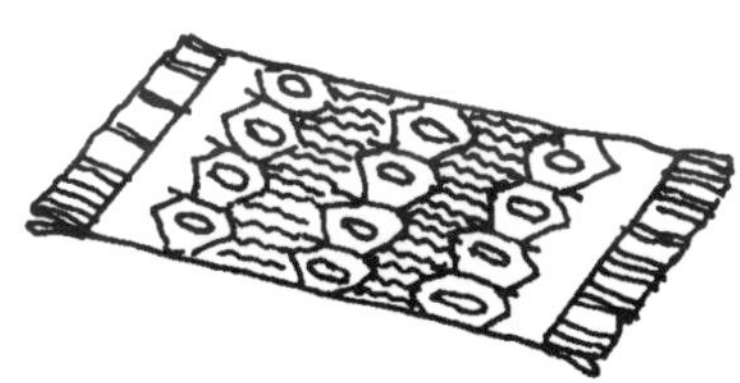

____

____

____

____

Name: ______________________ Date: ____________

Ss

Read the verse aloud and tell children to say "Sunday" when they hear the /s/ sound as in <u>sun</u>. *Read the verse again and tell children to circle all the letter* <u>s</u>*'s.*

On Saturday,
Sammy sat in the sun
And silently waited
For Sunday to come.
Grandma said,
"I am coming on Sunday
To sit with you and your sister
Till Monday."

Tell children to circle the letter that **begins** *the name of the picture.*

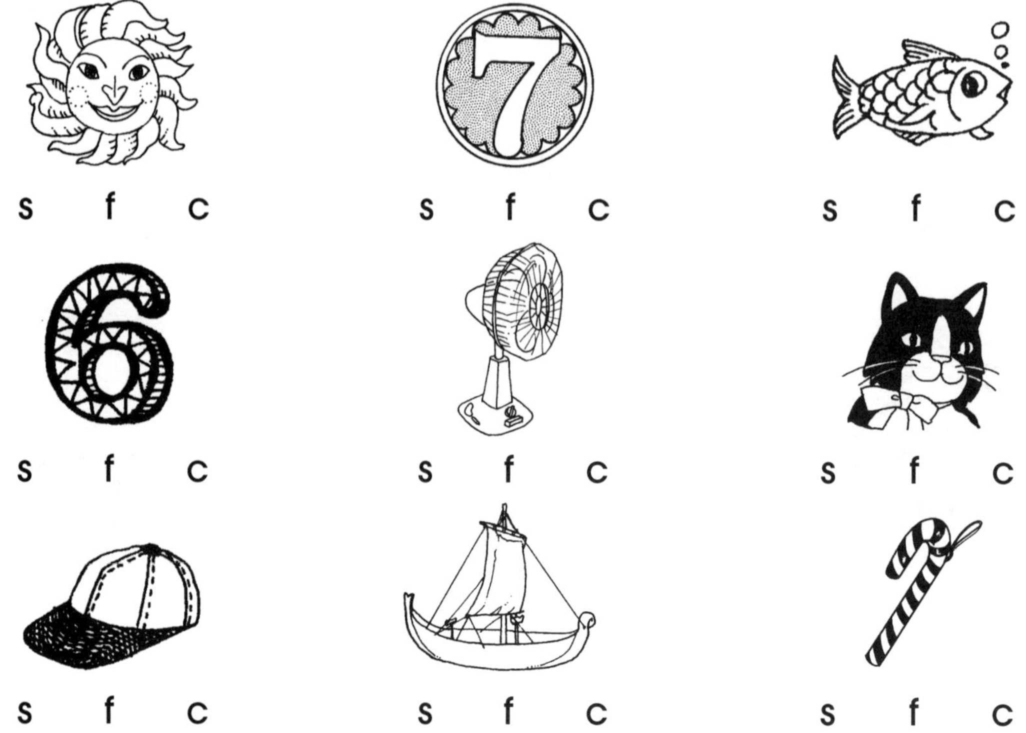

s f c s f c s f c

s f c s f c s f c

s f c s f c s f c

Tt 

Read the verse aloud and tell children to tap their toes when they hear the /t/ sound as in top. Read the verse again and tell children to circle all the letter t's.

Melanie Tompson,
Terry, and Fay
Played tic-tac-toe
On a fine summer day.
Who was the winner,
I really can't tell.
The game was a tie
Between Terry and Mel.

Tell children to print Tt below the picture if the picture begins or ends with the /t/ sound.

Name: ______________________________ Date: ______________

Vv

Read the story aloud and tell children to pretend they are playing a violin when they hear the /v/ sound as in van. Read the story again and tell children to circle all the letter v's.

Mr. Vinegar lived in a village in the valley. His house was covered with vines. He never smiled until Vicky Vincent visited him in her van and gave him a vase of violets. After Vicky's visit, he smiled very often.

Tell children to circle the pictures whose names begin with v.

Name: ______________________ Date: ____________ 1-22

Ww

Read the verse aloud and tell children to wave when they hear the /w/ sound in wig. Read the verse again and tell children to circle all the letter w's.

Willie waved to Wanda,
And Wanda waved to Willie.
But Wanda wouldn't wave
To her cousin Billie.
Willie winked at Wanda,
And Wanda winked at Willie.
And if anybody asks me,
I think both of them are silly.

Tell children to print a w in the box under the pictures whose names begin with w.

Name: ______________________ Date: ______________ 1-23

Yy 

Read the verse aloud and tell children to yell when they hear the /y/ sound as in yell. Read the verse again and tell children to circle all the letter y's.

If you see a yak
In your front yard or back,
I think you'd better tell
Your mom and dad and yell.
Who knows about a yak,
The critter might attack.

Tell children to circle the pictures whose names begin with the /y/ sound.

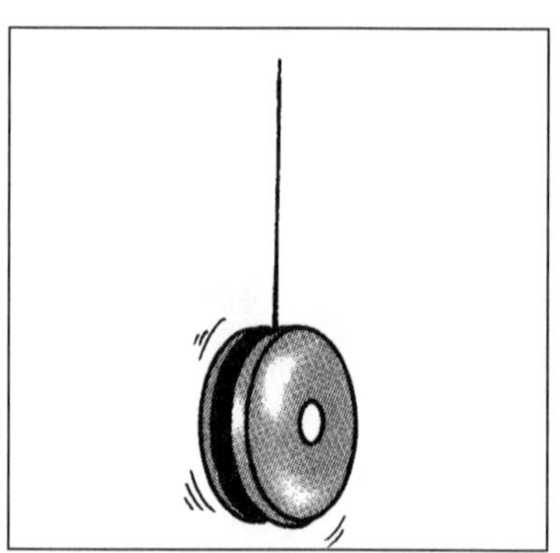

Name: ______________________ Date: ______________ 1-24

Zz

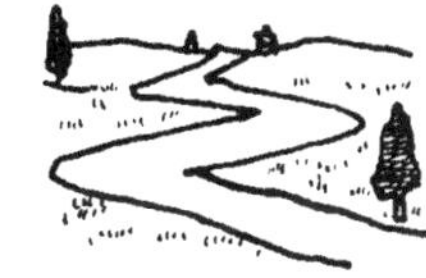

Read the verse aloud and tell children to draw zigzag lines in the air when they hear the /z/ sound as in zigzag. Read the verse again and ask children to circle all the letter z's.

Zachary Zack from Zanzibar

Went to New Zealand in his car.

But he didn't travel far.

The zigzag roads

Confused his car.

Tell children to blacken the circles below the pictures and words that begin with the /z/ sound.

Name: ______________________ Date: ______________ **1-25**

b, d, p

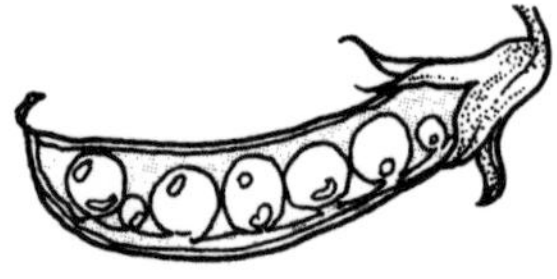

This is an initial /b/, /d/, /p/ differentiation activity. Ask children to print b, d, or p on top of pictures whose names begin with one of those letters.

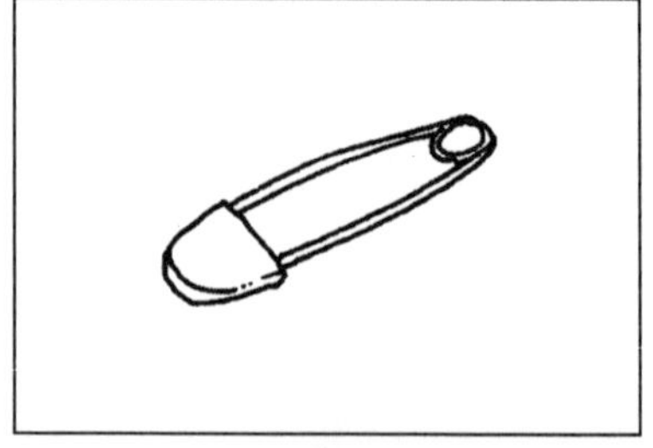

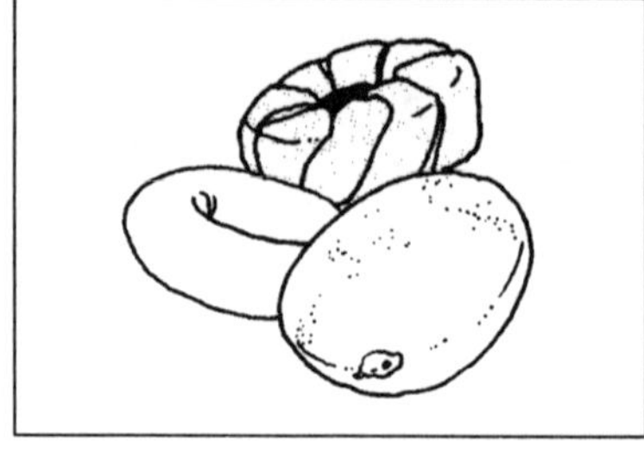

Name: ______________________ Date: ______________ 1-26

b, d, p 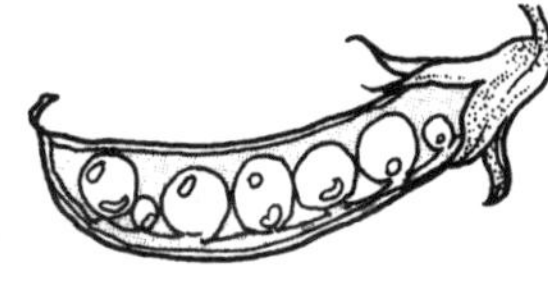

This is a final /b/, /d/, /p/ differentiation activity. Ask children to circle the correct words under the pictures.

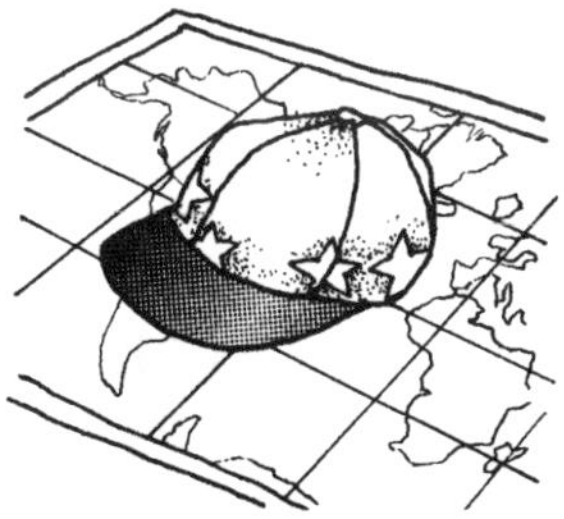

cab on mad
cap on map

bib bid

cob cod cop

dad dab

cab cap

rib rid rip

pub pup

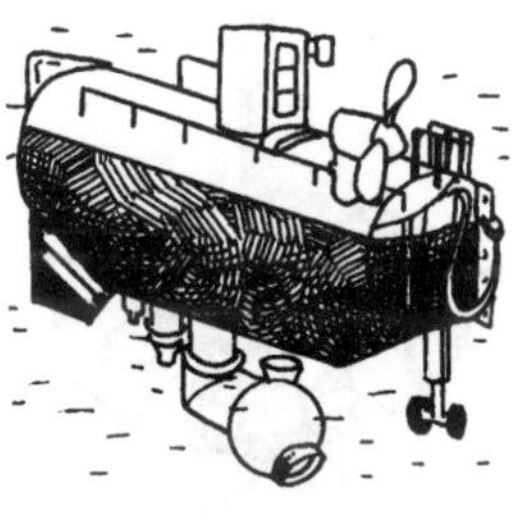

sud sub sup

mob mod mop

Police

Tod top

cob cod cop

sob sod sop

Name: ______________________ Date: ____________ 1-27

b, p, d, t 

This is a voiced and unvoiced initial consonant differentiation activity. Ask children to circle the beginning letter of the name of each picture. B *and* p *are one voiced and unvoiced pair;* d *and* t *are the other.*

b p	b p	b p
b p	b p	b p
d t	d t	d t
d t	d t	d t

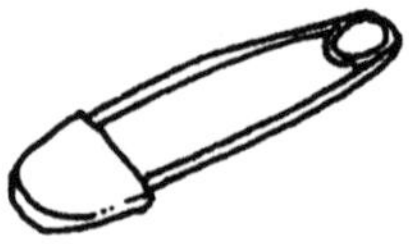

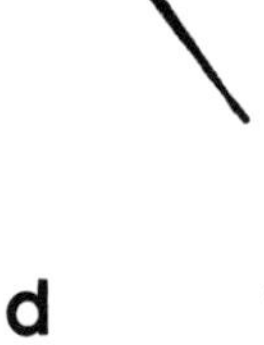

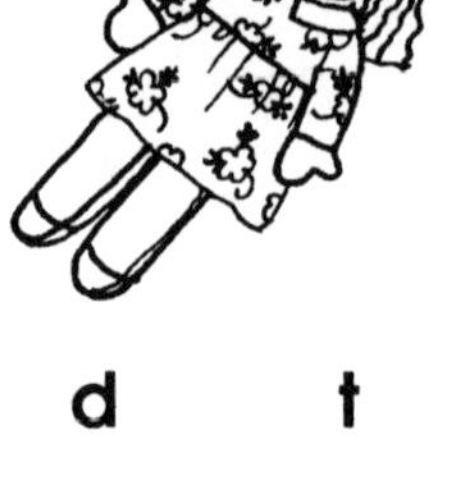

Name: ______________________ Date: ____________

b, p, d, t

This is a voiced and unvoiced final consonant differentiation activity. Ask children to circle the letter that ends the name of each picture.

b p

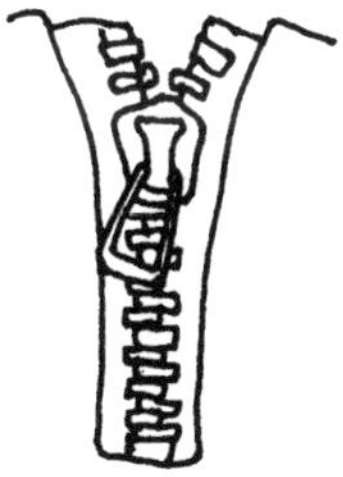

b p

b p

b p

b p

b p

d t

d t

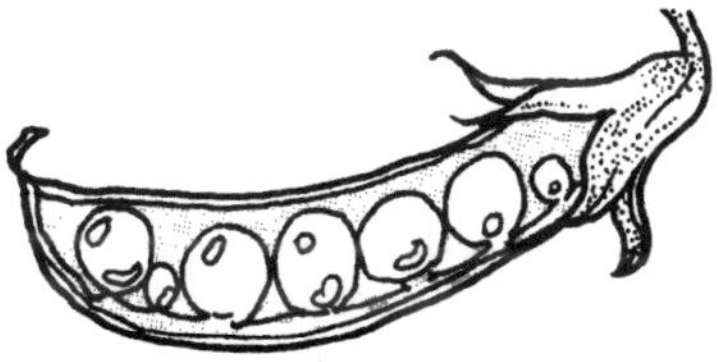

d t

d t

d t

cab	pod
cat	sob
dad	top
hat	web
hop	zip
mad	

Name: ______________________ Date: ______________

v, f

This is an initial /v/ and /f/ differentiation activity. Read the sentences below to children, and repeat the underlined word clearly. Ask children to circle the initial letter of the word they hear.

1. *The children are* very *happy.*
2. Fairies *are not real.*
3. *Mary wants to put her cat on a diet because he is too* fat.
4. *A* vat *is a big tub to store liquid.*
5. *A* fan *keeps you cool in the summer.*
6. *A* van *is bigger than a car.*
7. *Can you run* fast*?*
8. Vast *means very big.*
9. *I* feel *good today.*
10. Veal *is a kind of meat.*
11. *Who is the* fastest *runner in the class?*
12. *My dad always wears a* vest *to work.*
13. *I* feel *tired today.*
14. *A pretty* vine *is growing on the wall.*
15. *A* few *kids in the class were sick yesterday.*
16. *Did you have a good* view *from your hotel window in Seattle?*

1.	f	v	9.	f	v
2.	f	v	10.	f	v
3.	f	v	11.	f	v
4.	f	v	12.	f	v
5.	f	v	13.	f	v
6.	f	v	14.	f	v
7.	f	v	15.	f	v
8.	f	v	16.	f	v

Section 2
Short Vowels and Final Consonants

Gus and Russ
Never fight or fuss.
They sit together
On the bus.

Name: ______________________ Date: ______________

ab

Read the verse aloud. Tell children to wave their arms and pretend they are flying when they hear the /ăb/ sound as in <u>cab</u>*. Read the verse again and tell children to circle the letters that stand for the /ăb/ sound.*

In the magic land of Zab,
Doctor Fab
Had a magic lab
Where he built a magic cab
That flew in the air over Zab.

Ask children to draw a line from each word to the picture it names.

Lab
Bab
Cab

Gab
Dr. Fab
Nab

Name: ______________________ Date: ______________

ack

Read the verse aloud. Ask children to quack when they hear the /ăck/ sound as in tack. Read the verse again and tell children to circle the letters that stand for the /ăck/ sound.

Jack Black

Met Mrs. Mack.

He said, "Hi,"

And she said, "Quack."

He waved to her

And she waved back.

Tell children Mrs. Mack has many friends, but all their names rhyme with hers. Tell children to circle the names of Mrs. Mack's friends.

Dr. Fab	Jack	Bab
Zack	Tab	Dack

Name: ______________________ Date: ____________ 2-32

Read the verse aloud. Tell children to cry when they hear the /ăd/ sound as in mad. *Read the verse again and tell children to circle the letters that stand for the /ăd/ sound.*

Mom and Dad
Were very sad.
So they went to live
On a lily pad.
They had no door,
And they had no key.
But they had
My brother Tad
And me.

Tell children to print the correct word under each picture.

Add
Bad
Dad
Fad
Had
Lad
Mad
Pad
Sad

____

____

____

____

Name: ______________________ Date: ______________

ag 

Read the verse aloud. Ask children to pretend they are jumping out of a bag when they hear the /ăg/ sound. Read the verse again and tell children to circle the letters that stand for the /ăg/ sound.

There was a witch
Named Mag
Who was an ugly hag.
Her dress was
A torn-up rag.
She put a puppy
In a bag.
But his tail went
Wag, wag, wag
And he opened up the bag.

Tell children to put a big X on the pictures if their names do NOT rhyme with bag.

Name: ______________________ Date: ______________ 2-34

al

Read the verse aloud and tell children to hug each other when they hear the /ăl/ sound in pal. *Read the verse again and tell children to circle letters that stand for the /ăl/ sound.*

Sal was a neighbor.
Sal was a pal.
Al went to Sal's house
To visit Sal.
Al went to Sal's house.
Sal wasn't in.
So Al went to Sal's house
Once again.

Tell children to color the balloons that have rhyming words.

Name: ______________________ Date: ______________ 2-35

am

Read the verse aloud. Tell children to pretend they are washing their faces when they hear the /ăm/ sound as in jam. Read the verse again and tell children to circle letters that stand for the /ăm/ sound.

Little Pam
Spilled the jam
On her dress
And on her tam.
Little Sam
Washed the jam
Off of Pammy's
Dress and tam.

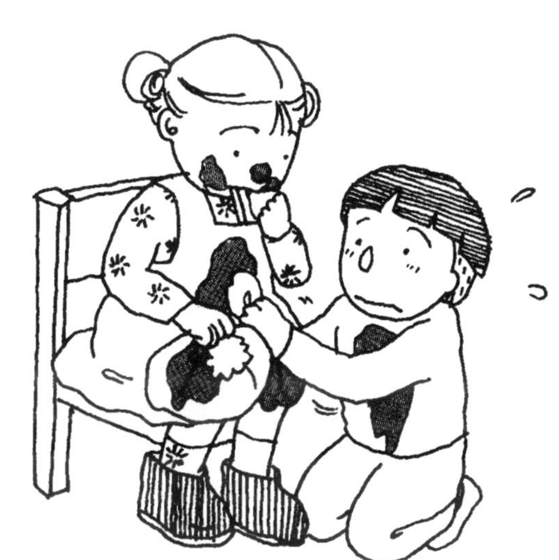

Tell children to print the correct words under each picture.

___ ___ ___

___ ___ ___

I ___ ___ ___ ___ ___

___ ___ ___

I ___ ___ ___ ___ ___

Am	Pam
Bam	Ram
Dam	Sam
Ham	Tam
Jam	Yam
M'am	

an 

Read the verse aloud. Tell children to fan their faces when they hear the /ăn/ sound as in pan. Read the verse again and tell children to circle the letters that stand for the /ăn/ sound.

Dan Van is a hungry man.
He puts an egg
In a frying pan
And cools it
Just as fast
As he can
With a folded
Paper fan.
He eats it up
With bread and jam.

Tell children to circle **yes** *if the words under the picture are correct and* **no** *if the words under the picture are wrong. Teach yes, no, in, and on as sight words if necessary.*

Dan on fan **YES** **NO**

Fan on Dan **YES** **NO**

Man in pan **YES** **NO**

Pan on man **YES** **NO**

Jan ran **YES** **NO**

Jan in can **YES** **NO**

Name: ____________________ Date: ____________ 2-37

ap

Read the verse aloud. Tell children to pretend they are sleeping when they hear the /ăp/ sound as in cap. Read the verse again and tell children to circle the letters that stand for the /ăp/ sound.

There was a boy named Hap
Who had a magic cap.
He took a nap
In his father's lap
And traveled alone
All over the map.

Tell children to circle **yes** *if the words under the picture are correct and* **no** *if the words are incorrect.*

Cap on Hap **YES** **NO**

Cap on Hap **YES** **NO**

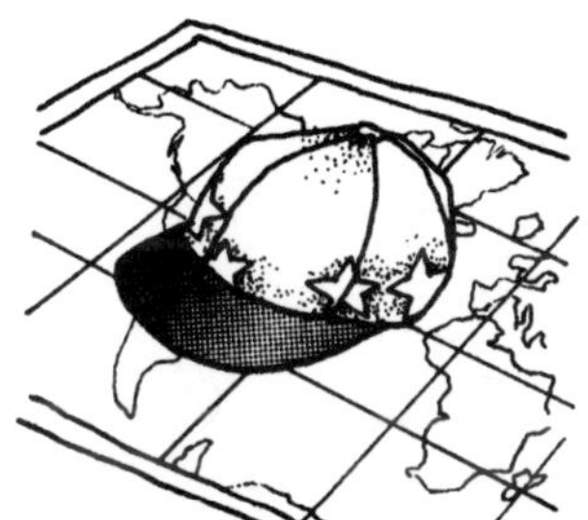

Cap on map **YES** **NO**

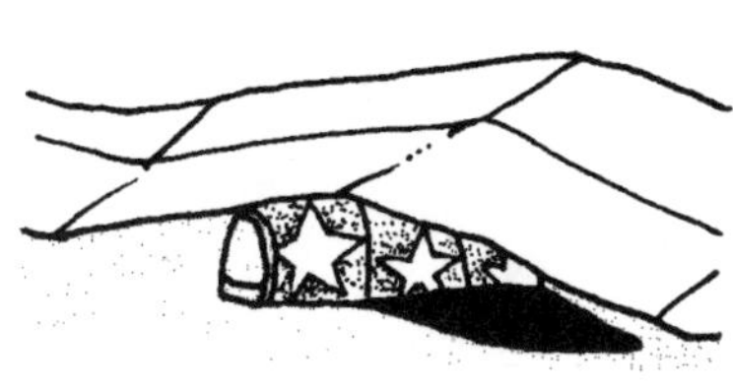

Cap on map **YES** **NO**

Hap on cap **YES** **NO**

Map on Hap **YES** **NO**

Name: ______________________________ Date: ______________

class

Read the verse aloud and tell children to raise their hands as if they were in class when they hear the /ăs/ sound as in class. *Read the verse again and tell children to circle the letters that stand for the /ăs/ sound.*

Children, children
Come to class.
Every boy
And every lass,
And the teacher
Never sass.
Then I know
That you will pass.

Tell children to circle the /ăs/ words in the grid. The words go across or down.

Words
bass
cass
gas
lass
mass
pass
sass

g	b	a	s	s	c
a	m	a	l	n	a
s	a	p	a	s	s
b	s	a	s	s	s
a	s	c	s	g	m
n	o	a	s	s	s

Name: ____________________ Date: ____________

at 

Tell children to stand up. Tell them to listen as you read the verse aloud and sit down whenever they hear the /ăt/ sound as in cat, then quickly stand up again. Read the verse again and tell children to circle the letters that stand for the /ăt/ sound.

A fat cat
Sat on a top hat.
The hat said,
"I'm not a top hat,
I'm a flat hat."

Tell children to circle the name of each picture below.

fat hat cat

can cat cab

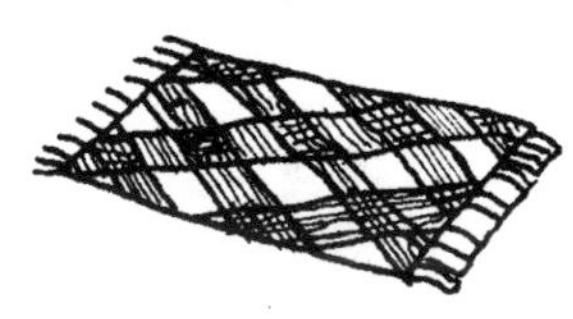

map mat man

bag bad bat

rat rag ran

pat fat pan

Name: ______________________ Date: ____________ 2-40

ax

Read the verse aloud and ask children to pretend they are chopping down a tree with an ax when they hear the /ăx/ sound as in wax. *Read the verse again and tell children to circle the letters that stand for the /ăx/ sound.*

If you want to send a letter,
I think you had better
Ask Mrs. Sax
How to use the fax.

Tell children to print the name of each picture.

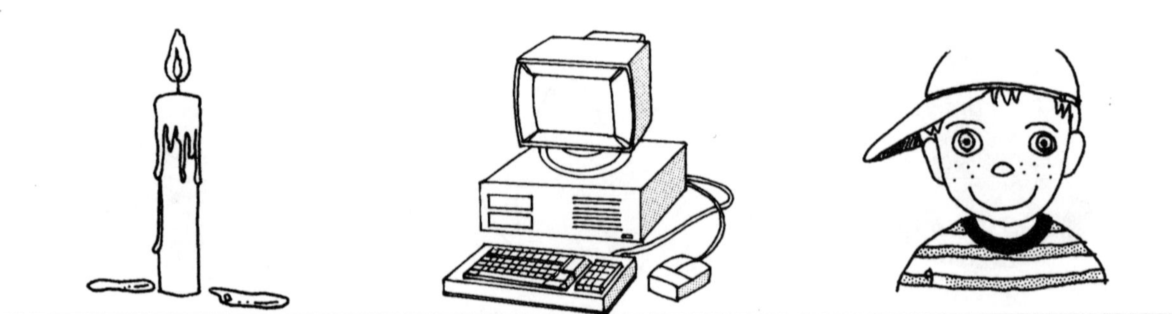

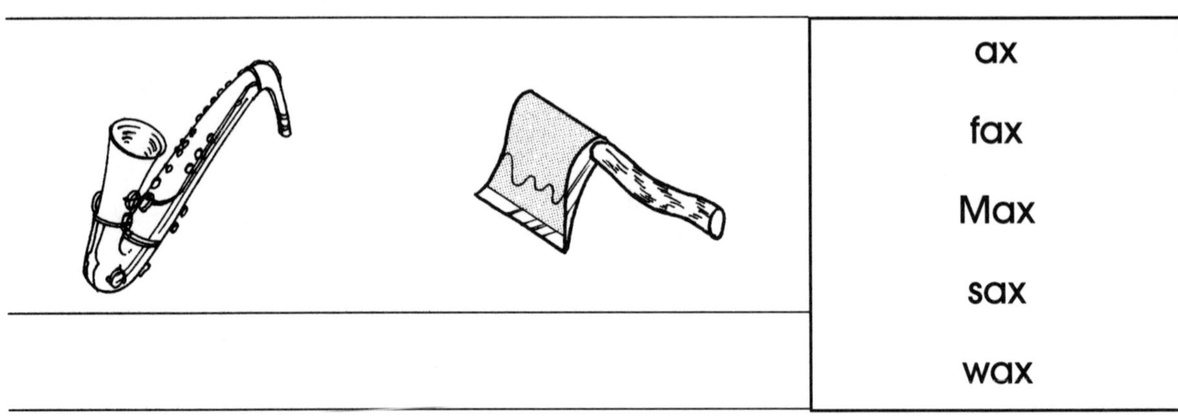

Short a Student Reading Selection

After children have studied all the short a sounds, they can read this story themselves. But first review the following sight words with them: the, is, says.

Scat Cat

Dan Dack, a fat man, sat. A tan cat sat at Dan's . The cat bats at Dan's . Dan is mad at the cat. Dan says, "Scat, cat!" The cat scats. The cat is sad. Dan says, "Back, cat." The cat is back at Dan's 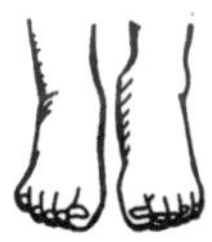 . The cat is glad.

Tell children to circle the pictures if their names have the short a sound as in apple.

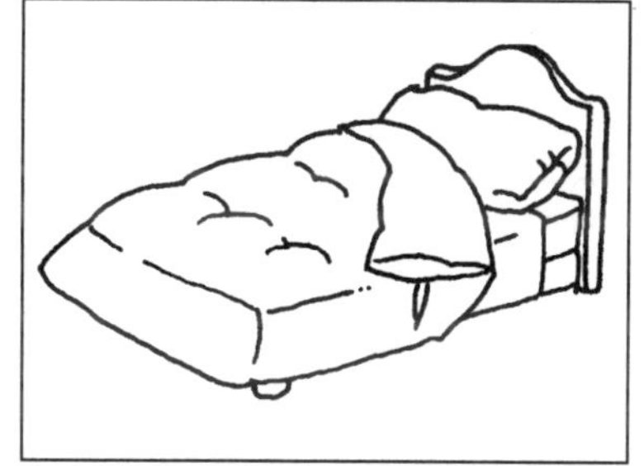

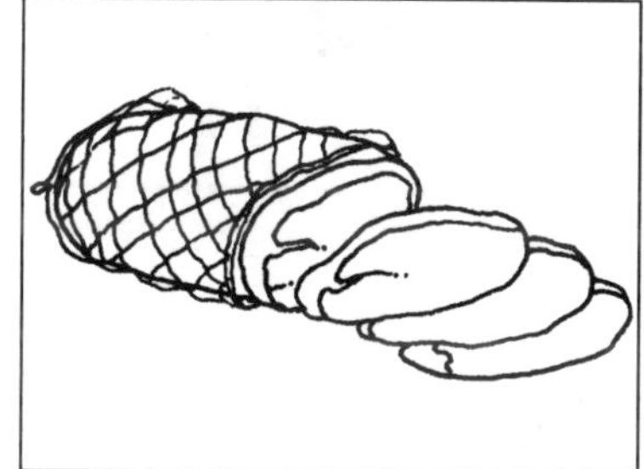

Short a Student Reading Selection

Children can read this story themselves after you teach with and say as sight words.

An Ant Can't

An ant can't whack a with an ax. An ant can't whack a with a bat. An ant can't bat at a cat. An ant can't bat at an ant. An ant can't gab with a gal. An ant can't gab with a pal. An ant can't say, "I am an ant."

Tell children to circle the name of each picture.

gal gas gab

pat fan fat

cap cat can

bag wag wax

ham had hat

tan tab tag

Name: ________________________ Date: ____________

Short a Student Reading Selection

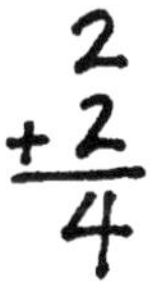

After you teach on, is, but, dog, *and* with *as sight words, children can read this story by themselves.*

Bad Cat

A fat cat and a black dog sat on a mat. The fat cat is Tab. The black dog is Sam. Sam had a  . Tab had a  . Sam pats Tab with a  . Tab bats Sam's back. Tab is Sam's pal, but Tab sat on Sam. Tab jabs Sam with a  . Sam is sad. Sam is mad. Tab is a bad cat. Sam  at Tab. At last, Sam ran.

Tell children to circle **yes** *or* **no** *beside each sentence.*

1. Tab is fat. **YES** **NO**
2. Tab had a  . **YES** **NO**
3. Sam had a rat. **YES** **NO**
4. Tab is Sam's pal, but Tab bats Sam. **YES** **NO**
5. Sam sat on Tab. **YES** **NO**
6. Tab sat on Sam. **YES** **NO**
7. Sam jabs Tab with a  . **YES** **NO**
8. Tab ran. **YES** **NO**
9. Sam ran. **YES** **NO**
10. Tab and Sam sat on a hat. **YES** **NO**

Name: ______________________ Date: ____________

ib

Read the verse aloud and tell children to pretend they are eating a rib when they hear the /ĭb/ sound as in bib. *Read the verse again and tell children to circle the letters that stand for the /ĭb/ sound.*

There was a boy
And his name was Tib.
He had a knife and a fork
And a bib.
He sat down to eat
A barbequed rib.
Don't you really
Envy Tib?

Tell children to print the beginning letter of a word that means to lie.

___ i b

Tell children to put an X in the box next to pictures whose names rhyme.

ick

Read the verse aloud and tell children to say "click" when they hear the /ĭk/ sound as in lick. Read the verse again and tell children to circle the letters that stand for the /ĭk/ sound.

Give me some words that rhyme with Nick.
If you're right, I'll tell you "click."
If you're wrong, I'll answer "ick."
Patty says, "The clock goes 'tick.'"
She is right, and I say, "Click."
Ricky says, "My name is Rick."
He is right, and I say, "Click."
Betty says, "I'm feeling sick."
Tommy's candle has a wick.
And I answer, "Click, click, click."

Tell children to circle **yes** *if the description under the picture is right and* **no** *if it's wrong.*

Rick YES NO

Dick licks. YES NO

Dick and stick YES NO

Mick is sick. YES NO

Tick, tick YES NO

Dick is sick. YES NO

Name: ______________________ Date: ______________ 2-46

id

Read the verse aloud and tell children to hide their faces in their hands when they hear the /ĭd/ sound as in lid. *Read the verse again and tell children to circle the letters that stand for the /ĭd/ sound.*

There was a little kid
Who ran away and hid
From a nasty dog
Named Sid
Because of what
He did.

Tell children they can pick some apples from the tree, but only apples with rhyming words. Tell them to color each picked apple red.

if, iff

Read the verse aloud and tell children to sniff loudly when they hear the /ĭf/ sound as in sniff*. Read the verse again and circle the letters that stand for the /ĭf/ sound.*

A mother lion sniffs the ground.
She thinks if I sniff and sniff
I'll find food for my cub, Cliff.
Then mother lion gets a whiff
Of something strange in the air.
She stands still and stiff
And sniffs and sniffs.
She thinks if it is food,
I will get it for Cliff.
If it is danger,
I will fight it for Cliff.

Tell children to circle **yes** *or* **no** *after each question. If necessary, teach* yes, no, get, *and* of *as sight words.*

1. Can Biff sniff? **YES NO**
2. Is a stick stiff? **YES NO**
3. Are stiff? **YES NO**
4. Can a van sniff? **YES NO**
5. If Griff can sniff, can he get a whiff of  ? **YES NO**

Name: ______________________ Date: ______________ 2-48

ig 

Read the verse aloud and tell children to say "oink" when they hear the /ĭg/ sound as in pig. Read the verse again and tell children to circle the letters that stand for the /ĭg/ sound.

As I was walking
In Pigland,
I saw a pig,
A big, fat pig,
A wonderful pig
Dancing a jig
And wearing a wig
In Pigland.
I had the most fun
In Pigland.

Tell children to circle the words that rhyme with pig.

Jig	Bag	Did	Fig
Bib	Wig	Lid	Hag
Big	Rib	Dig	Rig
Hid	Tag	Wag	Rag

Name: ______________________ Date: ______________

Read the verse aloud and tell children to stamp when they hear the /ĭl/ sound as in hill. Read the verse again and tell children to circle the letters that stand for the /ĭl/ sound.

The other night
In the moonlight
A boy named Will
Saw a great sight—
A herd of horses
On a hill
Tramping and stamping
And standing still.

Tell children to choose letters from the alphabet and from the list of consonant blends to make words ending in ill. Explain that they cannot use all the letters. Then ask them to read the words they have made and use them orally in sentences.

1. ___ill
2. ___ ___ill
3. ___ill
4. ___ill
5. ___ill
6. ___ill
7. ___ill
8. ___ill
9. ___ill
10. ___ ___ill
11. ___ill
12. ___ ___ill
13. ___ill
14. ___ill

a	q
b	r
c	s
d	t
e	u
f	v
g	w
h	x
i	y
j	z
k	ch
l	qu
m	sh
n	st
o	thr
p	

im 

Read the verse aloud and tell children to sing their favorite song when they hear the /ĭm/ sound as in brim. *Read the verse again and tell children to circle the letters that stand for the /ĭm/ sound.*

Jim Giraffe
Is tall and slim.
He wears a hat
Without a brim.
And when he cries,
I sing to him.

Tell children to print the correct word from the list under each picture.

slim
him
swim
dim
brim

____

____

Name: ______________________ Date: ______________

in 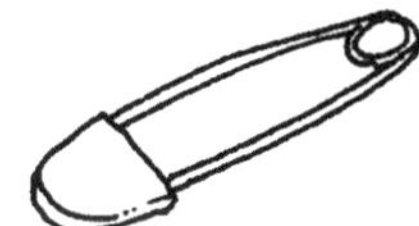

Read the verse aloud and tell children to whirl around when they hear the /ĭn/ sound as in pin. Read the verse again and tell children to circle letters that stand for the /ĭn/ sound.

Have you ever had
A tin cup?
Have you ever seen
A thin pup?
Have you seen a fish
With a silver fin?
Or angels dance
On the head of a pin?
Or played a game
You didn't win?
Or met a dog
Named Rin-tin-tin?

Tell children to print the **first** *letter(s) of each word under the correct picture.*

tin	fin	pin	bin	rin-tin-tin	chin

Coffee 8OZS.

ip 

Read the verse aloud and tell children to put their fingers on the tips of their noses when they hear the /ĭp/ sound as in lip. Read the verse again and tell children to circle the letters that stand for the /ĭp/ sound.

Dance, dance,
Prance, prance.
Put your hand on your hip.
Put a finger on your lip.
Put another on the tip
Of your nose.
Swing your clothes,

Touch your toes,
And zip, zip, zip
Through the rows
Of people watching
As you skip, dance, and dip
With your hands
Upon your hips.

Tell children to circle all actions in the picture that can be named by /ĭp/ words.

is, iss

Read the verse aloud and tell children to hiss when they hear the /ĭs/ sound as in sis. *Read the verse again and tell children to circle the letters that stand for the /ĭs/ sound.*

Sis, sis

Don't kiss

The snake.

The snake will hiss

If you kiss him.

Tell children to put the correct words from the list in the blanks.

hiss
kiss
miss
sis

1. A  can ____________.

2. A  can ____________.

3. ____________ Bell is mad. 

4. The [snake] can ____________ at ____________.

5. ____________ can ____________ the [snake].

it

Read the verse aloud and tell children to pretend they are hitting a fly when they hear the /ĭt/ sound as in <u>sit</u>. *Read the verse again and tell children to circle the letters that stand for the /ĭt/ sound.*

Riddle

Harry hit it.

Biff bit it.

An angel lit it.

What is it?

(*Answer*: A firefly)

Tell children to put a number in each circle. The number is for the word that tells about each picture.

1. it
2. bit
3. fit
4. hit
5. lit
6. pit
7. sit

ix 

Read the verse aloud and tell children to put six fingers up in the air when they hear the /ĭks/ sound as in six. *Read the verse again and tell children to circle the letters that stand for the /ĭks/ sound.*

Three plus three are six.
Six times six is thirty-six.
I have a game
Called "pick-up stix."
A broken door is
Hard to fix,
And if you buy
A pie crust mix,
You mix and mix and mix.

Explain to children that the letters ix *in* fix *and* icks *in* tricks *have the same sound—/ĭks/. Tell them that in this game they can catch fish. But they can catch only fish whose words rhyme with* ix *as in* fix. *Tell them to put a hook (* J *) through all the fish they catch.*

Short i Student Reading Selection

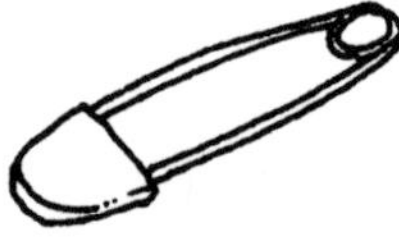

Teach in, on, and said as sight words. Then children can read the story by themselves.

Kit Cat and the Catnip

Kit Cat hid in a bag. Tim said, "Kit Cat, here's a catnip ___." Kit Kat sniffs the ___, taps it, sits on it, hisses at it. Kit Cat pats the ___, taps it, sits on it, hisses at it. Kit Cat rips the ___. The ___ is a rag. Jim is sad, but Kit Cat is back in the bag.

Tell children to complete the sentences with words from the list.

1. Sick is ___ ___ ___.
2. The ___ is ___ ___ ___.
3. A bag is a ___ ___ ___ ___.
4. Bill ___ ___ ___ ___ the .
5. A ___ has a ___ ___ ___.
6. The ___ ___ ___ ___ ___ ___ Kim.
7. Sid ___ ___ ___ the ___.
8. The ___ ___ ___ ___ ___.
9. Biff ___ ___ ___ the ___.
10. The ___ has a ___ ___ ___.

bib
fits
hid
hit
ill
licks
lid
lit
sack
sips

Name: ______________________ Date: ______________

Short i Student Reading Selection

After you review are, is, and say as sight words, children can read this story alone, either silently or aloud.

Nip and Pip

Nip and Pip are s. Biff and Sid are .

Biff's  is Nip. Sid's  is Pip.

Biff and Sid are pals. Nip and Pip are pals. Nip and Pip lick Biff and Sid. Biff and Sid kiss Nip and Pip. Lill is a cat. Pip licks Lill. Lill hisses at Pip. Pip is sad. Lill hisses at Nip. Nip is mad at Lill. Nip bit Lill. Nip is sad. Nip licks Biff.

Tell children to try to think of rhymes for each of the words below. Tell them not to use names.

1. sick: ______________________
2. lid: ______________________
3. wig: ______________________
4. ill: ______________________
5. rim: ______________________
6. tin: ______________________
7. dip: ______________________
8. hiss: ______________________

Name: ______________________ Date: ______________ 2-58

ob 

Read the verse aloud and tell children to cry or sob when they hear the /ŏb/ sound as in cob*.*
Read the verse again and tell children to circle the letters that stand for the /ŏb/ sound.

My Grandpa Rob
Roasts corn on the cob
With gobs of butter
While Grandma Cutter
Says that's his job
To roast corn on the cob
For a happy mob.

Tell children to draw a line from each word to the correct picture.

Bob
cob
job
mob
rob
sob

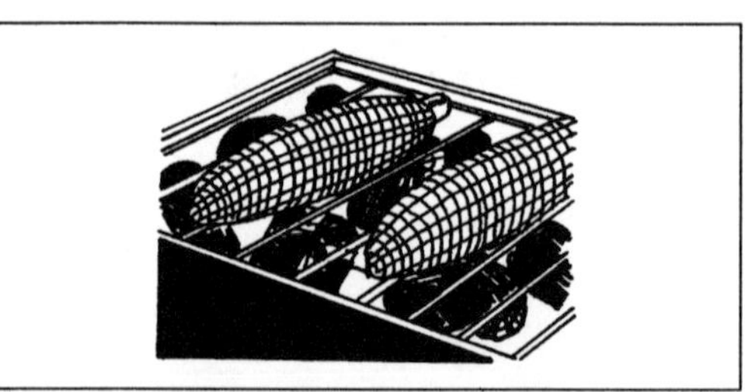

Name: ______________________ Date: ____________ 2-59

ock

Read the verse aloud and tell children to knock on their chairs when they hear the /ŏk/ sound as in sock. *Read the verse again and tell children to circle the letters that stand for the /ŏk/ sound.*

A little girl lives
Down the block.
When she comes to the door
She doesn't knock.
She just opens up the lock.
Sometimes she even
Throws a rock.
How I wish
That she would knock!

Tell children to put the number of the correct word in the circle next to the picture.

1. cock
2. frock
3. knock
4. lock
5. rock
6. sock

Name: ______________________ Date: ____________

od, odd

Read the verse aloud and tell children to nod their heads when they hear the /ŏd/ sound as in rod*. Read the verse again and tell children to circle the letters that stand for the /ŏd/ sound.*

"It's odd,"
Said Tod
With a funny nod.
Some hats are odd,
And some are mod.
"It's odd,"
Said Tod.

mod hat odd hat

Dictate the following words. Ask children to circle b *if the word ends in* b*, and* d *if the word ends in* d*: 1. cob, 2. cod, 3. job, 4. odd, 5. nod, 6. mob, 7. rod, 8. rob, 9. knob, 10. Bob, 11. Tod, 12. sob.*

1.	b	d	7.	b	d
2.	b	d	8.	b	d
3.	b	d	9.	b	d
4.	b	d	10.	b	d
5.	b	d	11.	b	d
6.	b	d	12.	b	d

Name: ______________________________ Date: ______________

og 

Read the verse aloud and tell children to say "Hi dog" when they hear the /ô/ sound as in dog. *Read the verse again and tell children to circle the letters that stand for the /ôg/ sound.*

A green dog
Sat on a log.
A hog came.
"Hi, dog,"
Said the hog.
"I'm a hog.
A hog is a big pig.
Is a green dog
A big frog?"

Tell children to circle the word that completes the sentence.

1. A _____ sits on a log.
2. A _____ sits on a log.
3. A _____ is on a hog.
4. A _____ is on a hog.
5. A _____ is on a dog.

1.	dog log hog
2.	hog dog fog
3.	log bog fog
4.	log hog dog
5.	dog log hog

Name: ______________________ Date: ______________

om, on 

Read the verse aloud. Tell the children to shiver with cold when they hear the /ŏn/ sound. Explain that the on in skeleton doesn't really have the sound of /ŏn/ in Don and that they'll learn why later.

Ron and Jon

Met a skeleton.

His name was Don.

He said, "I'm cold

With no clothes on."

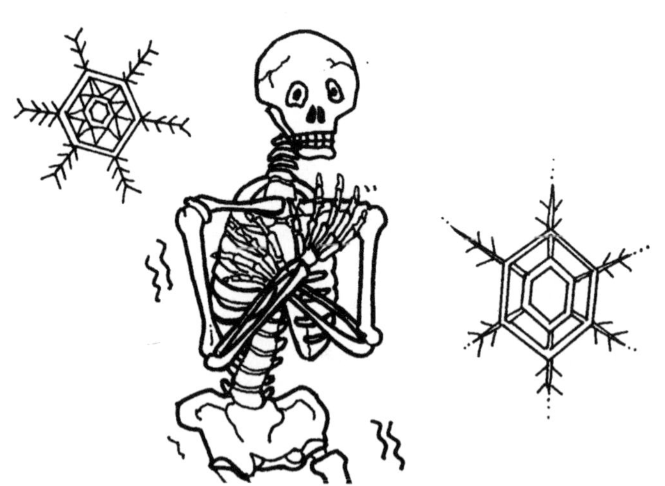

Tell children to fill in the letter that ends the word shown in each picture.

To_____ m n

Ro_____ m n

Do_____ m n

Mo_____ m n

Name: ______________________ Date: ____________ 2-63

Read the verse aloud and tell children to say "plop plop" when they hear the sound of /ŏp/ as in top. Read the verse again and tell children to circle the letters that stand for the /ŏp/ sound.

On house tops
And tree tops,
The rain falls
With plop-plops.
When I walk, I slip-slop.
When I run, I flip-flop.
When I slide,
I can't stop.

Tell children to circle the name of each picture. (This reinforces b, d, and r differentiation.)

Name: ______________________ Date: ____________ 2-64

OSS

Explain to children that o *in* boss *has the sound of /ô/ in* paw*. Read the verse aloud and tell children to pretend they are tossing a basketball into a basket when they hear the /ô/ sound. Read the verse again and tell children to circle the letters that stand for the /ôs/ sound.*

Tommy Ross was mad.
He shouted at his dad.
He said to Mr. Ross,
"You are not my boss!"
Mr. Ross just smiled and said,
"Sorry, Tom. It's time for bed."

Tell children to lightly fill in the letters over the words that have the /ôs/ sound as in toss *or* boss*. If their answers are right, they will make another /ôs/ word.*

l	p	a	l
Ross	hot	cot	not
b	o	t	v
dot	moss	Don	Ron
e	b	s	u
rob	sob	boss	sock
i	w	x	s
box	ox	hop	toss

ot

Tell children to pretend they are taking handfuls of gold out of a pot when they hear the /ŏt/ sound.

Some people say
At the end of the rainbow,
There is a pot
Filled with gold,
A lot, a lot.
Do you believe it?
I don't doubt it.
Because I know all about it.
I went in a dream.
Here's what I got.
Handsful of gold,
A lot, a lot.

Tell children to circle the letter that begins the word pictured.

b c d f
______ot

f g h j
______ot

n p r s
______ot

p r s t
______ot

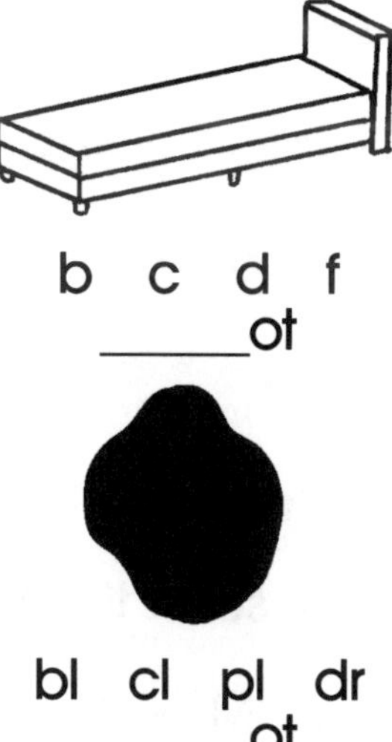

b c d f
______ot

bl cl pl dr
______ot

Name: ______________________ Date: ____________ 2-66

OX

Tell children to shout the name of Knox or Cox when they hear the /ŏks/ sound. If they think the fox belongs to Mr. Knox, they can shout "Knox." If they think the fox belongs to Mr. Cox, they can shout "Cox."

Mr. Knox had a box.
Mr. Cox had a fox.
Mr. Cox put the fox
In the box.
Knox's fox
Is in Cox's box.
Is the fox
Now Cox's fox?

Explain to children that the letters ox *in* fox *and* ocks *in* socks *have the same sound, /ŏks/. Read the poem aloud, and tell children to print all the words that have the /ŏks/ sound.*

Three old men of Mox ___ ___ ___
Went to sea in a box ___ ___ ___
With a fox and an ox ___ ___ ___ ___ ___
In ladies' frocks, ___ ___ ___ ___ ___ ___
With rocks and socks ___ ___ ___ ___ ___

___ ___ ___ ___ ___

And grandfather clocks, ___ ___ ___ ___ ___ ___
They sank the box ___ ___ ___
From Mox. ___ ___ ___

Name: ______________________ Date: ____________

OZ

Read the verse aloud and tell children to pretend they are bees saying "zzzz" when they hear the /z/ sound as in <u>oz</u>. Read the verse again and tell children to circle the letters that stand for the /z/ sound.

I want to go to Oz
To see the tin wood man
And Ozma of Oz.
I want to go with you.
So please come, too.

Tell children to draw lines around the <u>z</u> words in the grid. The <u>z</u> can be the first, middle, or last letter.

s	o	x	z	l	p	x	o	z
i	d	t	o	b	e	t	o	t
z	z	o	o	m	j	o	d	d
e	l	n	g	b	d	o	x	o
m	g	u	o	e	z	i	p	n
x	z	t	h	i	z	e	r	o
b	d	l	o	z	m	d	g	o
o	g	c	x	d	h	s	i	p
x	o	k	x	m	o	z	d	p

Short o Student Reading Selection 

Review *are*, *this*, *is*, *the*, *and* *to* *as sight words. Then children can read the story alone.*

Don and Lon

Don had on the cob. Lon is Don's big dog. Lon got the on the cob and ran to Dad's van and got in. Lon had the on the cob in his . Don said, "Lon, Lon, stop!" Not Lon. Lon bit the . Don got in Dad's van and sat on top of Lon. Lon licked his lips. The on the cob is in Lon's .

Tell children to circle the correct word under each picture. (This reinforces /ă/ and /ŏ/ differentiation.)

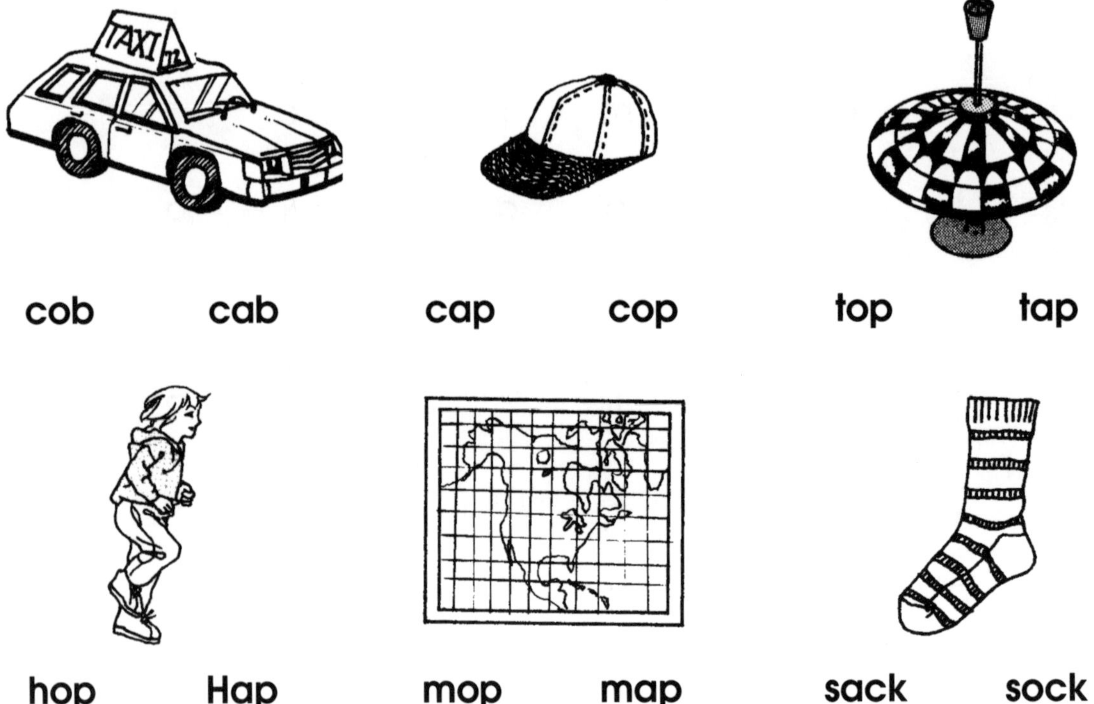

cob **cab** **cap** **cop** **top** **tap**

hop **Hap** **mop** **map** **sack** **sock**

Short o Student Reading Selection

After you teach he, is, says, and the as sight words, children can read this story themselves.

Tod Can Hop

Tod is a tot. He cannot sit. He has to hop. He hops on Ann's doll. He hops on Bob's sock. He hops on Mom's and mop. He hops on the . He hops on the clock. The clock says, "Tick tock." He hops on Pop's . Pop says, "STOP." Tod stops.

Tell children to underline the correct words under each picture.

Tod can hop.
Tod can stop.

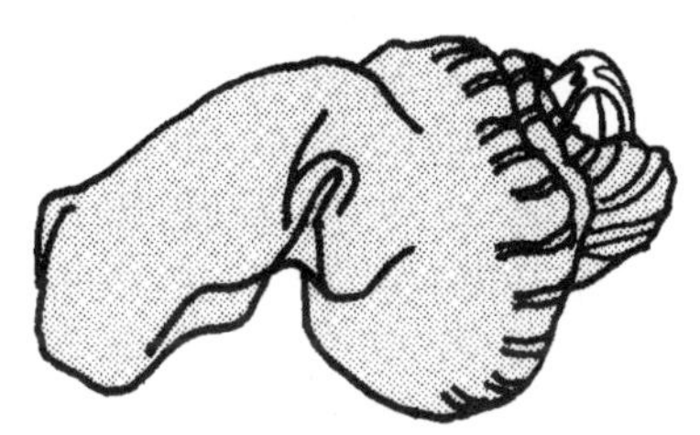

Sock in pot.
Pot in sock.

Hop!
Stop!

Pop on top.
Top on Pop.

Dog on hog.
Hog on dog.

Mom and Pop.
Mom and mop.

Short o Student Reading Selection 

Review I, says, and have as sight words. Explain that k in knock and know is silent. Then children can read this story alone.

Tick-Tock

The clock says, "Tick-tock." The  says, "Knock, knock."

The mop says, "Slip, slop." The  says, "Pop, pop."

The  says, "I am a cob."

The  says, "I have a knob."

Bob says, "I have a Pop and a Mom."

Tom says, "I am Tom."

The pot says, "I am hot."

The bed says, "I am a cot."

The hat says, "I am odd." 

The  says, "I am a cod."

The 

says, "I am a cop." The  says, "I can stop."

Ron says, "I can hop."

Name: ______________________ Date: ____________ 2-71

ub 

Tell children to growl like a lion cub when they hear the /ŭb/ sound.

Rub a dub dub
Three men in a tub
With a cat and a rat
And a lion cub.

Tell children to color the pictures that rhyme in each row.

cub

tub

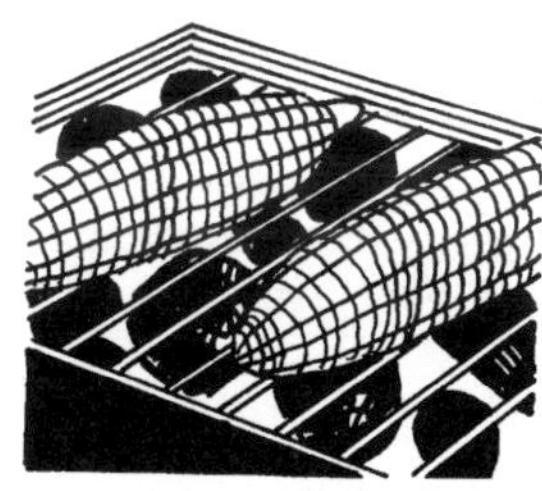
cob

cab

cub

sub

knob

sob

rub

Name: ______________________ Date: ______________ 2-72

uck 

Read the verse aloud and tell children to say "cluck cluck" when they hear the /ŭk/ sound as in duck. Read the verse again and tell children to circle the letters that stand for the /ŭk/ sound.

There was a truck
Named Buck.
There was a duck
Named Puck.
Buck said to Puck,
"I love you, duck,"
And Puck replied,
"Cluck cluck."

Tell children to print the word that will finish each sentence.

Buck
Cluck
duck
Puck
stuck
truck
tucks

1. ______________ is a truck.
2. ______________ is a duck.
3. Puck says, "______________."
4. A ______________ is big.
5. A ______________ is not big.
6. The truck is ______________ in the mud.
7. Mom ______________ Sam in bed.

Name: ________________________ Date: ____________

ud 

Read the verse aloud and tell children to stamp and make a thud-thud noise when they hear the /ŭd/ sound as in bud. Read the verse again and tell children to circle the letters that stand for the /ŭd/ sound.

Alone in the house
A boy named Bud
Heard a sound in the rain and mud.
A very soft thud, thud, thud.
The cow's in the barn
Chewing her cud,
But where oh where is Uncle Jud?
He looked out the window,
And what did he see?
The cow was under the apple tree,
Stomping her feet
With a thud, thud, thud.
"Get back in the barn,"
Said Uncle Jud.

Read the following numbered words. Tell children to listen for final consonants and circle b, d, or p: 1. bud, 2. cub, 3. cup, 4. dud, 5. Jud, 6. pup, 7. sub, 8. tub, 9. up.

1. b d p
2. b d p
3. b d p
4. b d p
5. b d p
6. b d p
7. b d p
8. b d p
9. b d p

Name: ______________________ Date: ____________ 2-74

uff 

Read the verse aloud and tell children to pretend they're putting their hands in a muff when they hear the /ŭf/ sound as in muff. *Read the verse again and tell children to circle the letters that stand for the /ŭf/ sound.*

When I was walking in
fairyland,
I met a girl with
silver hands.
She had a puff
Of silky stuff
Upon her cuff
And silver hands
In a silver muff
In fairyland.

Tell children to color the bubbles that have pairs of rhyming words.

Name: ______________________ Date: ______________

ug 

Read the verse aloud and tell children to say "ug" when they hear the /ŭg/ sound as in bug*. Read the verse again and tell children to circle the letters that stand for the /ŭg/ sound.*

Pug said,
"UG,
A bug
In my mug."

Tell children to circle the correct word next to each picture.

1. jug  hug

2. hug  rug

3. tug 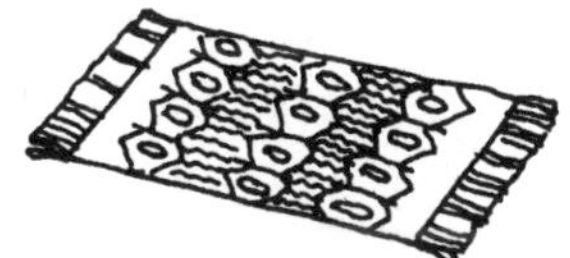 rug

4. mug  bug

5. mug  dug

6. snug  tug

Name: ______________________ Date: ____________ 2-76

uh 

Read the verse aloud and tell children to shake their heads "yes" when they hear uh huh and shake their heads "no" when they hear uh uh. Read the verse again and tell children to circle the letters that stand for the /ŭh/ sound.

Mom said,

"Pug, do you love me?"

Pug said, "Uh huh."

Mom said,

"Do you like to go to the dentist?"

Pug said, "Uh uh."

Mom said,

"Can you say, OWATAGOOSIAM?"*

Pug said, "HUH?"

---

*Oh, what a goose I am.

Ask children assorted questions with "yes" or "no" answers. Ask some to which children might reply with surprise. Children can answer "uh huh," "uh uh," or "huh." Sample questions are below.

1. Do you have a dog?
2. Do you like candy?
3. Do you like spinach?
4. Do you like bugs?
5. Do you like mud?
6. Do you want to go to the opera?

Name: ______________________________ Date: ______________ 2-77

ull

Tell children to pretend they're flying when they hear the /ŭl/ sound as in gull. *Read the verse again and tell children to circle the letters that stand for the /ŭl/ sound.*

In the lull of evening,
Against a dull sky,
A white gull
Flies beside a ship's hull.

Explain that ull *has the /o͝ol/ sound in* bull, full, pull *and the / ŭl/ sound in* gull, dull *and* hull. *Ask children to print the first letter of two words that rhyme with* bull *and the first letter of three words that rhyme with* gull.

bull

_____u l l

_____u l l

gull

_____u l l _____u l l

_____u l l

Tell children to print /ŭl/ words that complete each sentence.

1. A ____________________ is a  .
2. A ____________________ is on a ship.
3. The cup is ____________________.
4. The sun is not ____________________.
5. Bob and Jim can ____________________. 
6. A ____________________ is big.

Name: ______________________ Date: ______________ 2-78

um

Read the verse aloud. Ask children to say "Ho hum" when they hear the /ŭm/ sound as in gum. Read the verse again and tell children to circle the letters that stand for the /ŭm/ sound.

Old Mrs. Blum
Had a fine son.
He wasn't smart,
And he wasn't dumb.
He knew two and two
Was a sum.
He couldn't sing,
But he could hum.
He loved candy
And bubble gum.
When she asked him to work,
He said, "Ho hum."

Read the following words. Be sure to read the number before each word. Tell children to blacken the circle beside words that rhyme with gum: 1. sum, 2. Sam, 3. plan, 4. plum, 5. ham, 6. hum, 7. him, 8. bun, 9. m'am, 10. mum, 11. Mim, 12. chum.

1. ○
2. ○
3. ○
4. ○
5. ○
6. ○
7. ○
8. ○
9. ○
10. ○
11. ○
12. ○

Name: ______________________ Date: ____________

un

Tell children to pretend they're standing in the sun. Tell them to put their hands over their eyes when they hear the sound /ŭn/ as in sun. Read the verse again and tell children to circle the letters that stand for the /ŭn/ sound.

I like hamburgers on a bun.
I like to jump
And I like to run.
I like sitting
In the sun.
I like to read,
For books are fun.

Tell children to circle "yes" or "no" for each picture.

Gum in bun. **YES NO**

Sun on bun. **YES NO**

Run in sun. **YES NO**

Bun in gum. **YES NO**

Fun in sun. **YES NO**

Ron runs. **YES NO**

up

Read the verse aloud. Tell children to pretend they're drinking something in a cup when they hear the sound /ŭp/ as in cup. *Read the verse again and tell children to circle the letters that stand for the /ŭp/ sound.*

A baby dog is a pup.

A fancy word for eat is sup.

A glass is different from a cup.

And upside down

Isn't up.

Tell children to print the correct word under the first four pictures, and circle the correct word under the next four pictures. Tell children to draw a picture of an /ŭp/ word in the last box.

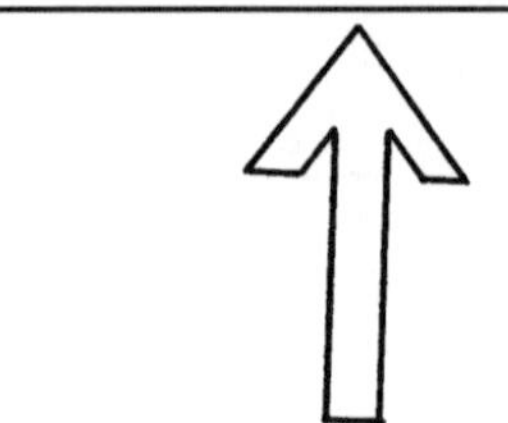

pop pup

cup cop

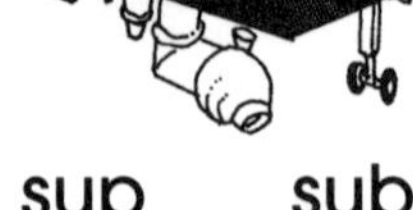

sup sub

cup cub

Name: ____________________ Date: ____________

US, USS 

Read the verse aloud and tell children to put their arms around children next to them when they hear the /ŭs/ sound as in bus. *Read the verse again and tell children to circle the letters that stand for the /ŭs/ sound.*

Gus and Russ
Never fight or fuss.
They sit together
On the bus
And say, "Together,
We are us."

Read the following words. Be sure to read the number of each word. Tell children to print an s *beside the numbers of words that end in* s: *1. bus, 2. kiss, 3. class, 4. if, 5. Russ, 6. stiff, 7. fuss, 8. pass, 9. puff, 10. stuff, 11. sniff, 12. snuff, 13. us, 14. sis, 15. sass.*

1. ___	6. ___	11. ___
2. ___	7. ___	12. ___
3. ___	8. ___	13. ___
4. ___	9. ___	14. ___
5. ___	10. ___	15. ___

Name: ______________________ Date: ____________ 2-82

ut 

Read the verse aloud and tell children to say "tut tut" when they hear the /ŭt/ sound as in nut. Read the verse again and tell children to circle the letters that stand for the /ŭt/ sound.

Old Mr. Ut
Lived in a nut.
He said,
"Tut tut,
I like my nut
But it's smaller
Than a hut."

Tell children to circle the correct word beside each picture.

nut
not

but
bat

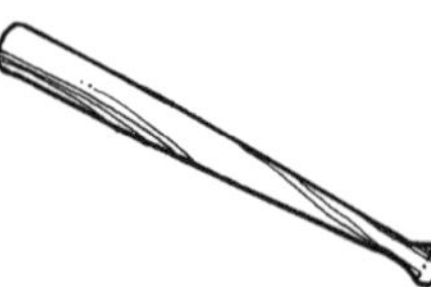

cot
cut

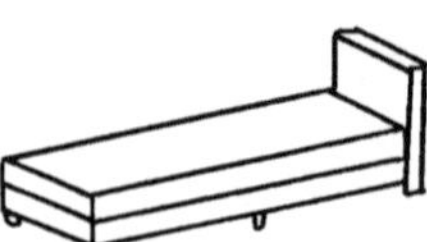

hat
hut

shot
shut

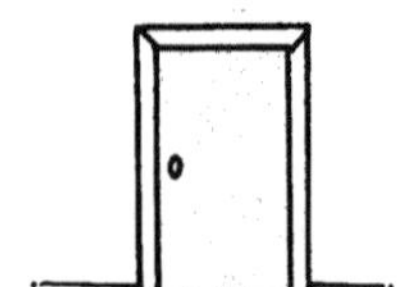

rat
rut

cat
cut

mutt
mat

Name: ____________________ Date: ____________ 2-83

uz

Read the verse aloud and tell children to buzz like bees when they hear the /ŭz/ sound. Read the verse again and tell children to circle the letters that stand for the /ŭz/ sound.

Bees buzz.

Sweaters fuzz.

Ask children what else buzzes. If they don't have ideas, suggest a doorbell, a power saw, a fly. Ask them what else has fuzz. If they don't have ideas, suggest a baby chick, a peach. Explain what's meant by a fuzzy picture. Ask them to draw their own ideas in the space below.

buzz **fuzz**

Name: ______________________ Date: ____________ 2-84

Short u Student Reading Selection 

Review comes, is, to, *and* the *as sight words. Then children can read the story alone.*

Bud and Mum

Bud is a cub. Bud rubs on Mum. Mum is not a cub. Mum is big. The sun is hot. Bud sits in the sun. The sun is fun. Bud gets a nut. A nut is fun. Bud runs and runs. To run is fun. Bud runs in the mud. But the mud is not fun. Bud sinks in the mud. The mud gets Bud. Bud is stuck in the mud. Bud sobs, "Mum, Mum, come!" Mum runs to Bud. Mum huffs and puffs. Mum gets Bud. Mum licks Bud. Bud is glad. Bud rubs on Mum.

Tell children to print the missing letters in the blanks.

1. _____ _____ b
2. _____ c k
3. _____ d
4. _____ g
5. _____ m
6. _____ f f

Buck	puff
bud	cub
bug	Mum

Name: ______________________ Date: ____________

Short u Student Reading Selection

Review a, of, and the as sight words. Then children can read the story independently.

Buck's Luck

Buck had a lot of luck. Buck and his dog, Bud, ran in the hot sun. Buck slid on a rock and sat in a rut. Bud had mud on his back. Buck had mud in his [eye]. But Buck had sat on top of a bag. Buck did not fuss. The bag had lots of gum and nuts. Yum, yum. Buck had luck.

Tell children to draw a line from each /ŭ/ picture to the tree.

eck 

Read the verse aloud and tell children to raise their heads pretending to look at something when they hear the /ĕk/ sound as in neck. *Read the verse again and tell children to circle the letters that stand for the /ĕk/ sound.*

Mrs. Beck
Came from Eck
Where she had
An auto wreck.
Mrs. Peck
Sprained her neck
Trying to see
The auto wreck.

Tell children to print the correct words under each picture.

back	sack
Mrs. Beck	tack
deck	wreck
neck	peck

ed

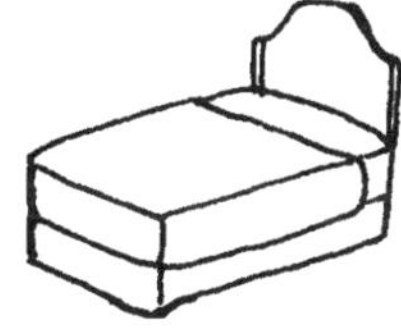

Read the verse aloud and tell children to pretend they're sleeping when they hear the /ĕd/ sound as in bed. Explain that aid in said is an unusual spelling of the /ĕd/ sound. Read the verse again and tell children to circle the letters that stand for the /ĕd/ sound.

Ted said,
"I've never slept
In a waterbed.
I never rode
On an old dog sled.
I never saw
The lions fed,
And yet I hope
To see it.
I've never cut my hand
And bled.
I hope I never do it."

Tell children to underline the correct word.

1. (Ed Led Bed) ran.
2. Mrs. Beck (fed Ted bed) the cat.
3. Ann is in (led red bed).
4. The [tulip] is (Ted red fed).
5. Dan (bed Ned led) the [dog].
6. (Ted Bed Fed) and (Wed Ed Bed) gab.
7. The [dog] sat on (Ed Fed Led).

Name: ______________________ Date: ____________ 2-88

eg, egg

Read the verse aloud and tell children to put out their hands as if they are begging for something when they hear the /ĕg/ sound as in egg. Read the verse again and tell children to circle the letters that stand for the /ĕg/ sound.

On Easter morning
Mom hides eggs in the yard.
Finding eggs isn't hard
But at 4 in the morning
My sister Meg wakes us up
and starts to beg.
"Let's go in the yard
and find the eggs."

Read the following directions and ask children to print the correct words in the blanks: Numbers one and two are names. Number three is a part of your body. Number four is something we eat. Number five is to ask for something you want very much.

1. ____ ____ ____

2. ____ ____ ____

3. ____ ____ ____

4. ____ ____ ____

5. ____ ____ ____

beg
egg
keg
leg
Meg
Peg

ell

Explain to children that an ell is a measurement that means four feet. An el with one l is a short word that means a train that runs above the ground in a big city. Read the verse aloud and tell children to extend their arms with as much space as they can get between each hand when they hear the /ĕl/ sound as in bell. Read the verse again and tell children to circle the letters that stand for the /ĕl/ sound.

An elephant of Zell
Had a nose
That was 14 ell.
Said Little Nell,
"How can you tell
If your nose is well
At the end of 14 ell?
And also, Mr. Elephant,
How can you smell?"

Tell children to color the circles under all the words that rhyme with ell.

bell ○	cab ○	el ○	fell ○	bad ○	back ○
well ○	bag ○	tell ○	pal ○	ham ○	bat ○
bed ○	leg ○	sell ○	Mel ○	lap ○	pass ○
hen ○	mad ○	swell ○	jell ○	pan ○	Nell ○

Name: ______________________________ Date: ______________

em 

Read the verse aloud and ask children to circle the letters that stand for the /ĕm/ sound as in gem. Explain to children that the final s in the plural gems has the /z/ sound.

The king had gems
in his crown.
The queen had gems
In the hem of her gown.
Were the people
Who bowed to them
Really bowing
To the gems?

Read the following words. Be sure to read the numbers. Tell children to circle m if the word ends in m, and n if the word ends in n: 1. Ben, 2. when, 3. then, 4. gem, 5. den, 6. Dan, 7. than, 8. them, 9. man, 10. men, 11. thin, 12. hem, 13. ham, 14. ten, 15. hen.

1.	m	n	6.	m	n	11.	m	n
2.	m	n	7.	m	n	12.	m	n
3.	m	n	8.	m	n	13.	m	n
4.	m	n	9.	m	n	14.	m	n
5.	m	n	10.	m	n	15.	m	n

en 

Read the verse aloud and tell children to cackle like hens when they hear the /ĕn/ sound as in ten. Read the verse again and tell children to circle the letters that stand for the /ĕn/ sound.

Two wise men
Of Zen
Wrote with
A ballpoint pen,
"Ten and ten
Are two times ten,
And a mother egg
Is a hen."

Tell children to circle the correct word under each picture.

hem hen | hen hem | hem ham | men man

Ken can | Dan den | pen pan | ten tan

es, ess

Read the verse aloud and tell children to nod their heads when they hear the /ĕs/ sound as in <u>mess</u>. *Explain that* <u>guess</u> *is pronounced /gĕs/. Read the verse again and tell children to circle the letters that stand for the /ĕs/ sound.*

"I guess"
Said Tess,
"I must confess,
I can't say, 'no.'
I must say, 'yes.'
I'm the one
Who made the mess."

Print the missing letter in the word under each picture.

lass
less

l _____ ss

mess
mass

m _____ ss

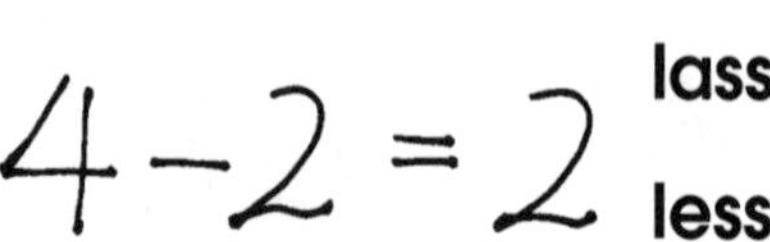

lass
less

l _____ ss

Bess
bass

B _____ ss

Name: ______________________________ Date: ______________

et 

Tell the children to listen as you read the verse aloud and open their mouths in surprise when they hear the /ĕt/ sound as in <u>net</u>. *Tell children to circle the letters that stand for /ĕt/ as you read the verse a second time.*

Dan Jet
Was a vet.
He treated dogs
And other pets.
He treated cats
Who've gotten wet.
But never ever
Had he met
A person
With a panda pet.

Tell children to print the missing letters.

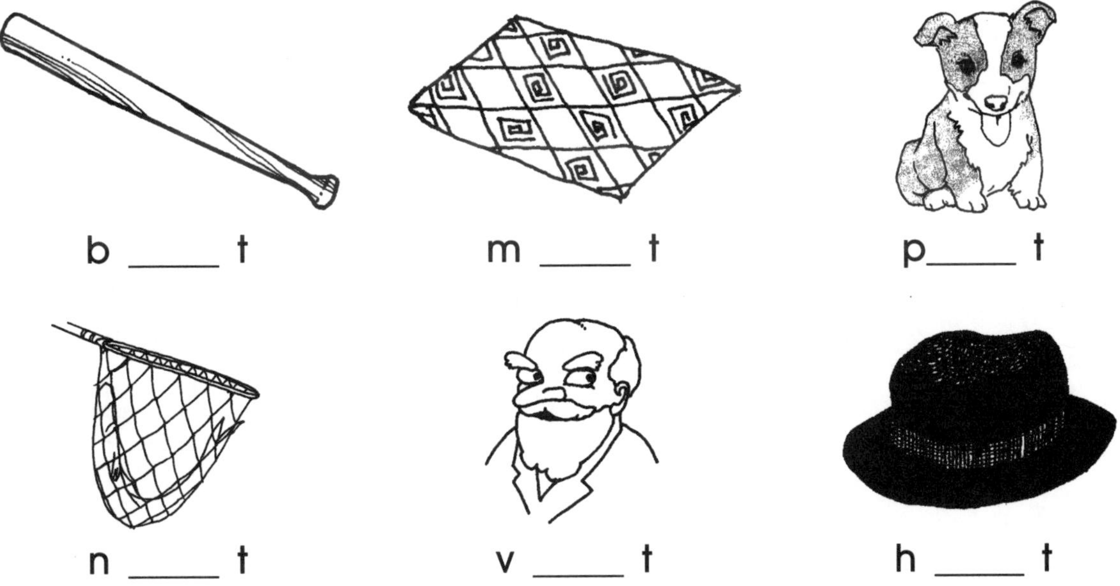

b ____ t   m ____ t   p____ t

n ____ t   v ____ t   h ____ t

ă, ĕ 

This is an /ă/ and /ĕ/ differentation activity. Tell children to circle the correct word under each picture.

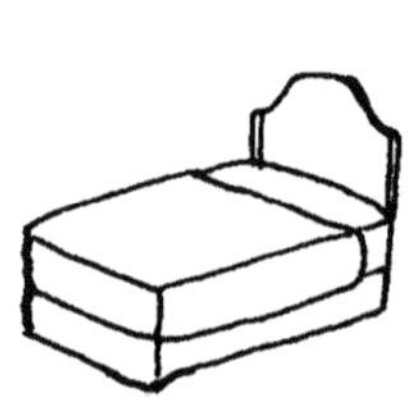

bad bed

jam gem

hat had

ham hem

lag leg

man men

pan pen

pat pet

tan ten

bat bet

bag beg

can Ken

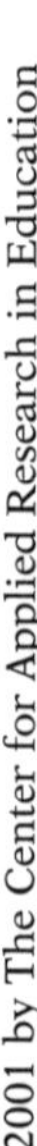

Name: ______________________ Date: ______________

Short e Student Reading Selection

Review a, has, is, says, to, and you as sight words. Then children will be able to read the story alone.

Jeff Has a Net

Jeff has a net to get a . Bess says, "It is bad to get a  in a net. The  is sad in a net. A  that is not in a net is glad. What if a big  had a net and got you?"

Read the following numbered words. Ask children to listen to the final consonants and circle b, d, or p: 1. bed, 2. cab, 3. dab, 4. fed, 5. lab, 6. led, 7. pep, 8. red, 9. step.

1. b d p	4. b d p	7. b d p
2. b d p	5. b d p	8. b d p
3. b d p	6. b d p	9. b d p

Short e Student Reading Selection

After you review he, is, said, and the as sight words, children can read this story themselves.

Mel in the Well

Mel is a big, black cat. Mel ran in the grass in the sun. Mel had fun till he fell in the well. Ed said, "Nell, run pell mell. Get Dad. Tell Dad Mel is in the well." Nell ran and got Dad. Dad put a net on a big stick. He put it in the well. Mel got in the net. Dad got Mel and put Mel in the grass. Mel is a wet mess, but he is well. Nell said, "A black cat is not bad luck. Mel had good luck."

Tell children to circle the correct word under each picture. (This activity reinforces /ĕ/ and /ă/ differentation.)

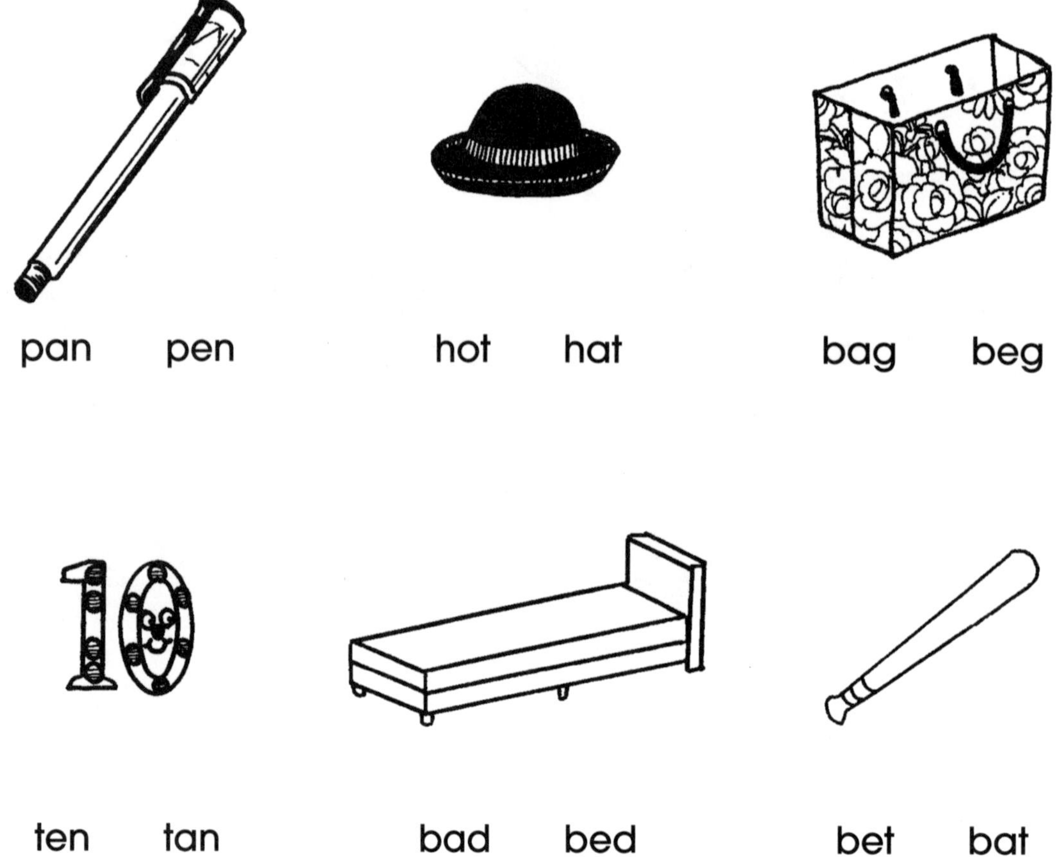

Short Vowel Student Reading Selection

Review a, I, is, said, the, *and* was *as sight words. Then children will be able to read this story alone.*

A Dog Is a Pal

Tess had a pal—Het. But Het's dad got a job in Japan, and Het left. Tess was sad, "I had a pal. Het and I sat in the sun and had a lot of fun." A black dog sniffs Tess's hand. Then the dog sniffs the hem of Tess's dress and licks Tess's chin and neck. Tess is glad. Tess said, "This dog is a pal. This dog and I can run and sit in the sun. A dog is fun!"

Tell children to circle the words that best describe each picture.

Het bats
Het bets

Big man
Big men

Black pen
Black pan

Bad kid
Big bed

Meg
Mag

Big bag
Man begs

Section 3

Long Vowels and Final Silent e

There was a zebra named Nate
who ate and ate and ate.

Name: ______________________________ Date: ______________ 3-98

ace 

Read the verse aloud and tell children to cover their faces with their hands when they hear the /ās/ sound as in face. Read the verse again and tell children to circle the letters that stand for the /ās/ sound.

There was a girl
Named Grace
Who covered her face
With flowers and lace
And people loved her
Everyplace.

Tell children to circle the name of the picture.

face race pace

place Grace trace

ice ace use

race lace face

race lace pace

Name: ______________________ Date: ______________ 3-99

ade

Read the verse aloud and tell children to pretend they are wading through deep grass when they hear the /ād/ sound as in wade. Read the verse again and tell children to circle the letters that stand for the /ād/ sound.

Let us wade
Through fields of jade
Where the flowers
Never fade,
And the sun is the
Color of lemonade.

Tell children to darken the circles under all words that rhyme with wade.

ade	made	race	place	sad	dad
○	○	○	○	○	○
ace	pad	glade	glad	lab	wade
○	○	○	○	○	○
jade	fad	Abe	fade	cab	came
○	○	○	○	○	○
mad	face	Babe	gab	cape	cane
○	○	○	○	○	○

Name: ______________________ Date: ____________

age

Read the verse aloud and tell children to pretend they're flying when they hear the sound of /āj/ as in cage. Read the verse again and tell children to circle the letters that stand for the long /a/ sound.

In a book
With many pages,
I read about birds
In golden cages.
They whispered to me,
"We want to be free,
We want to sit
In an apple tree.
We don't want to live
On a printed page.
We don't want to stay
In a golden cage."

Tell children to get to the playground by drawing a line between the words with long /a/ sounds.

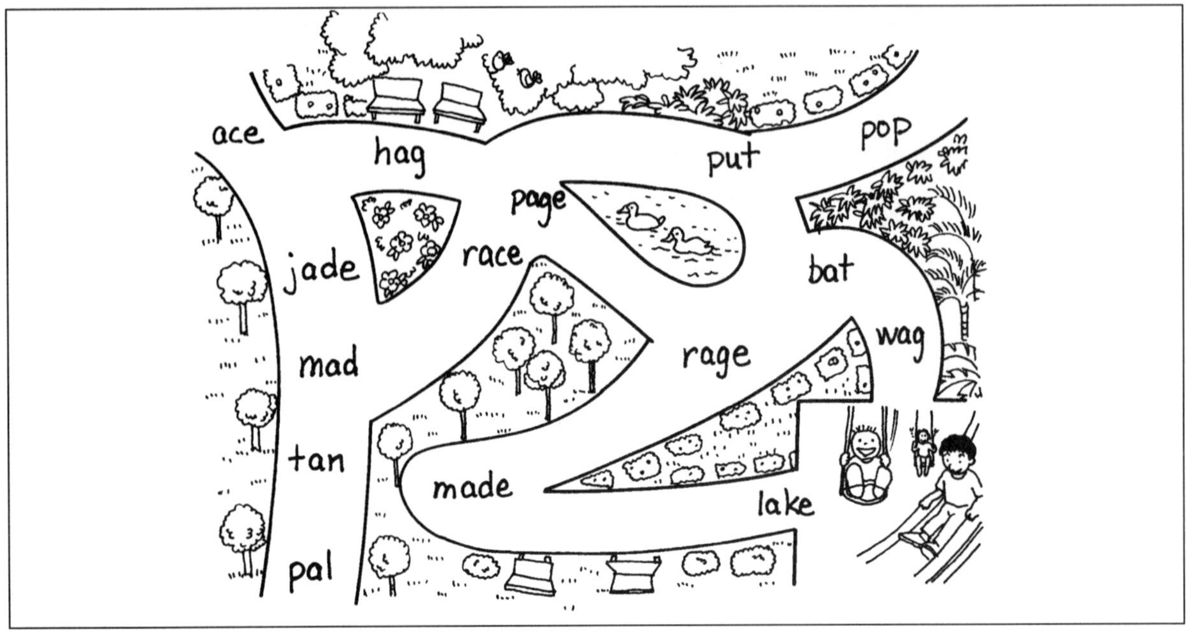

Name: ______________________ Date: ____________ 3-101

ake

Read the verse aloud and tell children to pretend they're shaking flour into a bowl when they hear the /āk/ sound as in <u>cake</u>*. Read the verse again and tell children to circle the letters that stand for /āk/.*

You take the sugar,
And I'll shake the flour.
And we'll make a cake
In half an hour.
We'll take it
And bake it
And mark it with J.
And then we will eat it,
Jake, Johnny, and Kay.

Tell children to circle all words that rhyme with <u>cake</u>*.*

bake Abe ace ade

age Babe cape

face fade page fake

lace lake

race made rage rake

pace wade wage

make wave ape take

Name: ______________________ Date: ____________ 3-102

ale

Read the verse aloud and tell children to blow as hard as they can when they hear the /āl/ sound as in <u>whale</u>. *Read the verse again and tell children to circle the letters that stand for the /āl/ sound.*

A whale is a mammal
Like you and like me.
A gale is a fast wind
On land and on sea.
A male is a person
We call him or he.
If you're white as a ghost,
You're certainly pale.
If your dad tells you a story,
He tells you a tale.
If mom wants to save money,
She goes to a sale.

Tell children to draw a line between each picture and the correct word.

bale
dale
gale
hale
male
pale
sale
tale
vale
whale

Name: ______________________ Date: ______________

ame

Read the verse aloud and tell children to scratch their heads when they hear the /ām/ sound as in game. Read the verse again and ask children to circle the letters that stand for the /ām/ sound.

I can't remember my teacher's name.
Is it Mr. Raner or Mr. Rame?
Mr. Fire or Mr. Flame?
I tried to remember.
It never came.
What in the world
Is my teacher's name?
Mr. Different or Mr. Same?
Mr. Wilder or Mr. Tame?
Well, tomorrow I'll hear
My teacher's name.

Tell children to complete the words under the pictures.

_____ ame

_____ ame

came
dame
fame
game
lame
name
same
tame

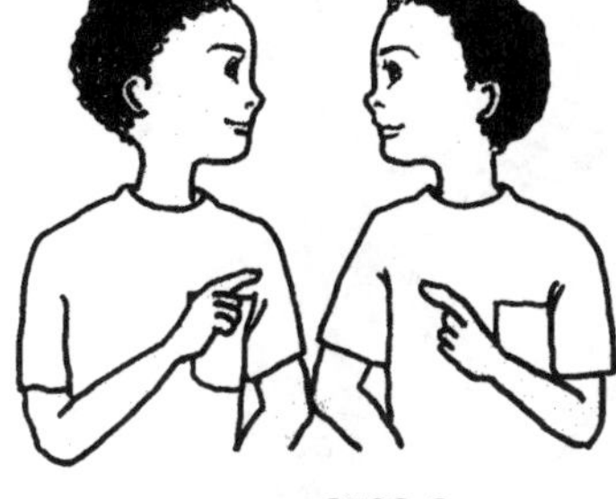

_____ ame

_____ ame

Name: ______________________ Date: ____________ 3-104

ane

Read the verse aloud and tell children to tap with their feet when they hear the /ān/ sound as in cane. Read the verse again and tell children to circle the letters that stand for the /ān/ sound.

Jane is six
And Dane's eleven.
Tommy Pane is eighty-
seven.
They're good friends
And like to talk.
Sometimes they even
Take a walk
Together down a sunny lane
With the tap, tap, tap
Of Tommy's cane.

Tell children to color the kites that have three rhyming words.

Name: ______________________ Date: ____________

ape

Read the verse aloud and tell children to open their mouths wide when they hear the /āp/ sound as in ape. *Read the verse again and tell children to circle the letters that stand for the /āp/ sound.*

At the circus
The children gape
At the clown
With the funny shape
And his friend
The dancing ape,
Who whirls and twirls
In a silver cape.

Tell the children to circle **yes** *if the words under the picture are correct, and* **no** *if they are wrong.*

Ape in cape. **YES NO**

Ape and grape. **YES NO**

Tape and ape. **YES NO**

Ape gapes. **YES NO**

Grapes and cape. **YES NO**

Shapes. **YES NO**

ase

Read the verse aloud and tell children to pretend they're batting a ball when they hear the /ās/ sound as in vase. *Read the verse again and ask children to circle the letters that stand for the /ās/ sound.*

Why is the red vase
On first base
With a suitcase?

Read the story aloud and ask children to circle the letters that stand for the /ās/ sound as in face *and* base.

Moving Day

On moving day, the mover said to Mom, "Do you have a place to put this case?"

Mom said, "Put the case anyplace."

I asked Mom, "What shall I do with Grandma's lace?"

Mom said, "Put the lace under the vase."

I said, "Here's the ace from our deck of cards. Where shall I put the ace?"

"For goodness sakes," Mom said. "Put the ace anyplace. Then go to the bathroom and wash your face. Walk slowly. Don't race. You're not running to first base."

ate

Read the verse aloud and tell children to open and close their mouths, pretending they are eating, when they hear the /āt/ sound as in gate. Read the verse again and tell children to circle the letters that stand for the /āt/ sound.

There was a zebra named Nate
Who ate and ate and ate.
He ate early and he ate late.
He ate a date
And a blackboard slate.
He ate a house,
And he ate the gate.
Finally he ate his crate,
This hungry zebra, Nate.

Tell children to circle **yes** *if the words under the picture are correct and* **no** *if they are wrong.*

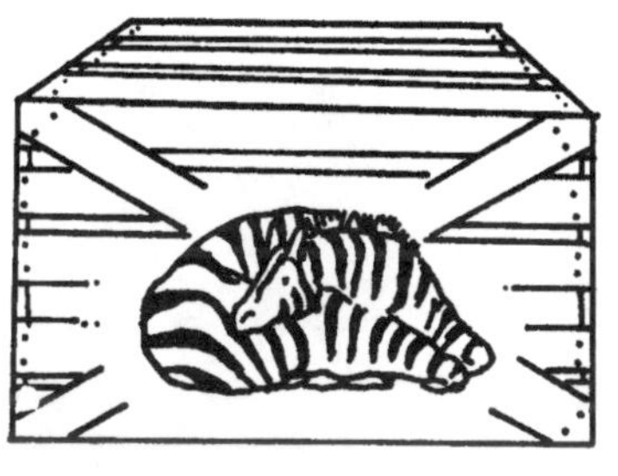

Nate in crate. **YES NO**

Nate ate crate. **YES NO**

Nate on gate. **YES NO**

Nate on crate. **YES NO**

Name: ______________________________ Date: ______________ 3-108

ave 

Read the verse aloud and tell children to pretend they are swimming in the sea when they hear the /āv/ sound as in Dave. *Read the verse again and tell children to circle the letters that stand for the /āv/ sound.*

In a cave
Near the waves
By the side of the sea,
Lived a boy by the name
Of Davy Dundee.
And here is what
He gave to me.
He gave me coral
That grows in the sea.
And he gave me fruit
From a mermaid's tree.

Tell children to circle the correct name of the picture.

aze 

Read the verse aloud and tell children to stare or gaze at the person next to them when they hear the /āz/ sound as in maze. *Read the verse again and tell children to circle the letters that stand for the /āz/ sound.*

The sun sets in a blaze of red sky.
I gaze and gaze
Dazed by the color of the sky
As the sun sets in a haze
Of orange and blue.
How about you?
Do you like to watch
The sunset too?

Tell children to put a circle around all the words that have the sound of /az/ as in maze.

gas	gaze		gab	gate
haze	hat		hate	ham
mate	mat		mad	made
date	dad	maze	dane	daze
back	blaze		base	bad

Name: ______________________ Date: __________ 3-110

Long a Student Reading Selection

Review have, said, and was as sight words. Tell children that the single, final s in as, is, and was has the /z/ sound. Children can read the story by themselves.

Jake

Nate had a big snake. His name was Jake. Kate said, "I hate snakes. I hate Jake." Nate was sad as Jake was his pal. Kate said, "Ick! It is sick to have a snake as a pet. A dog is a pet. A cat is a pet, not a snake." A [robber] came, a bad man. Kate and Nate ran, but Jake did not run. Jake sat on the red rug. The bad man said, "EEEE," and ran. Kate said, "Oh, Nate. I am glad Jake is a pal." Kate pats Jake and hugs him. Jake smiles.

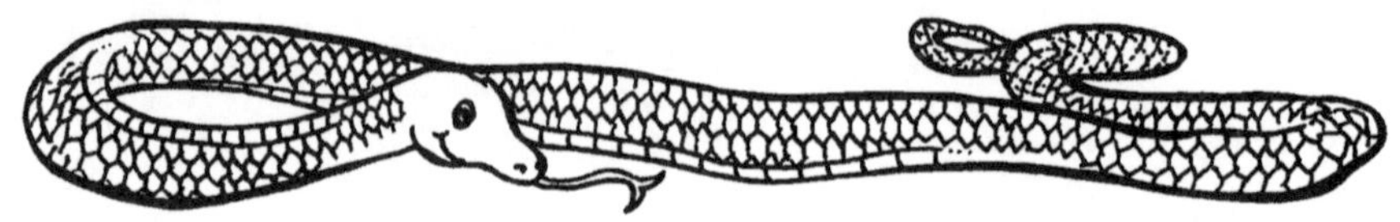

Tell children to look at the sets of pictures and words and circle D if they are different and S if they are the same.

1. [cap] cape D S
2. [hat] tame D S
3. [can] cane D S
4. [jam] James D S
5. [snake] snake D S
6. mat mate D S
7. snack snake D S
8. shake snake D S

Name: ______________________ Date: ____________ 3-111

ice

Read the verse aloud and tell children to pretend they are ice skating when they hear the /īs/ sound as in nice. *Read the verse again and tell children to circle the letters that stand for the /īs/ sound.*

The lake frosted with ice
Is very nice.
It looks like
A plate of rice
Or a field of white mice.
Take my advice
And look once or twice
Before warm weather
Melts the ice.

Tell children to print the correct word in each blank.

ice
dice
mice
nice
price
rice
slice

1. Ice is ______________.
2. ______________ can run.
3. ______________ are in a game.
4. ______________ is on my plate.

Tell children to print the correct word under each picture.

____

____

Name: ______________________ Date: ____________ 3-112

ide

Read the verse aloud and tell children to hide their faces in their hands when they hear the /īd/ sound as in bride. *Read the verse again and tell children to circle the letters that stand for the /īd/ sound.*

Did you ever hide in a wave?
Did you ever ride on a wave?
Did you ever ride with the tide
To the cool ocean side?
Did you ever find a shell
Shaped like a bell
On the cool sea side?
And another shell
With a mouth so wide
A baby bird could hide inside?

Tell children they are going to play bingo. They can shout "Bingo" when they draw a line between four rhyming words. The line can be up, down, or diagonal.

ride	ice	nice	rice
ace	tide	bride	slide
save	rave	wide	made
face	lace	case	hide

ife

Read the verse aloud and tell children to pretend they're running when they hear the /īf/ sound as in knife. *Read the verse again and tell children to circle the letters that stand for the /īf/ sound.*

If you see a pirate
With a knife,
Run for your life.
Would you like to meet
The pirate's wife?

Read the Mother Goose rhyme to the children and ask them to circle the letters that stand for the /īf/ sound as in knife *and the /īs/ sound as in* nice.

Three blind mice, three blind mice,

See how they run, see how they run.

They all ran after the farmer's wife.

She cut off their tails with a carving knife.

Did you ever see such a sight in your life,

As three blind mice.

Name: ______________________ Date: ____________ 3-114

ike 

Read the verse aloud and tell children to pretend they are pedaling a bike when they hear the /īk/ sound as in bike. *Read the verse again and tell children to circle the letters that stand for the /īk/ sound.*

Patty Pike
Likes to hike
In the woods
With her brother Mike.
Patty also likes to bike
To Grandma's house
Along with Mike.

Tell children to circle **yes** *if the words under the picture are correct and* **no** *if the words are wrong.*

Mike on bike. **YES** **NO**

Bike on Mike. **YES** **NO**

Ike and Mike. **YES** **NO**

Pat likes Mike. **YES** **NO**

Name: ______________________ Date: __________

ile

Read the verse aloud and tell children to smile when they hear the /īl/ sound as in smile*.*
Read the verse again and tell children to circle the letters that stand for the /īl/ sound.

Can a crocodile
smile?
Maybe for awhile,
Home on the Nile.

Tell children to circle the word in each group that doesn't fit. Then ask them why the words they circled don't fit. Tell them to make as many sentences as they can with the leftover words, using another sheet of paper. They can use is *or* are *in the sentences. Example: Bill is nice.*

ill fill Nile will	rake back sack tack	win fine dine mine	lick sick Dick Mike
ride hide hid wide	rim dim dime him	mile Nile dill file	Dick ice mice nice

Name: ______________________ Date: ____________ 3-116

ime

Read the verse aloud and tell children to pretend they are looking at their watches when they hear the /īm/ sound as in dime. *Read the verse again and tell children to circle the letters that stand for the /īm/ sound.*

I'll give you a dime
For every chime
From the big town clock
In summertime.

Read the following numbered words to the children. Ask them to circle **M** *beside the number if they hear the /īm/ sound as in* dime *and* **N** *if they hear the /īn/ sound as in* dine*: 1. dime, 2. dine, 3. fine, 4. lime, 5. line, 6. mine, 7. nine, 8. time, 9. summertime, 10. pine, 11. spine, 12. crime, 13. grime, 14. wine, 15. vine, 16. anytime.*

1. m n	5. m n	9. m n	13. m n
2. m n	6. m n	10. m n	14. m n
3. m n	7. m n	11. m n	15. m n
4. m n	8. m n	12. m n	16. m n

Name: ______________________ Date: __________

ine

Tell children to fill in the missing letters of /īn/ words as you read the verse. After the children have finished, read the verse again and tell children to circle the letters that stand for the /īn/ sound as in pine.

Let's think of words that
Rhyme with nine.
When something's good,
We say it's _ine.
Another word for eat
Is _ine.
Things in a row are in a _ine.
A kind of tree is a _ine.
It belongs to me,
So it is _ine.
If the sun is bright,
We watch it _ _ine.
I love you,
Be my valen _ine.

Tell children to put the listed words in the correct spaces in the grid.

dine

shine

pines

mine

line

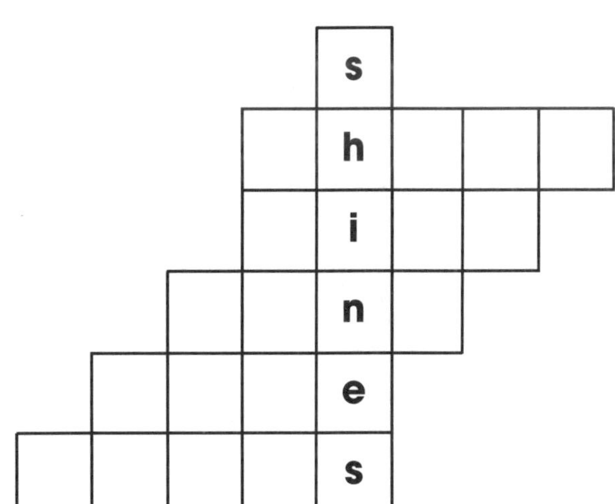

Name: ______________________ Date: ____________

ite

Read the verse aloud and tell children to pretend they are writing a letter when they hear the /īt/ sound as in kite. Read the verse again and tell children to circle the letters that stand for the /īt/ sound.

Our teacher, Mrs. White,
Taught us how to write
A letter that's polite.
It begins, "Dear Ted,"
And ends,

Sincerely,
Ned

Tell children to print the correct long i word under each picture.

dine
kite
knife
life
mice
mile
pine
ride
side
smile
vine

____

____

ive 5

Read the verse aloud and tell children to raise five fingers each time they hear the /īv/ sound as in five. Read the verse again and tell children to circle the letters that stand for the /īv/ sound.

Five Bees

It was sunny. They went for a drive. Mom and Dad and the kids made five. They were happy to be alive, until Dad saw a big beehive. Five bees came from afar. They flew buzzing into the car. Dad quickly hit the brake. How long did it take for a family of five to run for their lives? And the bees came after. They ran to a barn with open rafters. They dived right in, and the bees dived after. Then they ran out another door, and left five bees upon the floor.

Tell children to draw a circle around each word that has the same vowel sound as in the names of the pictures.

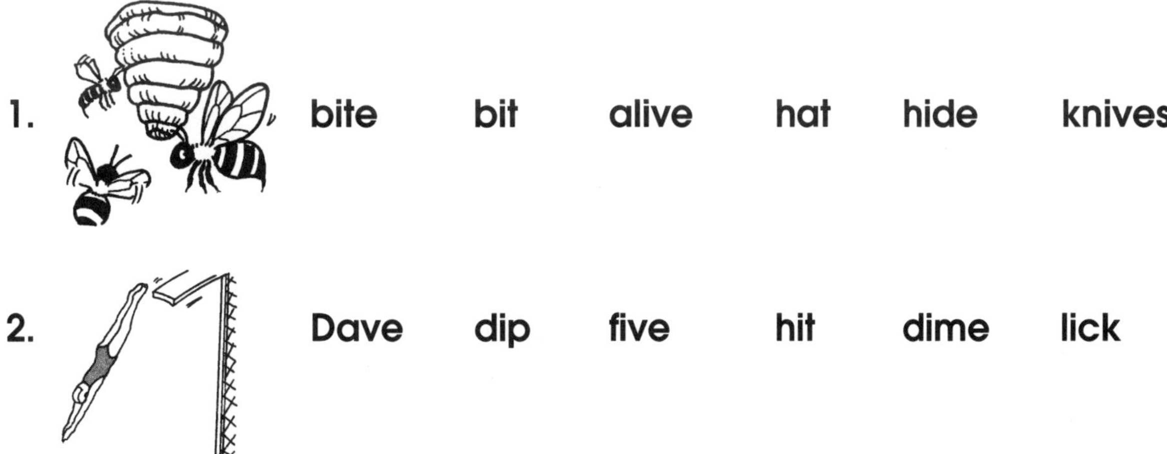

1. bite bit alive hat hide knives

2. Dave dip five hit dime lick

Name: ______________________ Date: ____________ 3-120

Long i Student Reading Selection

Review he, the, and to as sight words. Ask children to tell you things they like that have the /ī/ sound as in line. Then tell them they can read about all the things Mike likes.

Mike Likes

Mike likes to hike. He likes to pile rocks on top of rocks. He likes to suck on a lime. He likes to skate on ice. He likes to hide in the grass. He likes to get a dime when he cuts grass. He likes to wipe a ripe (apple) so it will shine. He likes to bite the (apple).

Tell children to work the puzzle below.

Across

1. 9

2. 

3. 

4. 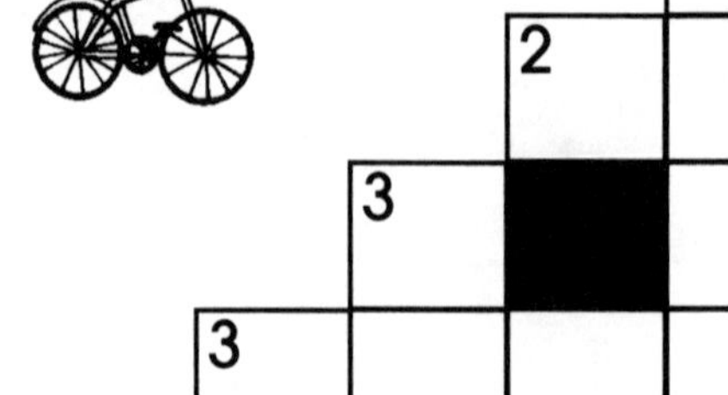

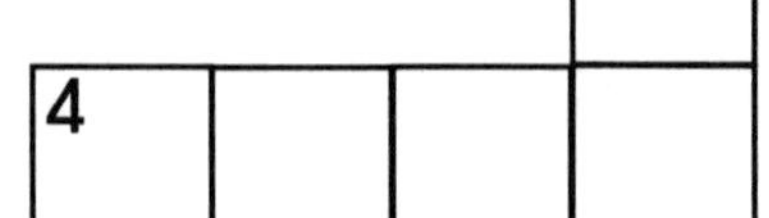

Down

1. 

2. 

3. 

oke 

Read the verse aloud and tell children to pretend they are lightly and playfully poking someone when they hear the /ōk/ sound as in broke. Read the verse again and tell children to circle the letters that stand for /ōk/.

My friend, Joe Bloke,
Gave me a poke.
When I got mad,
He smiled and spoke,
"Easy man,
It's just a joke."

Tell children to print rhymes for each word.

1. robe ___ ___ ___ ___ ___
2. code ___ ___ ___ ___
3. hole ___ ___ ___ ___, ___ ___ ___ ___,
   ___ ___ ___ ___, ___ ___ ___ ___ ___
4. spoke ___ ___ ___ ___ ___, ___ ___ ___ ___,
   ___ ___ ___ ___, ___ ___ ___ ___
5. home ___ ___ ___ ___, ___ ___ ___ ___
6. alone ___ ___ ___ ___, ___ ___ ___ ___

bone
broke
cone
dome
globe
joke
mole
poke
pole
rode
role
Rome
whole
woke

Name: ______________________ Date: ____________ 3-122

ole

Read the verse aloud and tell children to sing like birds when they hear the /ōl/ sound as in pole. Read the verse again and tell children to circle the letters that stand for the /ōl/ sound.

Shoe Sole and Jelly Role
Sat together on a pole.
They watched Mr. Danny Mole
Who lived below them in a hole.

Explain the marks for long and short vowels. Tell children to mark each vowel. They will have bingo if they have a line of long or short vowels going up, down, or diagonally.

hole	rob	sock	joke	home
rock	rose	Rome	on	hose
note	Tom	rode	dome	got
pot	sob	Don	mole	cone
not	bone	hot	cob	pole

Name: ______________________ Date: ____________

ome 

Read the verse aloud and tell children to pretend they are eating Italian ice when they hear the /ōm/ sound as in dome. Read the verse again and tell children to circle the letters that stand for the /ōm/ sound.

I went to Rome with Mom and Dad.
The nicest trip I ever had.
We ate food with funny spice,
And then we had Italian ice.
I saw a fountain and a dome
And things we do not have at home.

Tell children to print the name of each picture. Then have them circle the names in the list that have the long o sound that is in dome.

broke
cock
code
home
pole
rob
robe
rod
stone

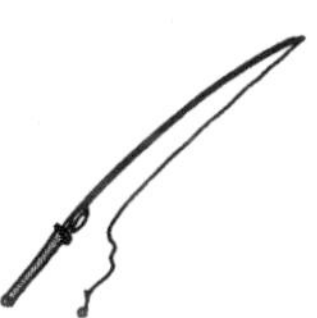

____

____

A = ○
B = □
C = ▽

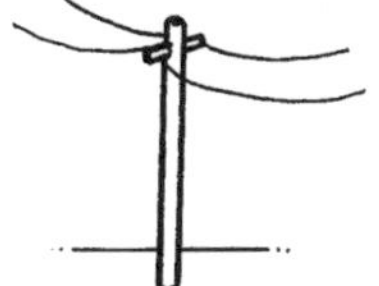

____

____

Name: ______________________ Date: __________ 3-124

one

Read the verse aloud and tell children to circle all words that have the long o sound as in bone or woke.

Yesterday I walked alone
And gave a hungry dog a bone.
I had a chocolate ice cream cone
But didn't want to be alone.
Then my friend came and walked with me
And smiled and laughed
And talked to me,
And I was happy as could be.

Read the following numbered words aloud and ask children to print **m** *or* **n** *in the blank space: 1. alone, 2. bone, 3. cone, 4. phone, 5. Rome, 6. home, 7. tone, 8. stone.*

1. alo___e
2. bo___e
3. co___e
4. pho___e
5. Ro___e
6. ho___e
7. to___e
8. sto___e

ope

Read the verse aloud and tell children to pretend they are whirling a lasso when they hear the /ōp/ sound as in rope. *Read the verse again and tell children to circle the letters that stand for the /ōp/ sound.*

The way to catch
An antelope
Is to do it
With a rope.

Tell children to circle the correct word under each picture.

rope mope vote

stone alone tone

hope hose rose

vote mole note

nose close rose

note nose pose

ose

Read the verse aloud and tell children to put their hands over their noses when they hear the /ōz/ sound as in rose. *Read the verse again and tell children to circle the letters that stand for the /ōz/ sound.*

Mom said,
"Let's go out and shovel snow
And make three snowmen in a row.
One can have a carrot nose.
And you and the snowmen
All can pose with a muffler
'Round your nose
So it won't get redder than a rose."

Tell children to put the short sound mark (˘) next to words that have the sound of /ŏ/ as in pot *and the long sound mark (–) next to words that have the sound of ō as in* rose.

Name: ______________________ Date: ____________

Long o and long u Student Reading Selection

Review her, said, the, you *and* your *as sight words. Explain that* s *as in* as *has the /z/ sound. Then children can read the story by themselves.*

The Note

Tom wrote a cute note to Rose. He put the note on an ice cube. He put the ice cube in a . He put the note and the ice cube in a tube. He put a rose in the tube. He wrote the note in code. He said, "I put the note on an ice cube as the sun is hot. I put a rose in the tube as your name is Rose. Put the rose in your . I ♡ you."

Tell children to circle the words that have the /ō/ sound as in rose *and the /u/ sound as in* cute.

cut

us

not

tub

rod

cub

tune

tube

note

robe

ton

tug

rode

mud

use

tone

rob

cube

cute

mule

Name: ______________________ Date: ______________

u

Read the sentences aloud and tell children to print the missing letters. Sometimes u has the sound of /yōō/ in cube, other times the sound of ōō in rude.

1. Toothpaste comes in a ___ube.
2. Ice can come in ___ubes.
3. If you're not polite, you're ___ude.
4. Have you ever broken a ___ule?
5. Have you ever ridden a ___ule?
6. Have you ever looked at the moon and sung a pretty ___une?

cubes
tubes
mule
rude
rule
tune

Tell children to print the correct missing letters in the blanks.

___ube **rst**

___ube **bcd**

___uge **fgh**

___ule **lmn**

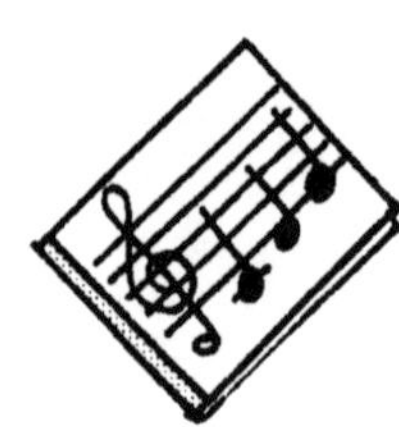

___une **rst**

___ute **bcd**

cube
cute
huge
mule
tube
tune

Name: ______________________ Date: __________ 3-129

a,e,i,o,u

This is a long and short vowel differentiation activity. Have children make long vowel words by adding e to short vowel words. Then have children read both words in each pair.

1. at	___ ___ ___	16. hid	___ ___ ___ ___
2. rat	___ ___ ___ ___	17. dim	___ ___ ___ ___
3. cat	K ___ ___ ___	18. bit	___ ___ ___ ___
4. can	___ ___ ___ ___	19. rip	___ ___ ___ ___
5. Dan	D ___ ___ ___	20. din	___ ___ ___ ___
6. fat	___ ___ ___ ___	21. fin	___ ___ ___ ___
7. fad	___ ___ ___ ___	22. rid	___ ___ ___ ___
8. gal	___ ___ ___ ___	23. hop	___ ___ ___ ___
9. hat	___ ___ ___ ___	24. rod	___ ___ ___ ___
10. mad	___ ___ ___ ___	25. not	___ ___ ___ ___
11. pan	___ ___ ___ ___	26. rob	___ ___ ___ ___
12. Sam	___ ___ ___ ___	27. cod	___ ___ ___ ___
13. cap	___ ___ ___ ___	28. pet	P ___ ___ ___
14. Jan	J ___ ___ ___	29. cut	___ ___ ___ ___
15. pin	___ ___ ___ ___	30. tub	___ ___ ___ ___

Name: ______________________________ Date: ______________ 3-130

a,e,i,o,u

This is a long and short vowel differentiation activity. Explain the long and short vowel symbols (¯ and ˘). Tell children to put the correct marks over the first vowel in each word.

can	same	cat
at	cap	cane
hat	**a**	cape
pan	Kate	pane
hate	Sam	ate

mop	hop	code
rod	note	robe
cone	**o**	mope
cod	hope	con
rode	not	rob

ride	pin	hid
fine	bit	dim
hide	**i**	ripe
rip	rid	bite
fin	dime	pine

cute	pet	cub
cube	**e**	dud
mete	**u**	cut
jut	dude	sun
Pete	jute	met

Section 4
Final Long Vowels

I climbed up the apple tree
To get some fruit for Bess and me.

Name: ______________________________ Date: ______________

e, ee

Tell children that both e *and* ee *stand for the /ē/ sound in* bee*. Read the verse aloud and tell children to buzz like bees when they hear the /ē/ sound as in* bee*. Read the verse again and tell children to circle the letters that stand for the /ē/ sound.*

I climbed up the apple tree
To get some fruit for Bess and me.
What did I see in the apple tree?
A great big honey bee!
He buzzed and buzzed and buzzed
  at me.
I was as scared as I could be
And climbed right down
  the apple tree.
I can remember to this day
How we screamed and ran away.

Tell children to circle the pictures whose names have the /ē/ sound.

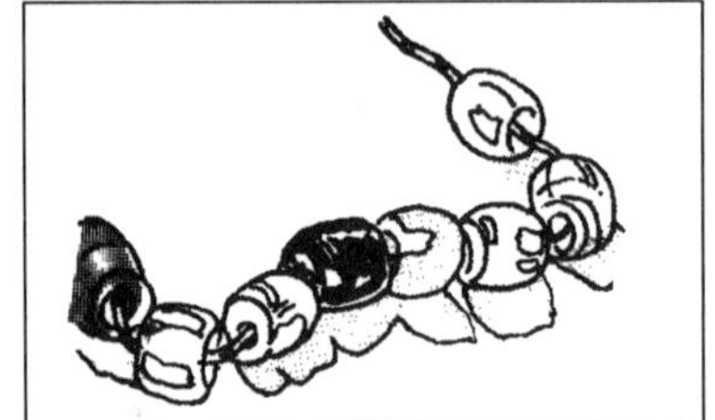

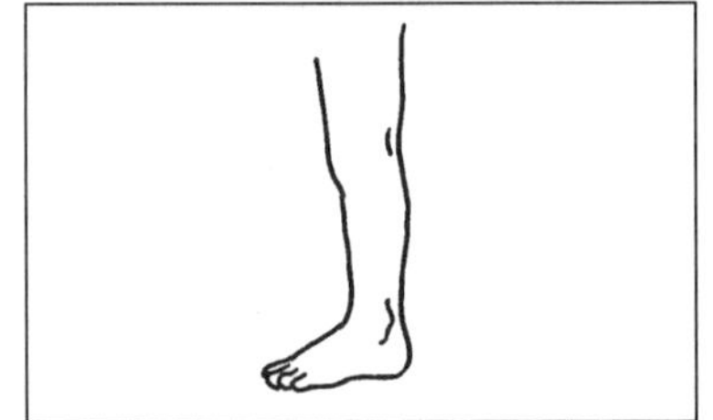

Name: ______________________ Date: ____________ 4-132

Read the verse aloud and tell children to shout "No" when they hear the /ō/ sound as in hippo. Read the verse again and tell children to circle the letter that stands for the /ō/ sound.

There was a hippo named Zo
Whose favorite word was NO.
He said,
"Before I go,
I first say no,
And then I go."

Tell children to circle the words that have the sound of /ō/ as in hippo and no. Tell them to circle the pictures whose names have the /ō/ sound.

Bob
go
rock

sock
loaf
so

load
rose
pole

hole
rope
hose

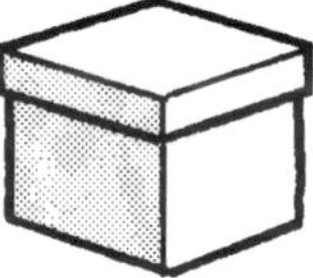

lock
road
hose

low
rode
ho ho

note
Rome
home

mow
dome
frock

Name: ______________________ Date: ____________

o, oa

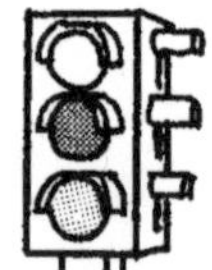

Read the verse aloud. Explain that both o and oa stand for the /ō/ sound in go. Tell children to say "whoa" when they hear the /ō/ sound. Read the verse again and tell children to circle letters that stand for the /ō/ sound.

A girl had a horse
By the name of Mo.
She said to her horse,
"Whoa, horsie, whoa."
But the horse said, "No,
I really want to go."
So the girl said,
"Giddy-yap, horsie, go."

Tell children to print a large O on all pictures whose names have the sound of /ō/ as in go.

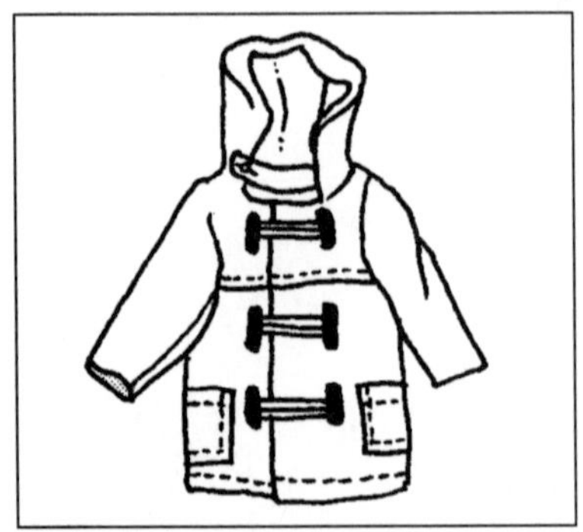

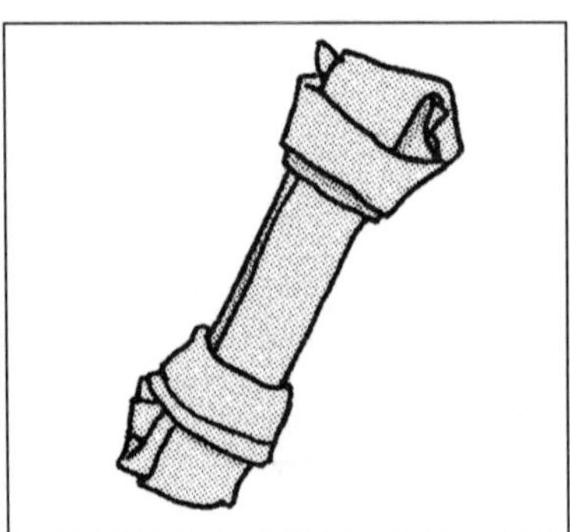

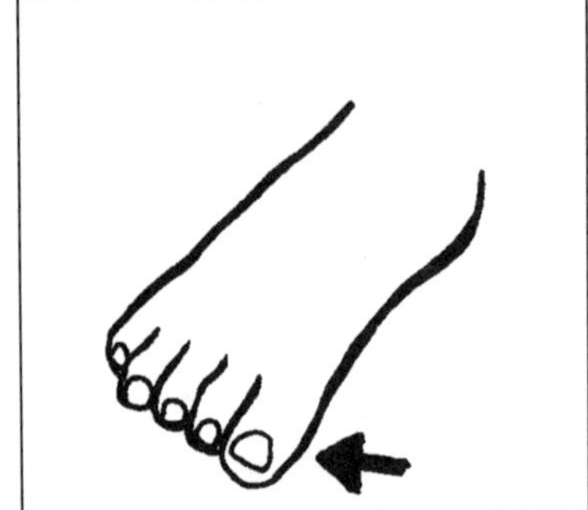

Section 5
Long Vowel Teams

It is really like a dream.
You see, we have a winning team.

Rule for children: Two vowels together came—
The second was silent,
The first said its name.

aid

Read the verse aloud and tell children to pretend they are afraid when they hear the /ād/ sound as in braid. *To show fear, they might open their eyes and mouths wide or put their arms over their faces. Read the verse a second time and ask children to circle the letters that stand for the /ād/ sound.*

I had a dream.
I was afraid
Of a big, bad man
In a pirate raid.
He had a patch on one eye.
I knew that I might even cry,
Until my dad came to my aid.
He said, "It's a dream.
Don't be afraid."

Tell children to print the correct words in the blanks.

afraid
aid
braid
laid
maid
mermaid
paid
raid

1. Dad ___ ___ ___ ___ the man.
2. I was af___ ___ ___ ___ in the 

   ___ ___ ___ ___.
3. A mer___ ___ ___ ___ has a  .
4. I ___ ___ ___ ___ the 

   on the 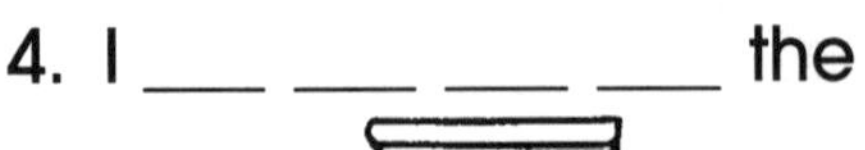 .
5. Kim has two ___ ___ ___ ___ ___s.

ail 

Read the verse aloud and tell children to pretend they are fish swimming in the water when they hear the /ā/ sound as in pail. *Read the verse again and tell children to circle the letters that stand for the /ā/ sound.*

At the Aquarium

I saw a fish with a polka-dot tail.
I saw a fish with fins like a sail.
I saw a fish shaped like a pail.
I saw a fish with a nose like a nail
And another fish as long as a rail
Who had a friend that belonged in jail
Because he had stripes on his back
And his tail.

Tell children to identify each fish in the space below the picture. Tell them to use the words sailfish, jailfish, nailfish, etc.

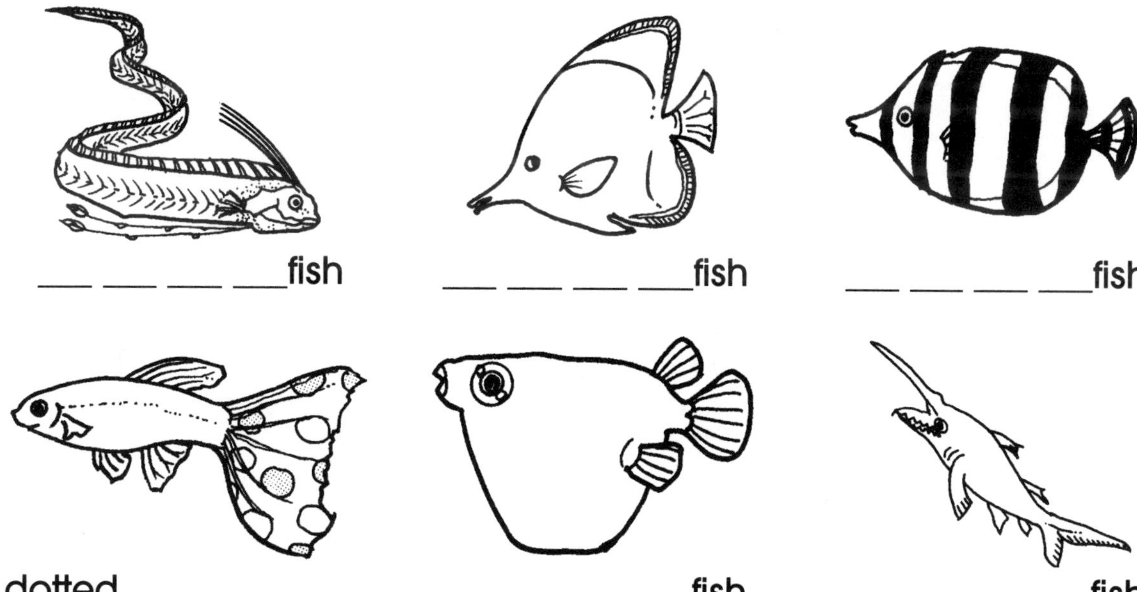

Name: ______________________ Date: ______________

ail, ale

Tell children that ail *and* ale *both stand for the /ā/ sound as in* pail. *Read the verses aloud and ask children to circle all letters that stand for the /ā/ sound.*

Dale went to the mailbox
To get the mail,
But he couldn't get it
Because of the hail.

Dale liked a sailboat
With a white sail,
But it blew away
In a furious gale.

Dale liked a puppy
Because of his tail,
But the owner told him
It wasn't for sale.

Dale went fishing
To catch a whale
But the water was in
His mother's pail.

Tell children to circle the correct word for each sentence.

1. Her face is (pale, pail).
2. I like to get (mail, male).
3. A man is (mail, male).
4. A runs on a (rail, hail).
5. Mom saves at a (sale, sail).
6. A dog has a (tale, tail).
7. A (wail, whale) is big.
8. I hit the (nail, male) with a .
9. 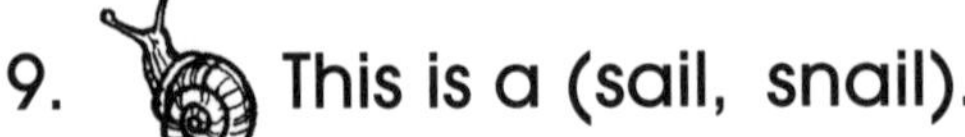 This is a (sail, snail).
10. I like to (sale, sail) on the lake.

Name: ______________________ Date: ____________ 5-137

ain

Read the verse aloud and tell children to make choo-choo train noises when they hear the /ān/ sound as in <u>train</u>. Read the verse again and tell children to circle the letters that stand for the ān/ sound.

Riding a train is lots of fun.
You get to meet most everyone.
But the main thing I really love,
My upper berth fits like a glove.
When I've lain down to sleep,
Best of all I like to peep
Out the window in the rain
As mountain tops and level plains
Fly past me on the speeding train.

Print the word that tells about each picture.

chain

pain

plain

rain

train

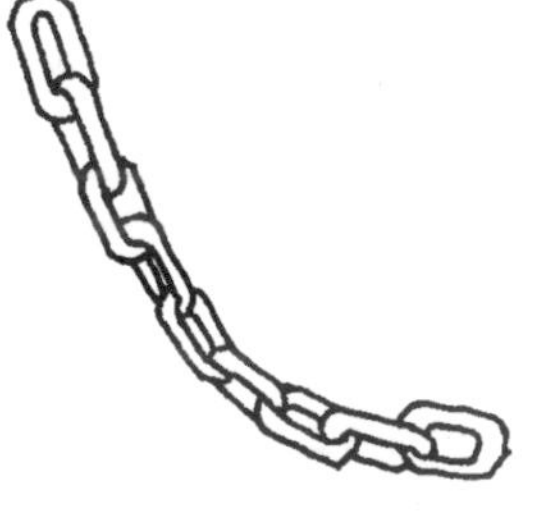

___ ___ ___ ___ ___

___ ___ ___ ___

___ ___ ___ ___ ___

___ ___ ___ ___

___ ___ ___ ___ ___

Name: ______________________ Date: ____________ 5-138

ai Student Reading Selection

Tell children that when you say, "Knock, knock. Who's there?" they must answer with ai words that have the /ā/ sound. After playing this game for a while, have each child read one of the answers below after you read the question. After you review you, of, with, who, and for as sight words, children can read the answers by themselves.

Knock, Knock. Who's There?

1. Gail
2. Mrs. Cain
3. Mrs. Lain
4. The mailman
5. The maid
6. A jail 
7. Rain and hail
8. A raid
9. A hen that laid an egg
10. A man in pain
11. A man who can't wait
12. A man you paid to get the mail
13. A man with bail for a son in jail
14. A man with a pail of nails
15. A pup that wags his tail and hits the 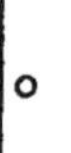
16. A man who needs aid
17. A man afraid of rain
18. The King of Spain 

Name: ____________________ Date: __________ 5-139

ay 

Read the verse aloud and tell children to pretend they're jumping in the hay when they hear the /ā/ sound as in hay. Read the verse again and tell children to circle the letters that stand for the /ā/ sound.

Jay said to May, "What do you say?
Would you like to play
Sometime today
In the barn, in the hay?"
May said, "Okay."
So they played all day
In mountains of hay.

Tell children to circle the word that best fits the picture.

bay pay gay

Jay hay say

hay Ray pay

day pay way

May pay way

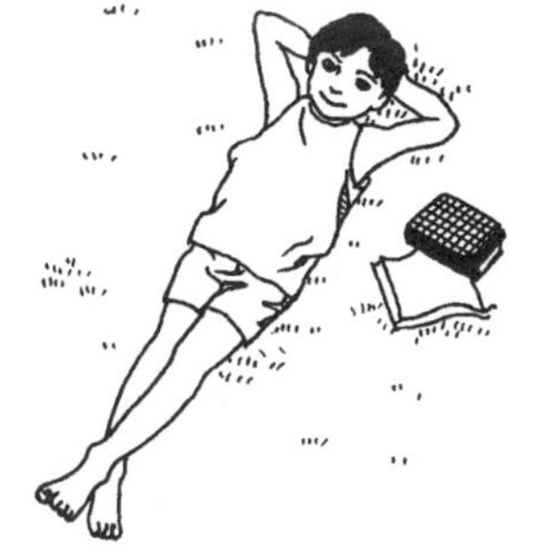

stay day pay

ea 

Read the verse aloud and ask children to clap when they hear the /ē/ sound as in tea. Read the verse again and ask children to circle the letters that stand for the /ē/ sound.

How many dolphins swim in the sea?

How many leaves make a cup of tea?

How many peas grow in a pod?

How many ladies' hats are odd?

Explain to children that different letters also stand for the /ē/ sound in tea. Ask children to circle the pictures whose names have the /ē/ sound.

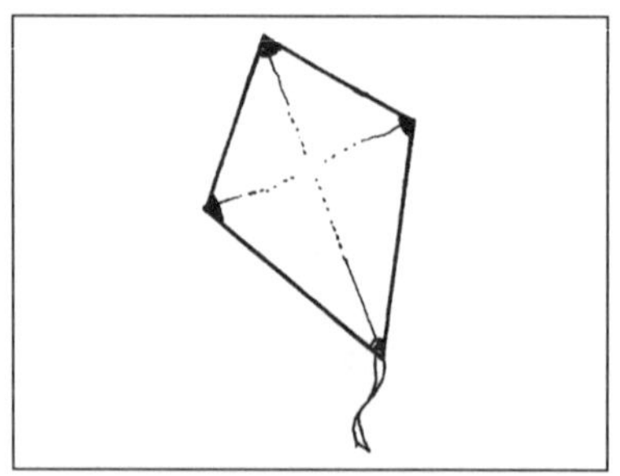

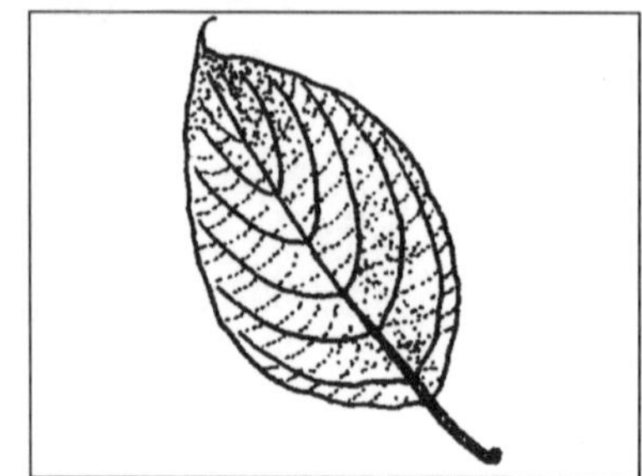

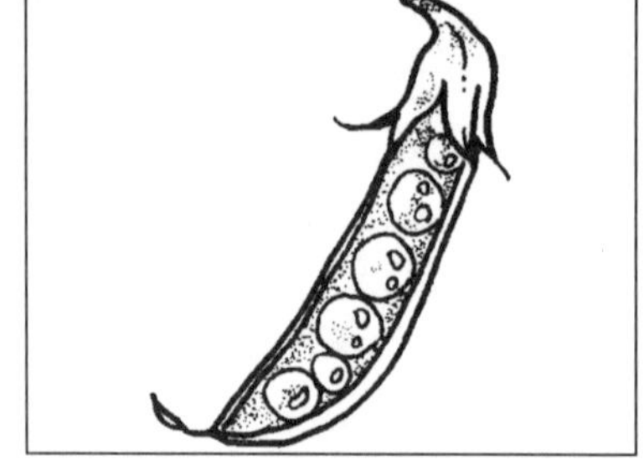

Name: ______________________ Date: ____________ 5-141

ead

Read the verse aloud and tell children to pretend they're reading a book when they hear the /ēd/ sound as in read. Read the verse again and tell children to circle the letters that stand for the /ēd/ sound.

I'll follow if you will lead.
All we want is a book to read.
If you'll lead, I'll follow,
And we'll be in Narnia tomorrow.

Tell children to circle the pictures whose names have the long e sound as in bead.

Name: ______________________ Date: ____________

eak

Read the verse aloud and tell children to make birdsong noises when they hear the /ēk/ sound as in beak. Read the verse again and tell children to circle the letters that stand for the /ēk/ sound.

In the cold and in the sleet,
A parrot with a yellow beak
Sat upon a mountain peak.
He was tired and he was weak.
He couldn't sing, but he could speak.
"Take me away
From this mountain peak.
Take me to the sun and flowers,
And I'll be singing in half an hour."

Tell children to print the correct /ēk/ words in the blanks.

1. The  has a ___ ___ ___ ___.

2. The top of a  is a ___ ___ ___ ___.

3. The  is ___ ___ ___ ___.

4. The  can ___ ___ ___ ___ ___.

beak
leak
peak
speak
weak

Name: ______________________ Date: ____________ 5-143

eal

Read the verse and tell children to squeal or yelp like a dog when they hear the /ēl/ sound as in meal. *Read the verse again and tell children to circle the letters that stand for the /ēl/ sound.*

Biff had dog food for his meal.
I had roasted corn and veal.
I left the table to answer the phone.
Biff was in the room alone.
He jumped on the table and tried to steal
My delicious corn and veal.
I said, "Biff, you mustn't steal.
You have your own delicious meal."
Then poor Biff began to squeal,
"Dog food simply isn't real,
Dog food isn't a real meal."

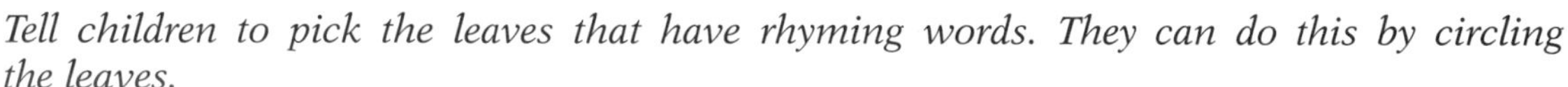

Tell children to pick the leaves that have rhyming words. They can do this by circling the leaves.

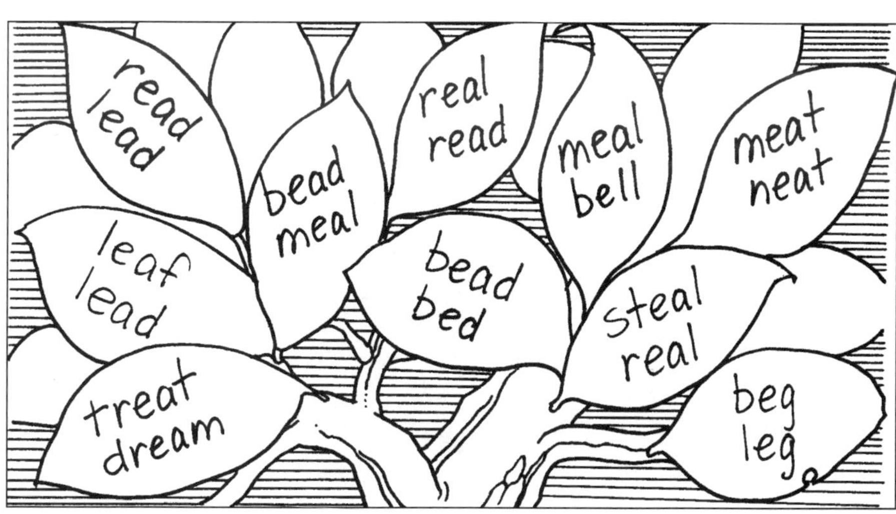

Name: ______________________________ Date: ____________ 5-144

eam 

Read the verse aloud and tell children to pretend they are batting baseballs when they hear the /ēm/ sound as in cream*. Read the verse again and tell children to circle the letters that stand for the /ēm/ sound.*

Patty Bream and Meg and Mo
Are the nicest kids I know.
It is really like a dream.
You see, we have a winning team.
Mom and Dad were in the bleachers.
I heard the screams and the screeches.
Pat hit the ball with all her might
And ran just like a beam of light.
A homer! And the bases loaded.
My poor head almost exploded.
I dropped my drink and my ice cream.
It was really like a dream.
You see, we had a winning team.

ean

Read the story aloud and tell children to pretend they're cleaning a room (sweeping or washing walls) when they hear the /ēn/ sound as in bean. Read the story a second time and tell children to circle the letters that stand for the /ēn/ sound.

Mom told Dean and Jean to clean their rooms. Dean said, "It's too nice a day to clean my room." Jean said, "I'll clean it tonight after we play." Mom said, "NOW! Clean your rooms now. Then you can play." Jean said, "Oh, Mom, you're mean." Dean said, "I think you're mean, too." But Dean and Jean cleaned their rooms. When they came back after playing baseball, they were hot and tired. They were glad their rooms were clean.

Tell children to draw lines between the pictures and the words that describe them.

- Beam ●
- Bean ●
- Clean ●
- Cream ●
- Dean ●
- Dream ●
- Gleam ●
- Jean ●
- Mean ●
- Scream ●
- Stream ●
- Team ●

Name: ______________________ Date: ____________ 5-146

eat 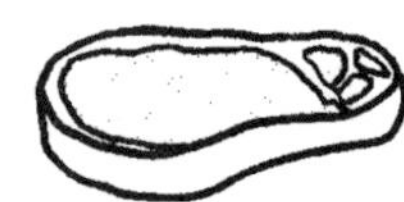

Read the verse aloud and tell children to pretend they are eating when they hear the /ē̄t/ sound as in meat. Read the verse again and tell children to circle the letters that stand for the /ēt/ sound.

I asked my mom for something to eat.
A really very special treat.
She said, "We'll make us
something neat.
You beat the eggs, and I'll add
the meat.
We'll go to the oven and turn on
the heat.
Then we'll sift some nice wheat
flour,
And we'll have meatballs in half
an hour."

Tell children to color the balloons that have two long e words, the sound of e as in meat.

ea Student Reading Activity

Children can do this activity by themselves as there are no unfamiliar words. Tell children to read each group of words and pick the word that doesn't belong. For example, in number 1, meat and veal are food. Seat is not.

Which Word Doesn't Belong?

1. meat veal seat
2. rain sea nail
3. pea bean read
4. beak tail bean
5. maid mailman deal
6. weak mean jail neat
7. Gail Jean Jake
8. heat rain hail real
9. leaf weed seal
10. Dean Jake Jean

Tell children to circle the pictures whose names have the /ē/ sound as in meat. Mention that the /ē/ sound can be spelled in different ways: /ē/ as in meat, seed, he, Pete.

bee	read
bread	seal
head	seat
meat	tea
pet	weed
Pete	

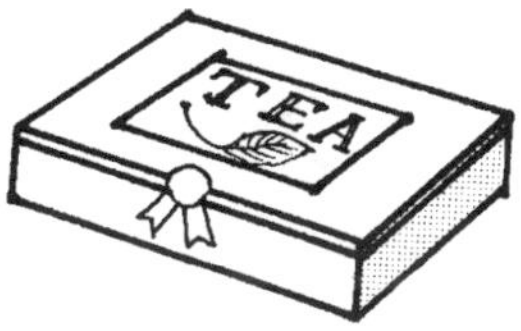

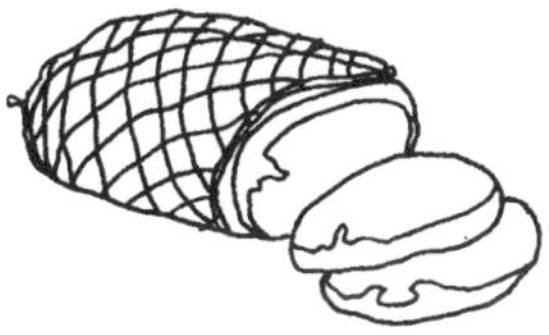

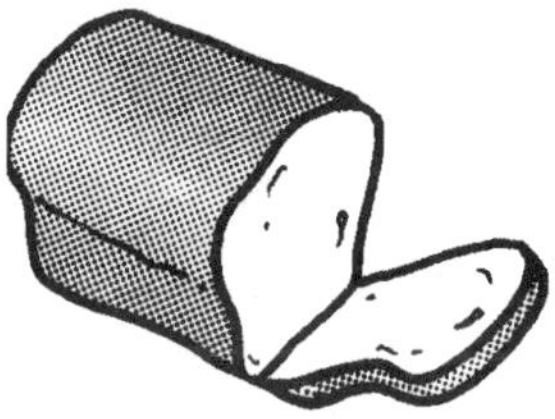

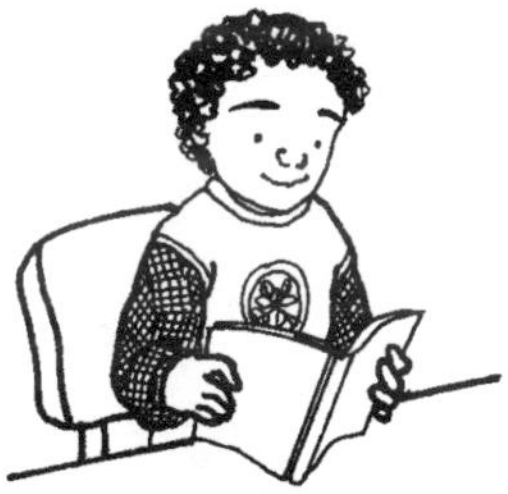

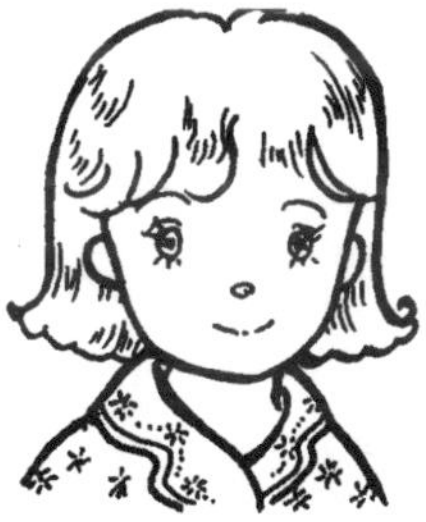

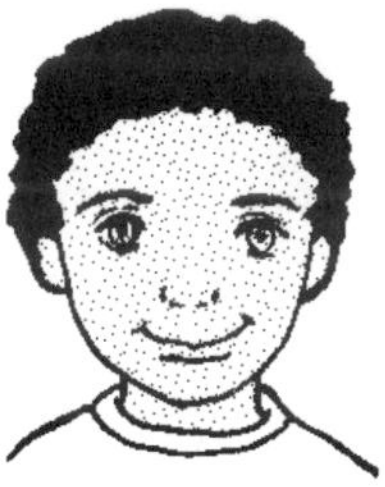

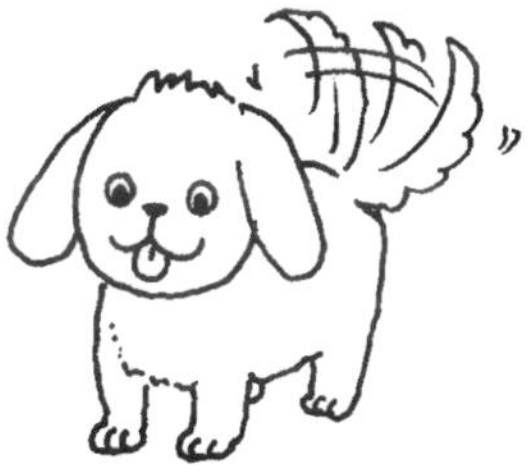

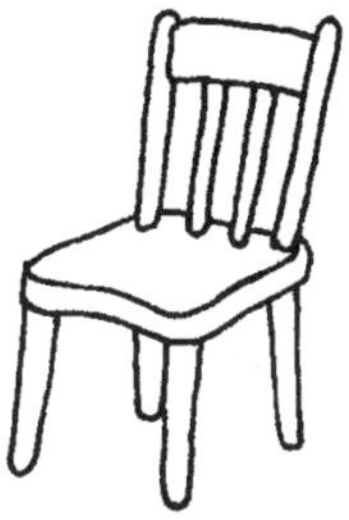

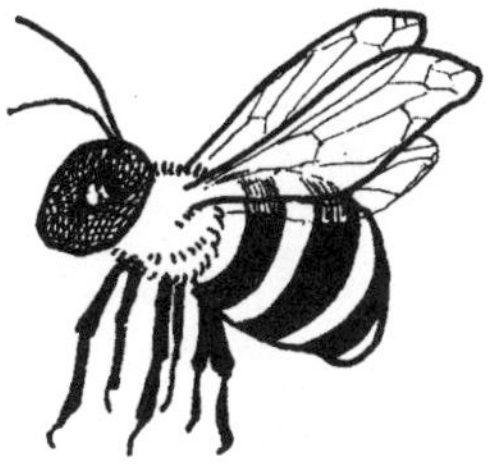

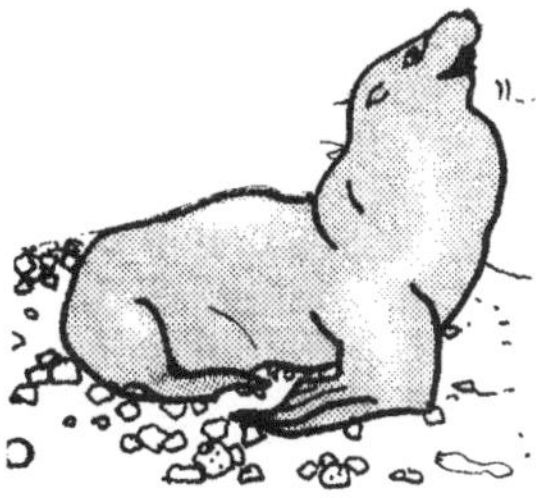

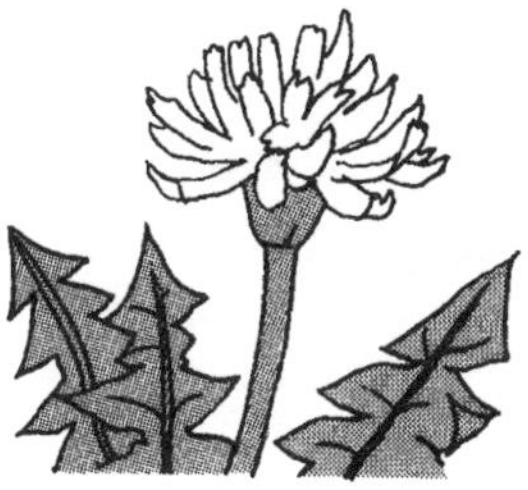

ea Student Reading Selection

Review are, does, is, of, says, and the as sight words. Remind children that creamed is pronounced /krēmd/, not /krēmĕd/. Then tell children to read the story by themselves.

Dean likes a real meal—meat, creamed peas, ice tea, white cake on a neat [table]. But Mom is sick. So Dad makes each meal. He makes a can of beans. The [table] is not neat. It is a mess. Dean hates beans in a can. So Dean makes the meal. He gets cake and ice cream. He and Dad take a seat. But Dad gets up. He gets a can of beans. Dean says, "A can of beans is not a real meal." Dad says, "Ice cream and cake are not a real meal." When Mom is well, she gets up. She is still weak, but she makes a real meal—lean veal chops, creamed peas, homemade cake. The [table] is nice and neat, not a mess. Dad is glad. Mom is well. He does not like to eat cake at mealtime. Mom is glad she is well. She likes Dean and Dad to eat a real meal.

Tell children to circle the names of things they can put in a grocery shopping cart.

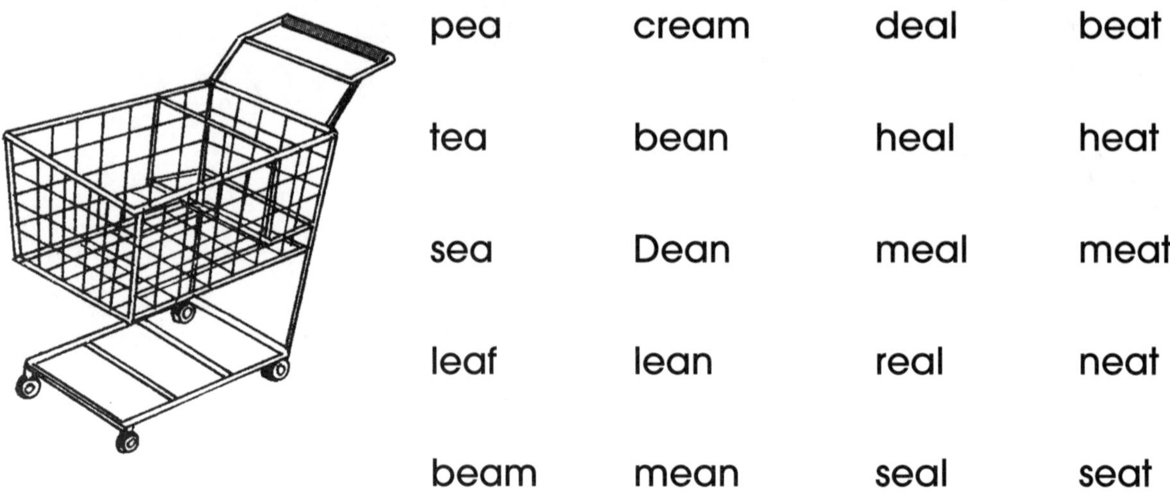

pea	cream	deal	beat
tea	bean	heal	heat
sea	Dean	meal	meat
leaf	lean	real	neat
beam	mean	seal	seat

eed

Read the verse aloud and tell children to pretend they are digging in the garden when they hear the /ēd/ sound as in <u>weed</u>. Read the verse again and tell children to circle the letters that stand for the /ēd/ sound.

Out in the garden
I planted a seed.
I asked my mom,
"What does it need?"
"You feed it water
And pull the weeds,
And a little sun
Are all it needs."

Tell children to color the pictures whose names have the long <u>e</u> sound. Remind them that both /ea/ and /ee/ can stand for the long <u>e</u> sound as in <u>weed</u>.

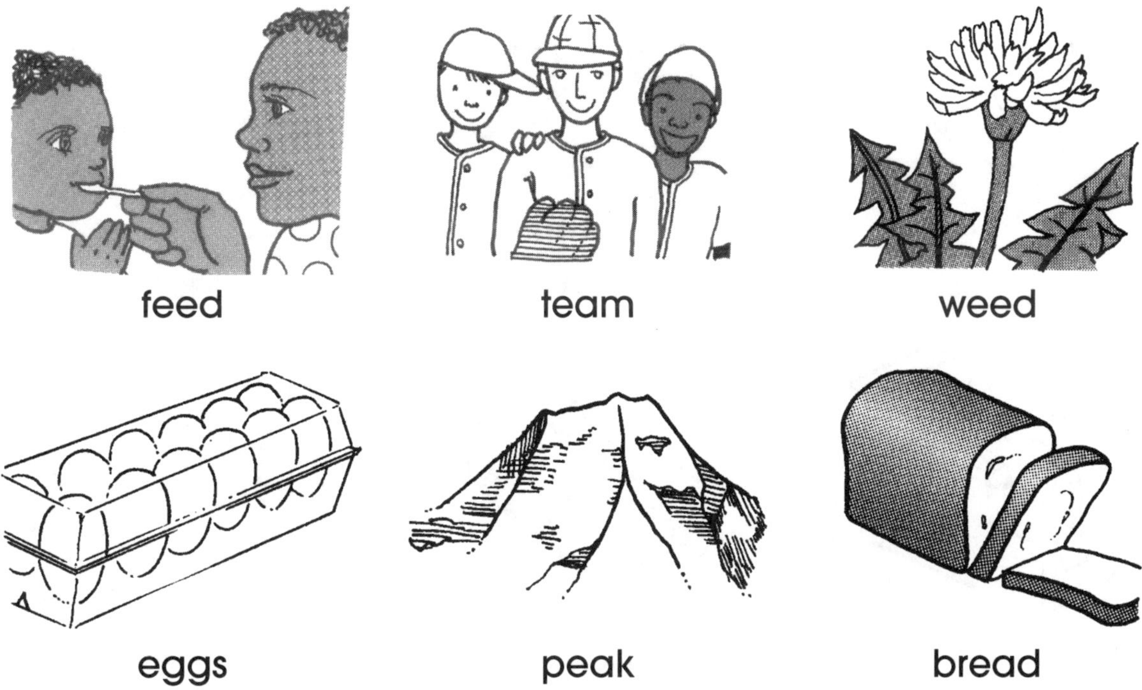

eek 

Read the verse aloud and tell children to cover their eyes with their hands when they hear the /ēk/ sound as in <u>peek</u>. *Read the verse again and tell children to circle the letters that stand for the /ē/ sound.*

We like to play hide and seek.
In fact, we play it every week.
But when you're IT,
you musn't peek!

Tell children to circle all the pictures whose names have the /ēk/ sound as in <u>peek</u>.

peck peak leak

bed deck week

Name: ______________________ Date: ____________ 5-151

eel

Read the verse aloud. Tell children to pretend they are throwing a fishing line into the water when they hear the /ēl/ sound as in eel. Read the verse again and tell children to circle the letters that stand for the /ēl/ sound.

Dad said,
"Danny, Danny, how do you feel?
Let's go to the lake
With your fishing reel.
The line is white
And the handle steel.
You can turn a little wheel
To pull in the fish
With your brand new reel.
Who knows? You might even
Catch an eel."

Tell children they can play tic-tac-toe by drawing lines through any three words that have the sound of /ēl/ as in eel.

tea	Ted	met
Bess	bean	pad
pail	bed	sea

sail	heat	neck
peck	bean	cube
cute	Pete	tail

Name: ______________________ Date: __________ 5-152

een

Explain to children that qu in queen has the /kw/ sound. Read the verse aloud and tell children to pretend they are ghosts saying "ooooo" when they hear the /ēn/ sound as in queen. Read the verse again and tell children to circle the letters that stand for the /ēn/ sound.

I'm really keen about Halloween.
I trick-or-treat for candy.
My sister is the queen of hearts,
And I am Jack-a-Dandy.
My brother Dean who is thirteen
Is the nicest ghost
 I've ever seen.
My friend Colleen walks between
Two goblin kings on Halloween.

Tell children to print the correct letters in the blanks.

1. Dean is ___ ___ ___ ___ ___ ___ ___ ___.
2. Pam is a qu___ ___ ___ on Hallo___ ___ ___ ___.
3. A leaf is ___ ___ ___ ___ ___.
4. Bob is seven___ ___ ___ ___.
5. This is a ___ ___ ___ ___ ___ ___:
6. The man is ___ ___ ___ ___ ___ ___ ___
 Dan and Jim.

between
fifteen
green
Halloween
queen
screen
seventeen
thirteen

Name: ______________________ Date: ____________ 5-153

eep 

Read the verse aloud and tell children to say "beep-beep" when they hear the /ēp/ sound as in Jeep. Read the verse again and tell the children to circle the letters that stand for the /ēp/ sound.

Cars say, "Beep-beep."
Chickens say, "Peep-peep."
In the night we always sleep.
In the ocean, water's deep.
A car is something like a Jeep,
And promises are made to keep.

Tell children to put the correct consonants in the blanks.

1. A [car] says "___eep." (B, P, D)

2. Dan is a___ ___eep. [sleeping boy] (pl, sl, tl)

3. The lake is ___eep. (b, d, t)

4. A [chick] says "___eep." (T, B, P)

5. A [broom] can ___ ___eep. (pl, sl, sw)

6. A [hill] is ___ ___eep. (st, bl, cr)

Name: ______________________ Date: ____________ 5-154

eet

Read the verse aloud and tell children to say "tweet, tweet" when they hear the /ēt/ sound as in feet. *Read the verse again and tell children to circle the letters that stand for the /ēt/ sound.*

Mary had a little bird
That always sang "Tweet, tweet."
It had yellow feathers
And little yellow feet.
But Danny had a bigger bird,
The best bird on the street.
It was green and had some red
The color of a beet.
It could walk and it could talk.
It was a parakeet.

Tell children to find the hidden picture by coloring words that have the /ē/ sound as in feet.

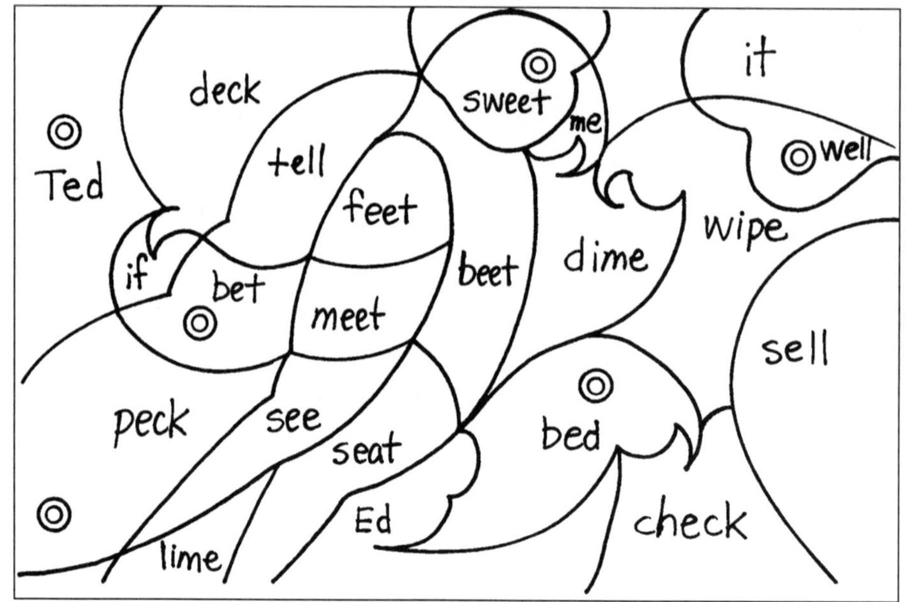

Name: ______________________ Date: ____________

ee Student Reading Selection

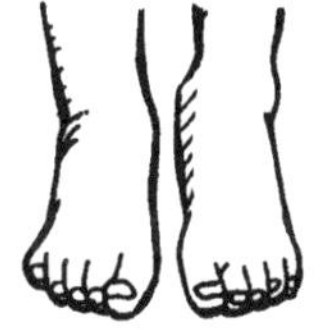

Review said, the, and was as sight words. Then children can read the story by themselves.

The Bad Jeep

Dee said to me, "Let's feed the s." One was as red as a beet. I gave the red an peel. He ate it. He sat on my knee. I gave the green a weed seed. He sat on my knee. Two s sat at my feet. We had fun. I feel glad. I said to the s "I you. I to feed you. We need you." Then a Jeep came. The Jeep said, "Beep, beep." The s left. I was mad at the Jeep and sad.

Tell children to circle the words that have the sound of /ē/ as in feet.

bead he

meet

head

bee

met fell need

bread

Pete Ned

meat

teen ten well

wheel feel

ie 

Read the verse aloud and tell children to pretend they are hugging Grandma when they hear the /ī/ as in pie. Read the verse again and tell children to circle ie words that have the /ī/ sound.

Mamma bakes an apple pie.
Daddy wears a brand new tie.
Puff and Towser always lie
Near the door
While Sue and I
Wait for Grandma
To come by.

Tell children that ie has the sound of /ī/, but other letters do, too. Tell children to circle the pictures whose names have the /ī/ as in pie.

oa

Tell children that oa *has the sound of /ō/ as in* boat. *Read the verse aloud slowly and ask children to fill in the missing letters as they hear the words pronounced. Read the verse again and tell children to circle the words that have the /ō/ sound.*

When you go to lots of places, you ___oa___.
If it looks like suds on the water, it's ___oa___.
A girl's name is ___oa___.
Money you borrow is a ___oa___.
A big frog is a ___oa___.
A big street is a ___oa___.
A big box is a ___oa___.
A big tree is an oa___.
We wash our clothes with ___oa___.
We buy bread in a ___oa___.
What we want to do is a ___oa___.
We can heat houses with ___oa___.
I can't swim but I can ___ ___oa___.
If it says, "maa," I think it's a ___oa___.
If you're cold, put on your ___oa___.

boat	goat	oak
coal	Joan	road
coat	load	roam
float	loaf	soap
foam	loan	toad
goal		

Name: ______________________ Date: __________ 5-158

oat

Read the verse aloud and tell children to run in place when they hear the /ō/ sound as in coat. Read the verse again and tell children to circle the letters that have the /ōt/ sound.

Things I Can Do

I can lie on my back in the water
And float.
I don't have a sail,
But I feel like a boat.
I may be a kid,
But can run like a goat.
I'm especially fast
If I don't have a coat.

Tell children to circle the pictures whose names have the long sound of ō as in coat.

goat

Mr. Cole

home

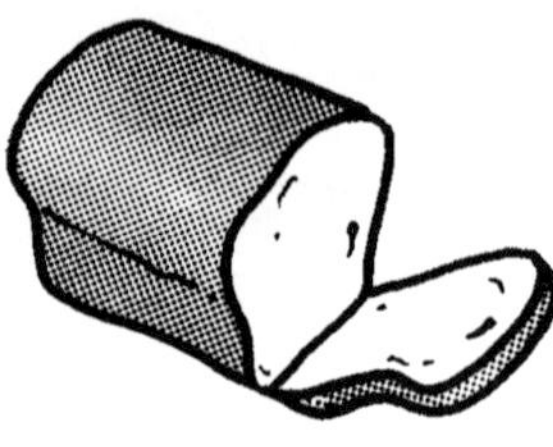

loaf

go

phone

Name: ______________________ Date: __________

Long o Student Reading Activity

Ask children, "Have you ever seen ____?" Each child answers, "No, I never saw____" and reads one of the answers below. Each answer contains long ō words children can read by themselves after you've taught the phonogram oa. *Ask children to describe each picture.*

Have You Ever Seen ___?

1. a goat on the road
2. a toad in a coat
3. a dome on a home
4. a goat eat soap
5. a load of goats in a boat
6. a rose on a nose
7. a mole in a hole
8. a nose on a pole
9. a road in Rome
10. a goat tell a joke
11. a goat write a note
12. a note in code
13. Mrs. Dole on a pole
14. a mole eat a bone
15. a load of toads in a boat
16. a loaf of soap
17. a nose on a rose
18. foam on a bone
19. a boat sail on a road
20. a goat vote
21. a stone moan

Name: ______________________ Date: ____________

Long Vowel Team Review 

Tell children to complete the names of the pictures by using long vowel teams—ai, ea, ee, or oa. Point out to children that the short and long vowel words have the same beginning and ending letters.

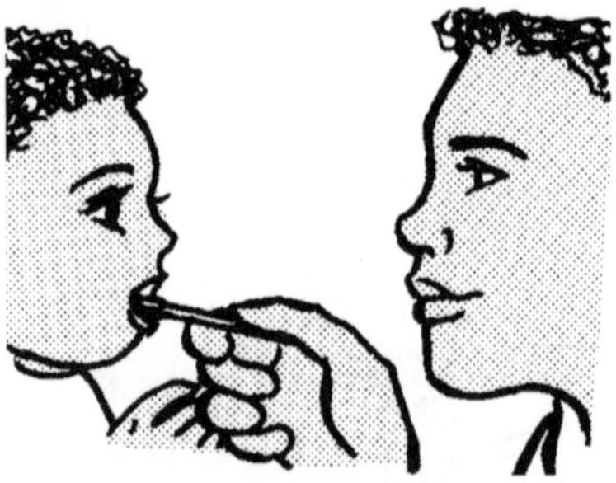

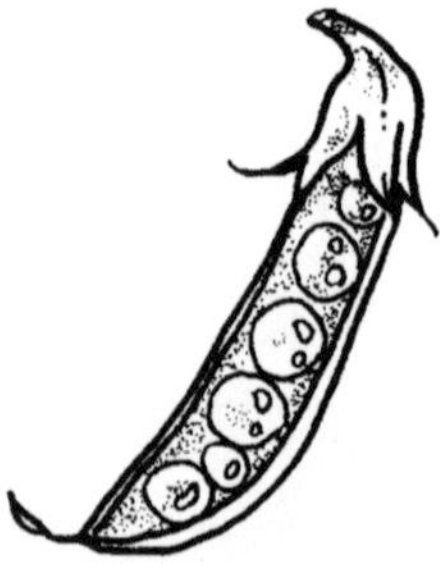

set	got	ran
s___ ___t	g___ ___t	r___ ___n
fed	**Ben**	**pal**
f___ ___d	b___ ___n	p___ ___l
cot	**Tod**	**met**
c___ ___t	t___ ___d	m___ ___t

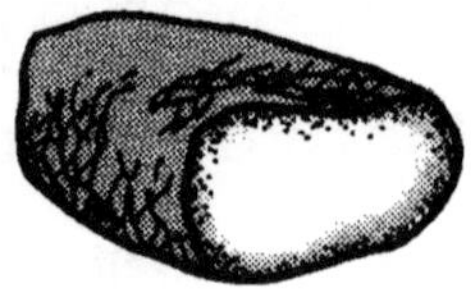

Name: ______________________ Date: ____________ 5-161

OW 

Read the verse aloud and tell children to blow like the wind when they hear the /ō/ sound as in bow. Read the verse again and tell children to circle the letters that stand for the /ō/ sound.

Daddy, daddy, do you know. . .
Why a turtle runs so slow?
Why the west winds always blow?
Why the roses bud and grow?
Where the rivers finally flow?
Tell me, Daddy, if you know.

Tell children to print the correct words in the blanks.

boat	float	pole
bone	hole	slow
bow	joke	

1. I laugh when Dad tells a ___ ___ ___ ___.
2. A red bird is sitting on a ___ ___ ___ ___.
3. Ted's ___ ___ ___ ___ can ___ ___ ___ ___ ___.
4. A (turtle) is ___ ___ ___ ___.
5. I can dig a ___ ___ ___ ___.
6. A dog likes a ___ ___ ___ ___.
7. Ann has a ___ ___ ___ in her  .

Name: ______________________ Date: ____________ 5-162

ow

Read the verse aloud. Tell children to say "whoo" like the wind blowing when they hear the /ō/ sound as in bow. Read the verse again and tell children to circle the letters that stand for the /ō/ sound.

When the north winds blow
In the ice and the snow,
It's hard to know
Flowers begin to grow
When winter ends
And summer sends
Sun to melt the snow.

Tell children to circle the pictures whose names have the sound of /ō/ as in no.

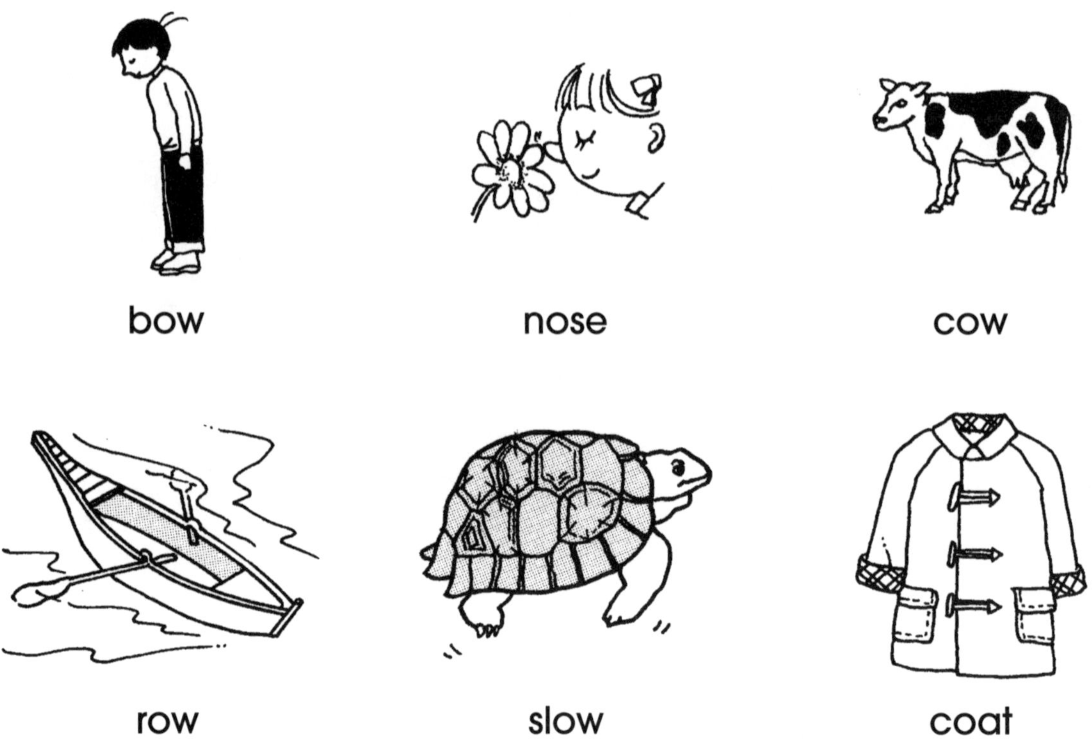

oe, ow

Explain to children that oe at the end of words has the sound of /ō/ as in toe. Also explain that o at the end of words has the /ō/ sound, and that ow also sometimes has the /ō/ sound. Read the verse aloud and tell children to stamp their feet when they hear the /ō/ sound as in toe. Read the verse again and tell children to circle all letters that stand for the /ō/ sound.

I wonder if you children know
oe words that rhyme with go?
On each foot's a little toe.
I have a pal whose name is Joe.
A lady deer is called a doe.
An enemy soldier is a foe.
We call a lot of sadness, woe.
Salmon eggs are salmon roe.
Now I've told you,
So you know.

Tell children to circle the underlined words that have the /ō/ sound as in toe.

1. A cow says, "Moo."
2. My foot has five toes.
3. A dog says, "Bow wow."
4. A cat says, "Meow."
5. In class we sit in a row.
6. The farmer has a hoe.
7. I will go now.
8. Mom said, "No!"
9. That car is slow.
10. That boy is Joe.

Section 6
Diphthongs

Let's boil water
For breakfast tea.
Let's broil bacon
For you and me.

Name: ______________________ Date: ____________ 6-164

aw 

Read the verse aloud and tell children to smile happily when they hear the /ô/ sound as in paw. *Read the verse again and ask children to circle the letters that stand for the /ô/ sound.*

Happiness

Little Bobby Shaw was happy when he saw a snow-white puppy with a jet black paw. Little Danny Daw was happy when he saw a jet black kitten with a snow-white claw. Officer McCullom was happy when he saw auto drivers who didn't break the law.

Tell children to print the correct /ô/ word under each picture.

claw
draw
jaw
law
paw
raw
saw

___ ___ ___

___ ___ ___

___ ___ ___

___ ___ ___ ___

___ ___ ___

___ ___ ___ ___

Name: ______________________ Date: ____________

Practice with More Difficult /ô/ Words

This activity is intended to help children master more difficult words in the /ô/ group, which includes such words as aw *in* claw, au *in* Paul *and* caught, all *in* ball, ou *in* bought, *and* al *in* talk. *Have children fill in the blanks with the words listed.*

1. bought — I ___ ___ ___ ___ ___ ___ a book.
2. caught — Bob ___ ___ ___ ___ ___ ___ the ball.
3. chalk — We write with ___ ___ ___ ___ ___.
4. fought — I ___ ___ ___ ___ ___ ___ with Tom.
5. haul — Dad ___ ___ ___ ___s wood in his truck.
6. mall — We shop in the ___ ___ ___ ___.
7. ought — I ___ ___ ___ ___ ___ to study.
8. shawl — Grandma wears a ___ ___ ___ ___ ___.
9. stalk — Corn grows on a ___ ___ ___ ___ ___.
10. stall — A horse sleeps in a ___ ___ ___ ___ ___.
11. taught — My mom ___ ___ ___ ___ ___ ___ school last year.
12. thought — I ___ ___ ___ ___ ___ ___ ___ I caught a fish.

Name: ______________________ Date: ____________

awn

Read the verse aloud and tell children to yawn when they hear the /ôn/ sound as in yawn. Read the verse again and tell children to circle the words that have the /ôn/ sound.

With a sleepy yawn,
Dad rose at dawn.
He had promised Mom
He'd mow the lawn.
He was sleepy and sad
And tired and mad
Until he saw through the glass
In the dew on the grass
A spotted fawn
Alone on the lawn.

Read the sentences aloud slowly. Ask children to circle words that have the /ô/ sound as in yawn. Explain to children that sometimes the /ô/ sound is spelled au as in Paul, all as in ball, as well as aw as in saw, ou as in bought, and al as in talk. **Note:** *Not all sentences have the /ô/ sound.*

1. Dad mowed the lawn.
2. I saw a bird.
3. The teacher is here now.
4. Mom bought a new hat.
5. Dad caught a fish.
6. Paul caught a ball.
7. Will you walk with me?
8. Will you talk with me?
9. A circle is round.
10. Dad thought about hauling the wood.

Name: ______________________ Date: ____________ 6-167

/ô/ Student Reading Activity

Review <u>*you*</u> *and* <u>*with*</u> *as sight words. Then ask children to read the questions by themselves, draw pictures of four of the words, and print the names of the pictures under each drawing.*

Can You Draw?

Can you draw a dog's paw? Can you draw a man with a big jaw? Can you draw a bird you saw? Can you draw a cat's claw? Can you draw a hawk? Can you draw a fawn? Can you draw grass on a lawn? Can you draw a girl—Shawn—in a shawl?

______________	______________
______________	______________

Name: ______________________ Date: ____________

oil

Read the verse aloud and tell children to circle the letters that stand for the /oil/ sound as in coil *and* boil.

Let's boil water
For breakfast tea.
Let's broil bacon
For you and me.
Let's keep hash browns
Warm in kitchen foil.
Let's make hot cakes
In a little oil.

Read these sentences to children and ask them to print the correct words in the blanks.

boil	coil	foil	oil	soil	spoil	toil

1. Put ___ ___ ___ in the pan.
2. Meat can ___ ___ ___ ___ ___.
3. Water can ___ ___ ___ ___.
4. Work is ___ ___ ___ ___.
5. Heat the meat in tin ___ ___ ___ ___.
6. Dirt is ___ ___ ___ ___.
7. Do you have a ___ ___ ___ ___ of wire?

Name: ______________________ Date: __________

oin 

Read the verse aloud and tell children to pretend they are eating something delicious when they hear the /oin/ sound as in coin. Read the verse again and tell children to circle the letters that stand for the /oin/ sound.

Riddle

If you join
Sir and loin,
What kind of meat
Do you get to eat?

Tell children to circle the words that rhyme with the picture.

1. join boy loin boil
2. toy join Roy coil
3. oil loin soy foil
4.  cone joint coin join

Name: ______________________ Date: ____________ 6-170

oy

Read the verse aloud and tell children to pretend they are sailors shouting "ship ahoy" when they hear the /oi/ sound as in toy. Read the verse again and tell children to circle the letters that stand for the /oi/ sound.

A is an apple.
B is a boy.
C is a cucumber.
J is for joy.
S is a soybean.
T is a toy.
And **H** is a sailor
Who cries "ship ahoy."

Tell children to try to unscramble the 12 /oi/ words in the list.

boil	coin	oil	soil
boy	foil	point	toil
coil	join	Roy	toy

1. ilbo ___ ___ ___ ___
2. oyt ___ ___ ___
3. ijon ___ ___ ___ ___
4. ory ___ ___ ___
5. inco ___ ___ ___ ___
6. oils ___ ___ ___ ___
7. ybo ___ ___ ___
8. ilto ___ ___ ___ ___
9. ocli ___ ___ ___ ___
10. optin ___ ___ ___ ___ ___
11. iflo ___ ___ ___ ___
12. loi ___ ___ ___

Name: ______________________ Date: ____________ 6-171

/oi/ Student Reading Activity

Review is *as a sight word. Then have children take turns reading things they can and cannot do. They can read all the sentences by themselves.*

I Can. I Can't

1. I can smile in joy.
2. I can make a toy fan.
3. I can say, "Ship ahoy."
4. I can say, "Roy is a boy."
5. I can say, "Joy is not a boy."
6. I can say, "Mom and Dad will not spoil me."
7. I can boil an egg.
8. I can boil soybeans.
9. I can get a coin.
10. I can join a club.
11. I can coil a hose.
12. I can dig in the soil.
13. I can put oil in a pan.
14. I can use tin foil.
15. I cannot toil in a coal mine.
16. I will not be a bad boy.
17. I will not steal a coin.
18. I will not boil a coin.
19. I will not join a bad boy and steal a coin.
20. I will not hit Joy.
21. I will not hit Roy.
22. I will not spoil a toy.
23. I will not soil a rug.
24. I will not spill oil on a rug.

out

Read the verse aloud and tell children to shout when they hear the /out/ sound as in shout. *Read the verse again and tell children to circle the letters that stand for the /out/ sound.*

Mom said,
"What is this racket all about?
Danny Jones, don't you shout!
If you want to be noisy,
Then please go out!"

Tell children to choose the correct sentence for each picture and put the sentence number in the circle. Read sentences if necessary.

1. Dan read a book about cats.	3. Dan is a Boy Scout.
2. "Go out and play."	4. "I got a trout!"

Name: ______________________ Date: ____________ 6-173

ow

Read the verse aloud and tell children to say "meow" when they hear the /ou/ sound as in <u>cow</u>. *Read the verse again and tell children to circle the letters that stand for the /ou/ sound.*

The cat said,
"Can you meow?"
The dog replied,
"I don't know how."
The cat said, "Well,
I'll teach you how,
Meow, meow, meow."
The dog said, "Oh,
I've got it now,
Bow-wow, bow-wow, bow-wow."

Tell children to circle the word that goes with the picture.

bow how now

cow sow bow

wow plow pow

wow pow meow

Name: ______________________________ Date: ______________

own

Read the verse aloud and tell children to put their hands on their heads to look like a crown when they hear the /oun/ sound as in gown. Read the verse again and tell children to circle the letters that stand for the /oun/ sound.

Mrs. Brown comes to town
With purple feathers in her gown
And diamonds in a little crown.
She always smiles
When she doesn't frown.
When she isn't standing,
She's sitting down.
Her closest friend
Is a circus clown
Who follows her all over town.

Tell children to circle YES if the sentence describes the picture and NO if it doesn't.

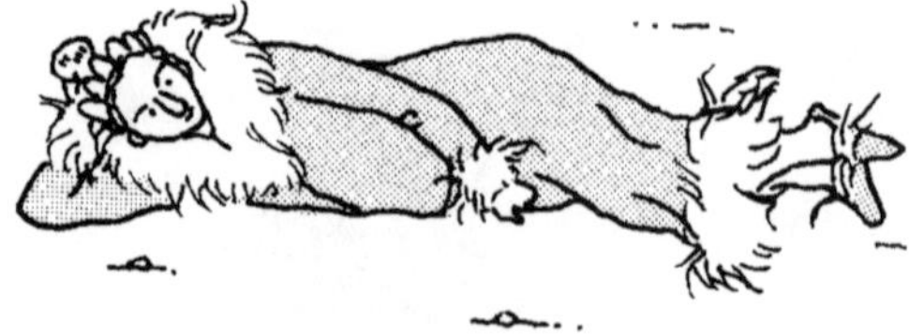

Mrs. Brown is down. 

The crown is down. 

This is a crown. YES NO

Here are Mrs. Brown and Mr. Clown. YES NO

/ou/ Student Reading Selection

Review are, said, the, want, and you as sight words. Remind children that ed after howl is pronounced /d/ and ed after shout is pronounced /ĕd/. Then children can read the story by themselves.

Chow Time

The dog howled and said, "Bow-wow." The cow said, "Moo." The owl said, "Who." The sow said, "Oink, oink." The fowl said, "Cluck, cluck." The cat said, "Meow." The boy shouted, "Now." Mom said, "Wow, you are loud." The boy said, "Now, Mom, now. We want chow."

Tell children to put the number of each scrambled word in the circle beside the correct picture.

1. noipt
2. low
3. lioc
4. wolcs
5. wolcn
6. ows

Name: ______________________________ Date: ______________ 6-176

Diphthong Review

This is a diphthong review activity. Tell children to circle the words that have the same vowel sound as the one in the name of the picture.

1. paw — saw — talk — how — toy

2. 
coil — boil — jaw — oil — Roy

3. 

coin — raw — join — joy — point

4. 
boy — soil — soy — boil — paid

5. 
cow — out — how — shout — law

6. 
down — wow — gown — dawn — town

Section 7

r-Controlled Vowels

Mork, the stork,
Flew to New York
With a baby basket
For Mrs. Bork.

Name: ______________________ Date: ____________ 7-177

ar 

Read the verse aloud and tell children to say "Honk, honk" when they hear the /är/ sound as in car. Read the verse again and tell children to circle the letters that stand for the /är/ sound.

Danny's dad bought a big, new car.
He said,
"We'll travel near and far."
Danny said,
"Can we travel to the stars?
Can we take a trip to Mars?"

Tell children to print ar words on the blanks in each petal of the flower.

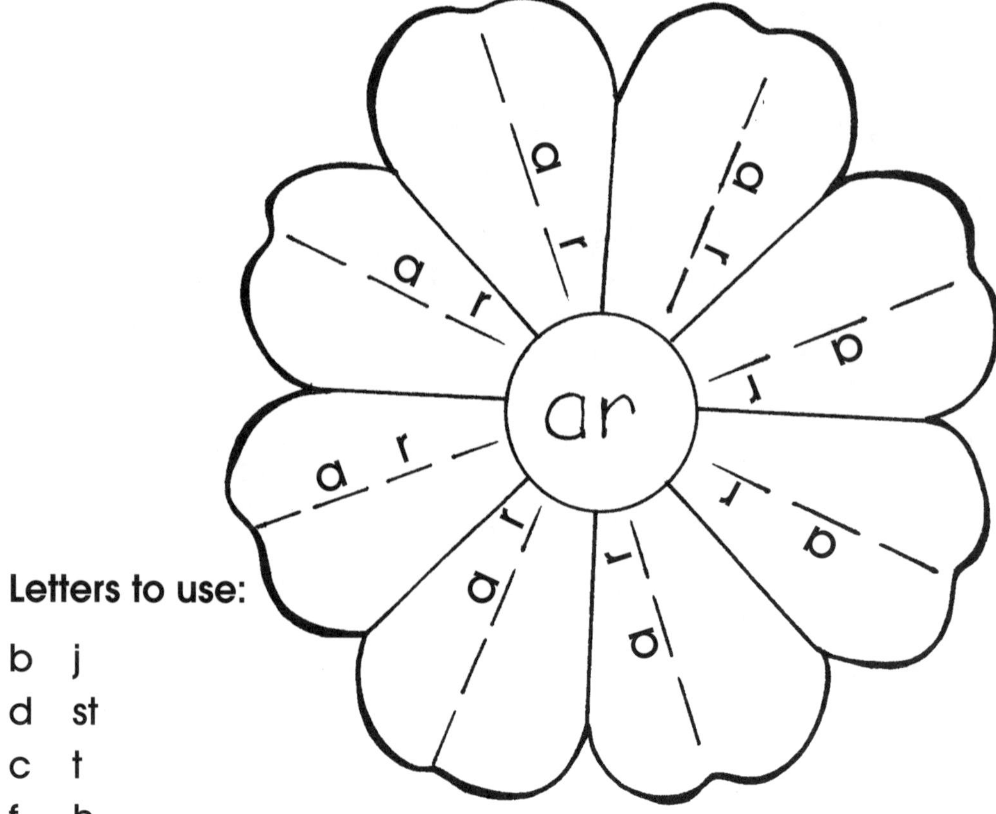

Letters to use:

b j
d st
c t
f h

Name: ______________________ Date: ____________ 7-178

ard

Read the verse aloud and tell children to circle the letters that stand for the /ärd/ sound as in card. Explain that u in guard is silent.

Mary's daddy is a guard.
His days are long.
His work is hard.
But he has a shiny card
With his name, Irving Pard,
Security at Scotland Yard.

Tell children to fill in the circle next to the word that completes each sentence.

1. Japan is _____. ○ jar ○ far ○ bar
2. I have a glass _____. ○ car ○ star ○ jar
3. _____ is black. ○ Lard ○ Far ○ Tar
4. My house has a big _____. ○ jar ○ yard ○ hard
5. I cut my hand. I have a _____. ○ scar ○ guard ○ star
6. A jail has _____. ○ stars ○ cars ○ bars
7. A stone is _____. ○ hard ○ card ○ lard
8. Mary's dad is Mr. _____. ○ Lard ○ Star ○ Pard

Name: ______________________ Date: ____________

ark

Read the verse aloud and tell children to bark when they hear the /ärk/ sound as in bark. *Read the verse again and tell children to circle the letters that stand for the /ärk/ sound.*

Meg and her mama, Mrs. Stark,
Went for a walk in a pretty park.
It was just beginning to get dark,
When their little dog began to bark.
Then they heard a meadow lark
Singing a happy summer tune
To its dear old friend,
The man in the moon.

Tell children to circle the letters that **end** *each word.*

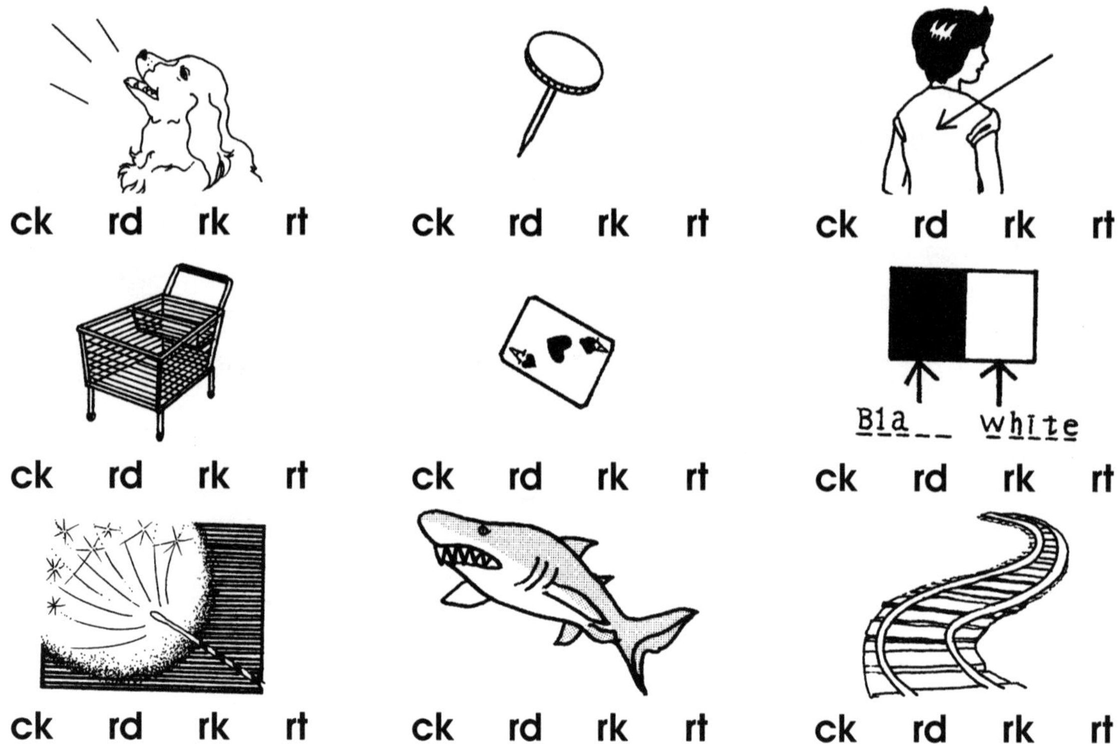

Name: ______________________ Date: ____________ 7-180

arm, arn 

Read the story aloud and tell children to circle the letters that stand for the /är/ sound as in charm or yarn.

The Charm

Barb visited her uncle's farm. She found a little box while she was playing in the yard near the barn. It was tied with yarn. There was something small and hard in the box: a little silver four-leaf clover. There was a card in the box. It said, "This is a lucky charm. If you wear it on your arm, you will have good luck and never come to harm."

Tell children to say the name of each picture and circle the **last** *letter of each name.*

arm	Barb	barn	card	charm	yarn

b d m n 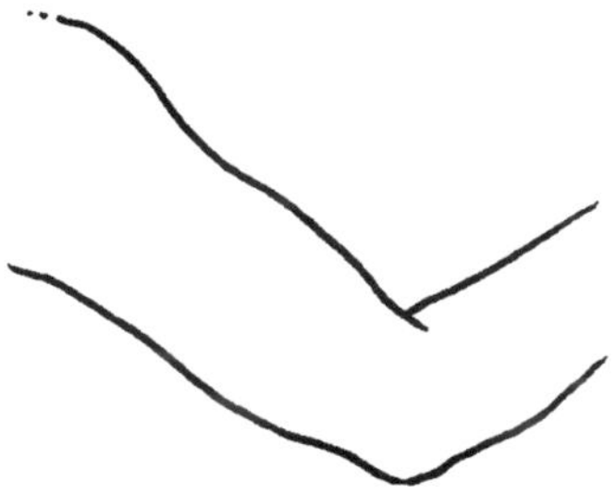   b d m n    b d m n

b d m n    b d m n    b d m n

Name: ______________________ Date: ____________ 7-181

arp

Read the verse aloud and tell children to pretend they are playing a harp when they hear the /ärp/ sound as in harp. Read the verse again and tell children to circle the letters that stand for the /ärp/ sound.

Little Mary Carp

Had a silver harp.

Everytime

She plucked a string,

The sound was clear and sharp.

Tell children to circle the ending letters of each picture's name.

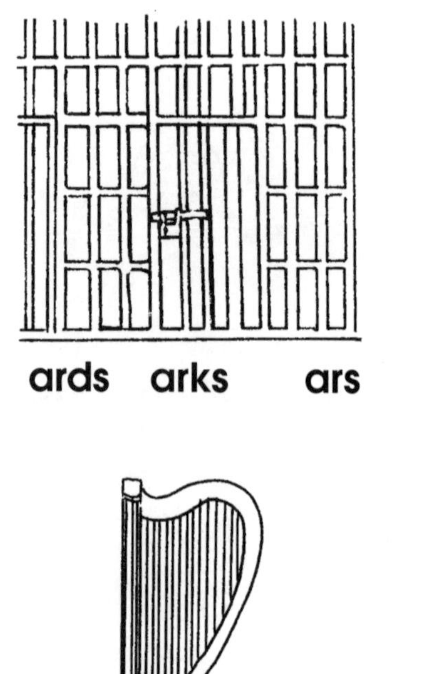

ards arks ars

ard ark arn

ard ark arp

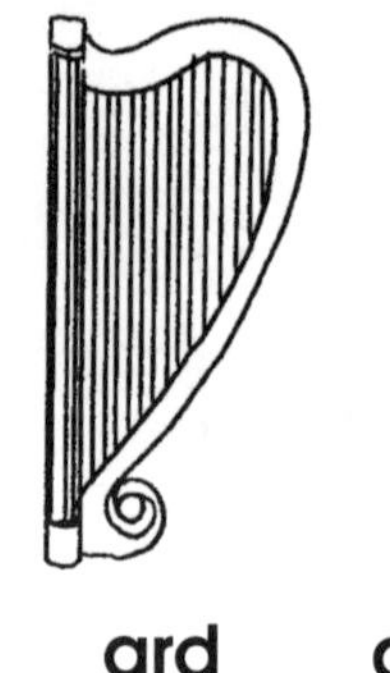

arb ard arp

ard ark arm

bars
card
harp
park
shark

Name: ______________________ Date: ____________

art 

Read the verse aloud and tell children to pretend they are throwing a dart at a dartboard when they hear the /ärt/ sound as in dart. *Read the verse again and tell children to circle the letters that stand for the /ärt/ sound.*

Mrs. Hart said to Art,
"Always finish what you start.
Don't do anything in part.
Suppose *I* stopped
Each time I start
And gave you half a cherry tart?"

Tell children to blacken the circles next to phrases that describe the pictures correctly.

Art in park ○

Park in dark ○

Shark in cart ○

Dart in art ○

Bark at lark ○

Part of Art ○

Name: ______________________ Date: ____________ 7-183

Hidden Pictures 

Tell children to circle the hidden pictures of these /är/ words.

arm	car	cart	jar
bar lock	card	harp	shark

Name: ______________________ Date: __________

/är/ Student Reading Selection

Review of, said, the, and was as sight words. Remind children that the final s in was has the /z/ sound. Then children can read the story by themselves.

Bark at the Stars

Carl had a dark dog. His name was Tar. Tar liked to ride in the car, but he did not ride far. He got car sick. Dad said, "Get Tar out of the car. Let's stop at the farm." Tar liked the farm. He saw a lark. He barked at the lark. He saw a cart. He barked at the cart. He saw a hoe on the farm. He barked at the hoe. He said, "Arf, arf." He saw a cow. He snarled at the cow. Carl said, "Let's take him far. Let's take him to Mars. He can bark at the stars."

Tell children to spell ar words with the first letter of each picture.

___ ___ ___

___ ___ ___ ___

___ ___ ___ ___

___ ___ ___ ___

___ ___ ___ ___

Name: ______________________ Date: ____________

or 

Explain to children that the /ôr/ sound in roar can be spelled in different ways: or as in for, oor as in door, ore as in more, and oar as in roar. Read the story aloud and tell children to circle all the letters that stand for the /ôr/ sound.

Mom said, "What did you do that for? You spilled honey all over the floor. Why didn't you ask me to pour it for you, or ask me to get some more of it for you? Your father will shout. Your father will roar, 'Tommy, what did you do that for?' Now you hurry up and run to the store! You get something to clean up this mess!" Tommy said sweetly, "Sure, Mommy, yes."

A four-part spinner and colored marker are needed for this game. One die from a pair of dice can also be used. Players move the number of spaces indicated if they can pronounce the words. Otherwise, they must return to start.

pour	or	for		FINISH boar
sour		four		boat
roar		out		floor
oar		door		foot
coat		ore		nor
oat		shore	soar	soap
START				

Name: ______________________________ Date: ______________

Read the verse aloud and tell children to pound their knees with their fists when they hear the /ôrk/ sound as in fork. Read the verse again and tell children to circle the letters that stand for the /ôrk/ sound.

Mork, the stork,
Flew to New York
With a baby basket
For Mrs. Bork.

Tell children to complete the words under the picture with either an a or an o.

Name: ______________________ Date: ____________ 7-187

orm, orn

Read the verse aloud and tell children to pretend they are blowing a horn, "toot-toot," when they hear the sounds of /ôrm/ as in storm *and /ôrn/ as in* horn. *Read the verse again and tell children to circle the letters that stand for /ôrm/ and /ôrn/.*

Have you seen a rose without a thorn?
A pair of jeans that were not torn?
A bull that didn't have a horn?
A pair of shoes no one had worn?
A waving field of purple corn?
A person who was never born?
A pretty shape without a form?
Your older brother's college dorm?
A dry and sunny thunderstorm?

Tell children to fill in the circle next to the phrase that describes each picture.

Corn with a thorn ○
Corn in a storm ○

A form in a dorm ○
A storm in a dorm ○

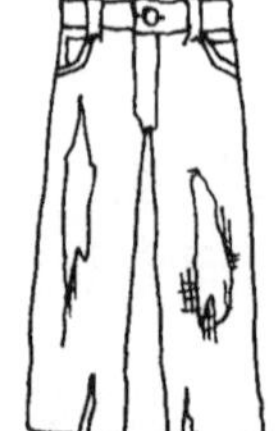

Torn pants ○
Ants on pants ○

Corn in a dorm ○
Corn in a storm ○

A bike in a dorm ○
A bike with a horn ○

She has worn the hat ○
She has torn the hat ○

Read the verse aloud and tell children to squat on the floor as if they are very short when they hear the /ôrt/ sound as in fort. Read the verse again and ask children to circle the letters that stand for the /ôrt/ sound.

Mort Port was very short.
Other kids would always snort,
"He's too short for any sport."
Then the kids built a fort,
A little fort upon the floor,
And only Mort got in the door.

Tell children to fill in the beginning letters of the words under the pictures.

davenport
fort
port
short
sport

____ort

daven____ort

____ ____ort

____ort

____ ____ort

Name: ______________________ Date: ____________ 7-189

/ôr/ Student Reading Selection 

Review my, said, and was as sight words. Explain that th as in this has the same sound as in the. Also explain that children can sound out the two parts of sunshine separately. If necessary, explain how the abbreviation Mr. is pronounced.

Dad's Sunshine

Jan Ford was born on a hot day. Dad said, "This is a big day. Let's blow a horn, for Jan was born. Mork the Stork came in the sun and heat." So Mr. Ford said, "Jan is my sunshine."

Tell children to draw lines from the words to the correct pictures.

corn

fork

fort

horn

port

short

sport

stork

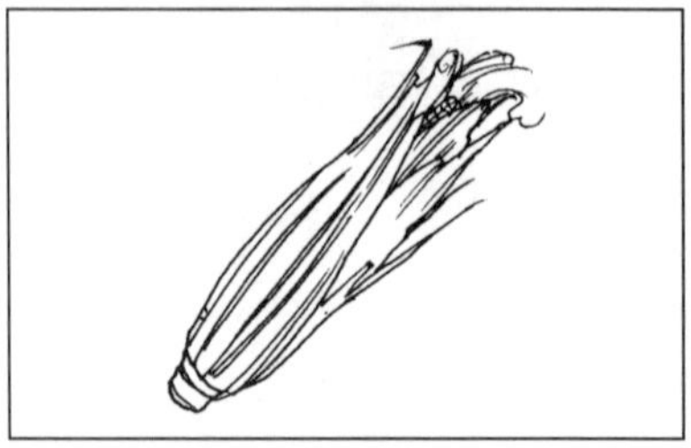

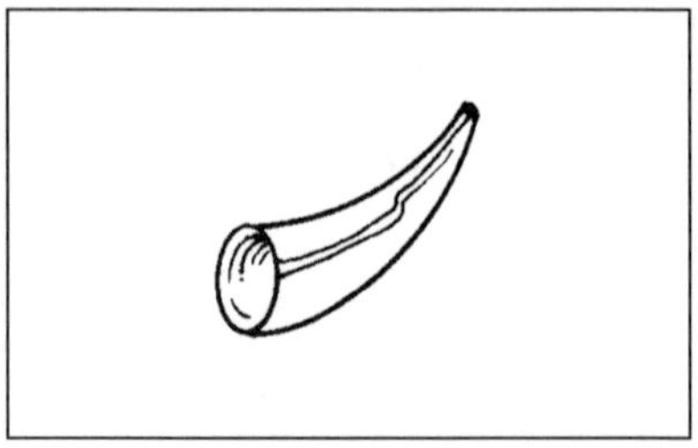

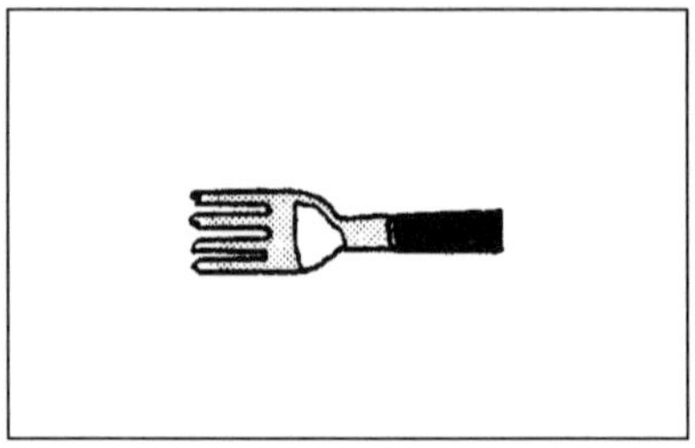

Name: ______________________ Date: ____________

er

Tell children that the /ûr/ sound can be spelled in different ways: er as in herb, ir as in sir, or as in work, and ur as in Burt. Read the verse aloud and ask children to purr when they hear the /ûr/ sound. Read the verse again and tell children to circle all the letters that stand for the /ûr/ sound.

Herb was a clerk in a department store.
Sometimes he thought his work was a bore.
Until the day a mermaid came to the store.
She was the prettiest girl in the world.
Her eyes burned bright,
And her hair was curled.
When she talked, she seemed to purr,
"Please, will you help me, sir?"
He thought he'd do anything for her.

Read the definitions below slowly. Tell children to put the letter of each definition beside the correct word.

____ 1. Burt	A. sound a cat makes
____ 2. clerk	B. an animal's hair
____ 3. fur	C. can grow in a garden
____ 4. germ	D. a sudden movement
____ 5. her	E. a person who sells in a store
____ 6. herb	F. a girl or woman
____ 7. jerk	G. makes you sick
____ 8. purr	H. a boy's name

Name: ______________________ Date: ____________ 7-191

irt 

Read the verse aloud and ask children to think of /ûr/ words that tell what Johnny might have gotten on his shirt. Read the verse again and tell children to circle the letters that stand for the /ûr/ sound as in skirt.

Johnny and Mary played in the dirt.

Mary got mud all over her skirt.

What did Johnny get on his shirt?

Tell children to print the correct word under each picture.

bird	fir	sir	third
dirt	shirt	stir	

Yes, ___ ___ ___

___ ___ ___ ___ ___

___ ___ ___ ___

___ ___ ___ ___ on a ___ ___ ___ ___ ___

___ ___ ___

___ ___ ___ ___

Name: ______________________________ Date: ______________

ur, urn, urp

Read the verse aloud and tell children to pretend they are turning a steering wheel when they hear the /ûr/ sound as in burn. *Explain that sometimes the letters* ir *stand for the /ûr/ sound, as in* whirl *and* girl. *Read the verse again and ask children to circle the letters that stand for the /ûr/ sound.*

Can a knight hurl a spear?
Can a driver turn a wheel?
Can a baby burp?
Can a dog slurp?
Do matches burn?
Can the weather turn?

Is a dog a cur?
Do weeds have burrs?
Can hair curl?
Can a dancer whirl?
You don't have to guess.
The answer is yes.

Tell the children to print the first and last letters of each word.

Name: ______________________ Date: ____________ 7-193

/ûr/ Student Reading Selection

girl

Review come, of, said, and was as sight words. Explain that the two parts of mermaid and murmur can be sounded out separately. If necessary, help children with dish, fish, hand, and want, if you haven't yet taught final blends and final s's. Then children can read the story by themselves.

The Mermaid

A mermaid lived in the tide and surf. She had a tail, but she had no skirt. She had scales and she had no shirt. She liked to swim and whirl in the waves. The sea was her joy and her own green turf. She was part a fish and part a girl. So she had a wish—to meet a boy and not a fish. One day a boy swam in the sea. His name was Bert. He did not want to hurt her, but he was a flirt. He smiled at her and murmured, "Come out of the sea." She came, but the sand and dirt hurt her [eye] s. When she was out of the sea, the sun burned her. She turned and ran back to her own sea home.

Tell children to draw lines from the words to the correct picture.

bird	fir	hurt	sir
burr	girl	purr	skirt

Name: ________________________ Date: ____________ 7-194

air 

Read the verse aloud and tell children to pretend they are riding a donkey. They can bounce up and down and hold the pretend-reins when they hear the /âr/ sound as in chair. Read the verse again and ask children to circle the letters that stand for the /âr/ sound.

Won't you come to the county fair
To see a clown with orange hair,
A zebra sitting in a chair,
And a pair of monkeys
Riding donkeys
Down a winding stair?

Tell children to place air words in the correct spaces in the puzzle.

air	fair	hair	pair	stair

C
H
A
I
R
S

air, are, ear, ere

Tell children that the /âr/ sound in air can be spelled in different ways: are as in hare, ear as in wear, and ere as in there. Read the verse aloud and tell children to pretend they are hiding when they hear the /âr/ sound. Read the verse again and ask children to circle different letters that stand for the /âr/ sound.

Where is Bobby Lew? Did he go to the City Zoo? Did he run away with a giant hare? Did he ride away on the old gray mare to fight a dragon who wasn't there? Did he get a scare from a polar bear, or take a trip to the county fair? Is he underneath the stair? Wait a minute! I see him *there!* He's hiding right behind the chair.

Name: ______________________ Date: ____________

ear

Read the story aloud and tell children to put their hands on their ears when they hear the /îr/ sound as in ear. *Read the story again and tell children to circle the letters that stand for the /îr/ sound.*

A tear ran down Tammy's face. Her brother Tom had lost the race though Mom said he'd win first place. Tom is very big and dear, and he only races once a year. Friends said, "Tammy, did you hear? Your brother wasn't even near. He finally pulled up in the rear." Tammy thought she'd never cheer her brother who was kind and dear. But Tommy came home with a smile on his face. "Tammy," he said, "I can't win every race."

Tell children to put the correct ear *word beside each definition. Read the definitions aloud if necessary.*

		Word box
1. ___ ___ ___ ___	A sign of sadness	ear
2. ___ ___ ___	A part of your body	fear
3. ___ ___ ___ ___	You feel this when afraid	hear
4. ___ ___ ___ ___	Close	near
5. ___ ___ ___ ___	Your ears can do this	rear
6. ___ ___ ___ ___	Back of a room	tear

Name: ______________________ Date: ____________ 7-197

earl

curl

Explain to children that the /ûrl/ sound in girl can be spelled in different ways: url as in curl, irl as in girl, earl as in pearl, and orl as in world. Read the verse aloud and ask children to whirl around when they hear the /ûrl/ sound. Read the verse again and tell children to circle the letters that stand for the /ûrl/ sound.

Pretty Mandy Pearl
Had a little curl
Right in the middle of her forehead.
She liked to dance and whirl,
And her only brother, Earl,
Loved to see her twirl.
He said to all the world,
"She's my sis, the ballet girl."

Tell children to put the number of the correct word in the circle of each picture.

1. curl
2. Earl
3. pearl
4. whirl
5. world

Name: ____________________ Date: ____________

oar

Read the verse aloud and tell children to roar like lions when they hear the /ôr/ sound as in roar. Read the verse again and ask children to circle the letters that stand for the /ôr/ sound.

I'd like to hear a lion roar.
I'd like to see the wild birds soar.
I'd like to touch a wild boar's tusk
And dip oars in a river at dusk.

Tell children to circle air, ear, or oar under the pictures whose names have those letters.

boar	ear	fear	hair	roar	stairs

air ear oar | air ear oar | air ear oar

air ear oar | air ear oar | air ear oar

are

Read the verse aloud and tell children to pretend they are walking in the rain when they hear the /âr/ sound as in hare. Read the verse again and tell children to circle the letters that stand for the /âr/ sound.

He walked in the rain and didn't care that his head and hands were bare. He walked even though he had the fare to ride a bus or take a train. He just liked walking in the rain. Sure some people look and stare, maybe because they wouldn't dare to do anything strange or rare.

Tell children to put the correct beginning letters in each blank. Review about, do, is, and you as sight words. Then children can do this activity by themselves.

bare	hare	rare
care	mare	stare
fare	pare	wares

1. His head is ____are.
2. A store sells ____ares.
3. On a train, we need ____are.
4. A ____are is like a  .
5. Dad likes ____are meat.
6. When I peel an (apple), I ____are it.
7. A girl (horse) is a ____are.
8. Mom said, "I ____are about you."
9. Mom said, "Do not ____ ____are. It is rude."

ire 

Read the verse aloud and tell children to pretend they are acrobats balancing on a wire when they hear the sound of /īr/ as in fire. *Read the verse again and tell children to circle the letters that stand for the sound /īr/.*

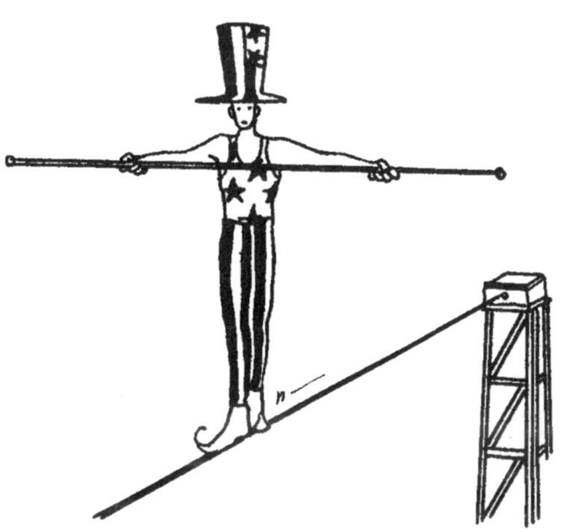

Mr. Mire, the acrobat,
Wears a flag-colored hat.
He can swallow flaming fire.
He can balance on a wire
And walk upon a rolling tire.
All circus owners want to hire
The amazing Mr. Mire,
Acrobat.

Tell children to draw a line between words that have the /īr/ sound. If the line goes up and down, across, or diagonally, they have made BINGO.

hire	him	her	fur
line	fire	fine	mine
fit	fir	wire	sir
are	car	care	tire

Name: ______________________ Date: ____________ 7-201

ore 

Read the verse aloud and ask children to hold out their hands as if asking for more when they hear the /ôr/ sound as in store. Read the verse again and ask children to circle the letters that stand for the /ôr/ sound.

I saw a sight
I never saw before,
A pelican in a candy store.
He ate some gumdrops
And asked for more
And drank lemonade
Until his throat was sore.

Explain to children that different letters can stand for the /ôr/ sound as in store. Ask them to circle the words that have the /ôr/ sound. Read the sentences to them if necessary.

1. An apple has a core.
2. I want more meat.
3. Who is at the door?
4. Lemons are sour.
5. Mom needs flour for the cake.
6. A lion can roar.
7. Dad went to the store.
8. Pam wore a red hat.
9. I will go in an hour.
10. I tore my dress.
11. The cat is on the floor.
12. Your hat is cute.

arry, erry

Explain to children that the final y in words like ferry has the sound of /ē/ as in bee. In words like ferry, erry has the sound of /ĕrē/. In words like Larry, arry has the almost identical sound of /ărē/. Read the verse aloud and ask children to circle the letters that stand for the /ărē/ and /ĕrē/ sounds.

Merry Christmas, Jerry.
Merry Christmas, Harry.
Will you help me carry
Presents home to Mary?
We have to catch the ferry.
It will really be so jolly
With a Christmas tree and holly,
Fruit cake with candied cherry
And mistletoe white berry
And friends like Uncle Jerry
Who make Christmas day so merry.

Tell children to circle the words in which the final y has the sound of /ē/ as in bee.

berry say merry
play carry May
Mary Kay Gary
day ferry clay
way shy
very cherry Larry
why Harry fry
honey money
hay bunny buy

Name: ______________________________ Date: ____________ 7-203

arch, irch, urch

Read the verse aloud and tell children to put their hands over their heads to form an arch when they hear the /ärch/ sound as in arch or the /ûrch/ sound as in birch and church. Read the verse again and tell children to circle the letters that stand for the /ärch/ and /ürch/ sounds.

On the fourth of July
The soldiers march
Around the square
And under the arch.
Each is straight
As a tall young birch.
Thumpety-thump past the church.
All their collars
Are stiff with starch.
To the beat of the drums,
The soldiers march.

Tell children to put the letter of the word in the correct blank.

1. A ___ is a tree.
2. My house has a ___.
3. Fire on a stick is a ___.
4. An ___:
5. A ___:
6. Spring starts in ___.
7. A bird can ___ in a tree.

A. arch
B. birch
C. church
D. March
E. perch
F. porch
G. torch

Name: ____________________ Date: __________ 7-204

war, wor

Tell children that an initial w changes the sound of r-controlled vowels. For example, ar in war has the sound of /ôr/ in for, and or in worm has the sound of /ûr/ in fur. Read the story aloud and ask children to circle the letters that stand for /ôr/ and/ ûr/ sounds.

Willy Worm

The war between Willy Worm and Bertha Bird began on a warm day. Willy's worm friends whispered the warning words, "Run anywhere in the world. Run for all you're worth." She was tired and worn, but Bertha Bird had morning work. She would not rest until she brought a worm to her babies in the nest.

Tell children to circle the words that have the /ôr/ sound as in for and to underline the words that have the /ûr/ sound as in fur. Then tell children to put each w word in the correct spaces.

war

warm

warn

wart

word

worm

work

world

worth

W o

ld
t
n
m
r
d
m
k
h

Section 8

Irregular Vowel and Vowel Consonant Combinations

The brave knight,
Sir Thomas Dwight,
Saddled his horse
And rode into the night.

Name: ______________________ Date: ____________ 8-205

able

Read the story aloud and tell children to circle the letters that stand for the /ābəl/ sound as in table.

We went looking for Chuck, a black and white duck that lived in a pool not far from the school. We looked in the barn and we looked in the stable. We even looked right under the table. We looked and looked, but we were unable to find our pet in the house or the stable. We looked behind every garden shrub and found him at last in the big bathtub.

Read the following definitions to the children. Fable: *A story usually with animals that teaches us something about life.* Sable: *A meat-eating animal whose fur is used for coats.* Cable: *A heavy rope or chain.* Gable: *A triangular upper part of a wall at the end of a roof. Next, ask children to put the number of the correct word in the circle next to each picture.*

Name: ______________________ Date: __________ 8-206

alk 

Read the verse aloud and tell children to raise their hands when they hear the /ôlk/ sound as in chalk. Read the verse again and tell children to circle the letters that stand for the /ôlk/ sound.

In my class
We raise our hands to talk
And ask permission before we walk.
If we forget, our teacher, Mrs. Falk,
Writes our names in chalk
On the big blackboard.
But if we're good all day,
We get to have play.
Then we dance and talk
And draw with colored chalk
On the big blackboard.

Tell children to draw lines between words that have the /ô/ as in talk or tall. If the line goes across, up, down, or diagonally, this is BINGO.

ball	paw	talk	yawn	hawk	tall
tan	cat	cab	tan	gab	bad
old	gold	told	fold	hold	cold
rock	sock	clock	knock	block	frock
male	sale	tail	rail	fail	jail
bone	cone	alone	stone	Joan	hope

Name: ______________________ Date: ____________ 8-207

all 

Read the verse aloud and tell children to bang one hand against the other when they hear the /ôl/ sound as in ball. *Read the verse again and tell children to circle the letters that stand for the /ôl/ sound.*

Billy Big Bat

Went to the mall

To buy himself

Another ball.

Tell children to use words that rhyme with all *to describe each picture.*

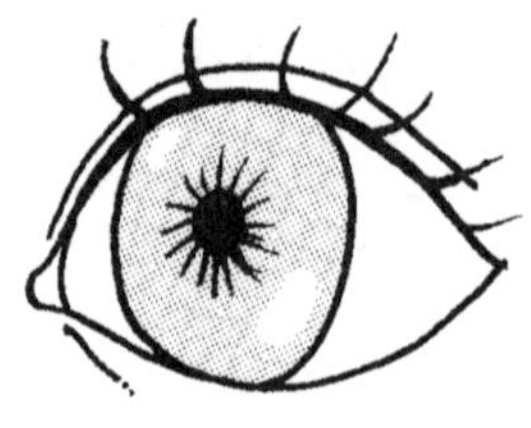

__ __ __ __ __ __ __ __ __

Bob is __ __ __ __

Eye__ __ __ __

Phone __ __ __ __

Shopping __ __ __ __

Water__ __ __ __

ight 

Explain to children that ight *has the sound of /ī t/ in* light *and* kite*. Also explain that the* k *in* knight *is silent. Read the verse aloud and tell children to pretend they are throwing spears at the dragon when they hear the /ī t/ sound. Read the verse again and tell children to circle the words that stand for the /ī t/ sound.*

The brave knight,
Sir Thomas Dwight,
Saddled his horse
And rode into the night.
He knew in the morning
He must fight
The dragon king
With breath of flame.
Out of the east
The monster came.
From his nose
Smoke rings rose.

Green eyes flashed
In the morning light.
Sir Thomas was brave,
But he shook with fright.
"Maybe I'm wrong,
And maybe I'm right,
But, Mama, I don't want to fight."
His mama said, "You've been
Tossing all night.
Are your pajamas a little tight?
Wake up
And I'll get you a frost delight."

Name: ______________________ Date: ____________ 8-209

ould

Tell children that the letters ould *have the sound of /o͝od/ as in* could, would, *and* should. *Read the verse aloud and tell children to circle the letters that stand for the /o͝od/ sound.*

I wish I could,

I wish I would

Do all the things

A good kid should.

Tell children that if they draw lines between words with the sound of /o͝o/ as in could, *they will reach the woods for a picnic with friends.*

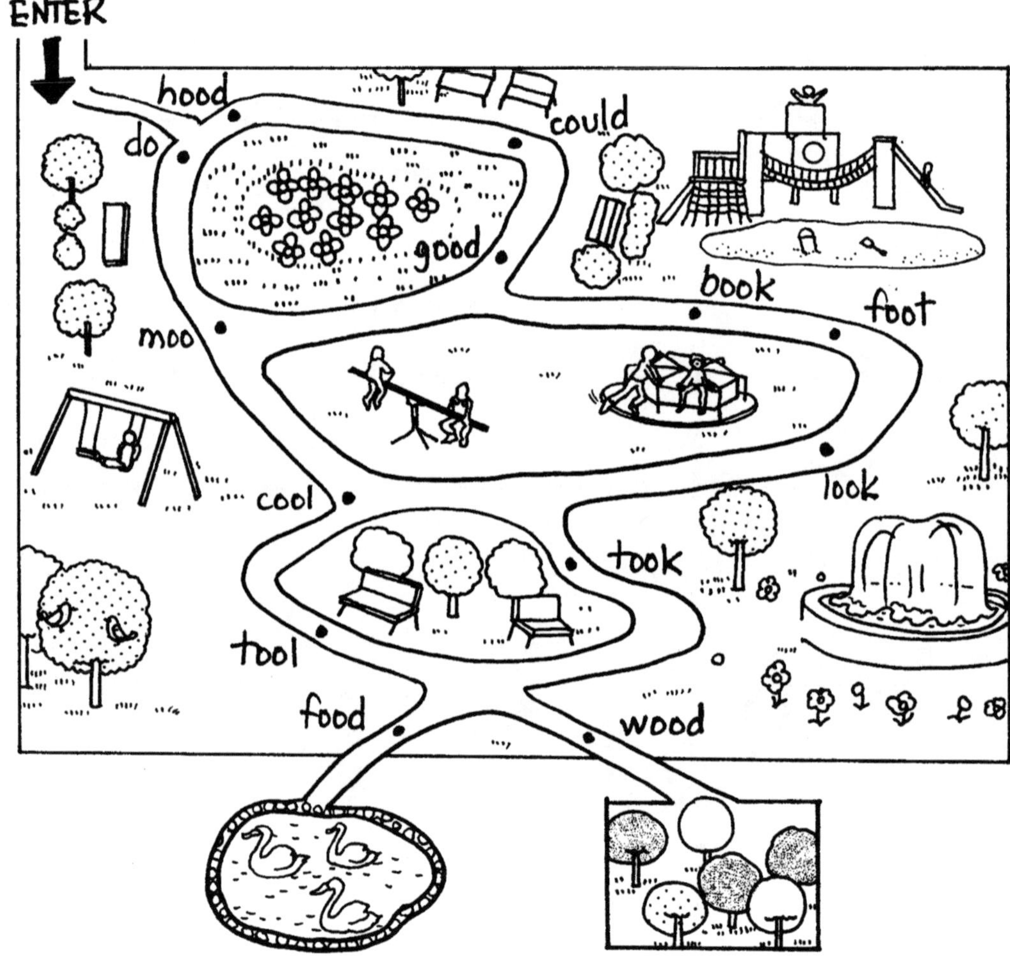

Name: ______________________ Date: ____________ 8-210

y 

Read the verse aloud and tell children to pretend they're crying when they hear the /ī/ sound as in shy. Read the verse again and tell children to circle the letters that stand for the /ī/ sound.

Mom said, "Pam, try not to cry."

Pam said, "Why, Mom, why?"

Mom said, "If I dry your eyes

You can see the sun and sky.

You can see the small birds fly.

That's why."

Tell children to circle pairs of words that describe each picture.

Dad in tie Dad, why

big sky big fly

Mike's bike big Mike

tie in sky pie in sky

ice cube ice mice

fry rice try pie

Name: ______________________ Date: __________ 8-211

Long i Review

Tell children to color those spaces with words that have the /ī/ sound as in kite.

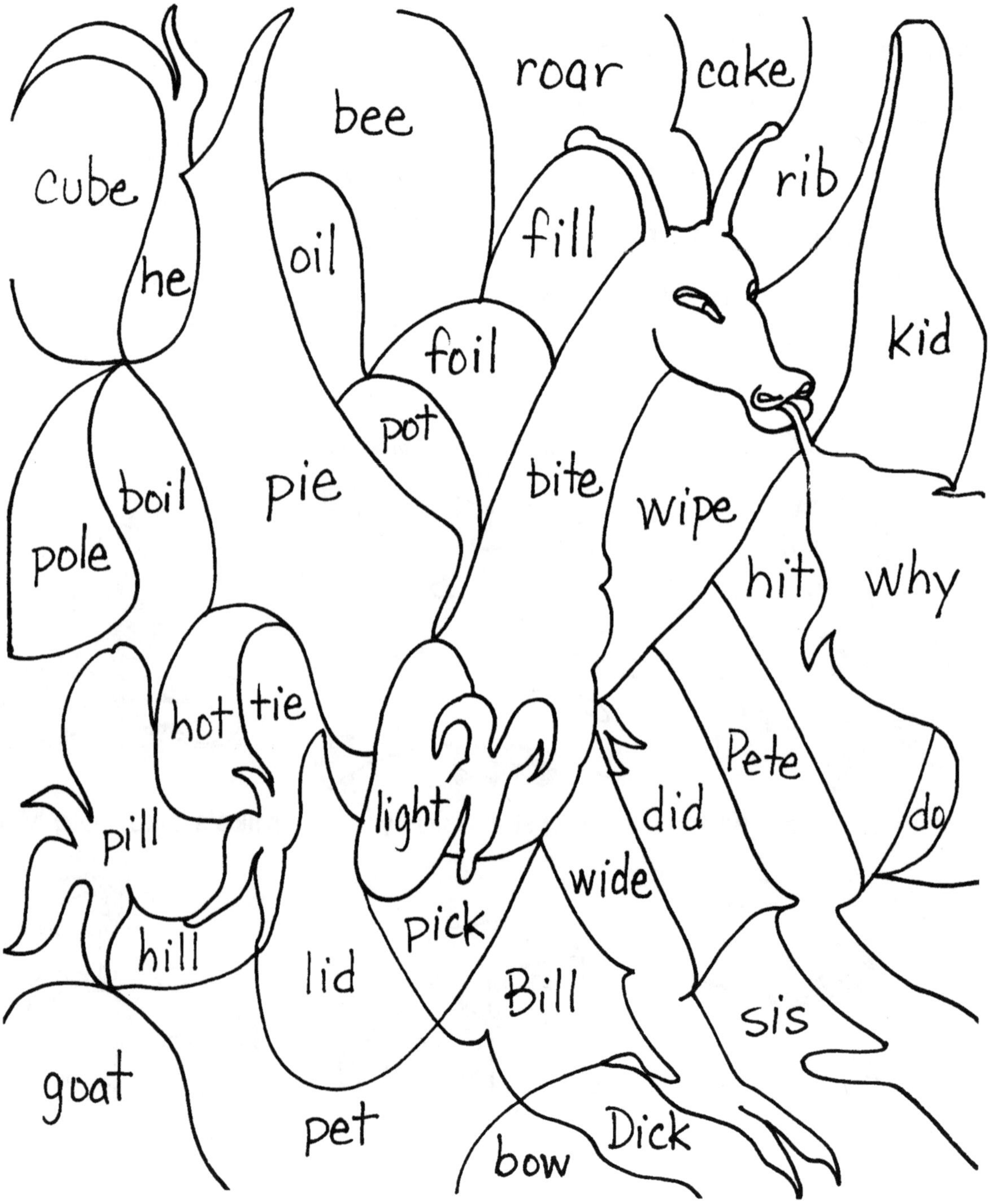

cube
he
bee
roar
cake
oil
fill
rib
foil
kid
pot
boil
pie
bite
wipe
pole
hit
why
hot
tie
Pete
light
did
do
pill
wide
pick
hill
lid
Bill
sis
goat
pet
Dick
bow

Long Vowel Review

This is an activity in long vowel identification. Tell children to circle the pictures of the long vowel words. Some of the pictures will be easy to see and some will be hidden.

cake	sky	cube	pole	wheel
kite	tie	goat	bow	bee

ĕad

head

Explain to children that on this page the letters ead have the sound of /ĕd/ as in bed, not /ē/ as in meat. Read the story aloud and ask children to pretend they are putting bread on their heads each time they hear ead pronounced as /ĕd/. Read the story again and ask children to circle ead each time these letters stand for the /ĕd/ sound.

Bread on Head

Roy liked to play at meals. He put bread on his head. Mom said, "Don't put bread on your head. Eat your bread!" Roy said, "Yes, Mom," and ate his bread. Roy put a pencil on his ear. Mom said, "Don't put a lead pencil on your ear. Write a note instead." So Roy wrote a note to Dad. Dad read the note and was glad. Roy read a book in bed. Mom said, "That's okay, Roy. You can read in bed." So Roy read a book about a boy named Roy.

Tell children to circle the pictures whose names have the /ĕ/ sound as in bed.

bread	**net**
feet	**tea**
head	**ten**
lead	**thread**
meat	**tree**
	web

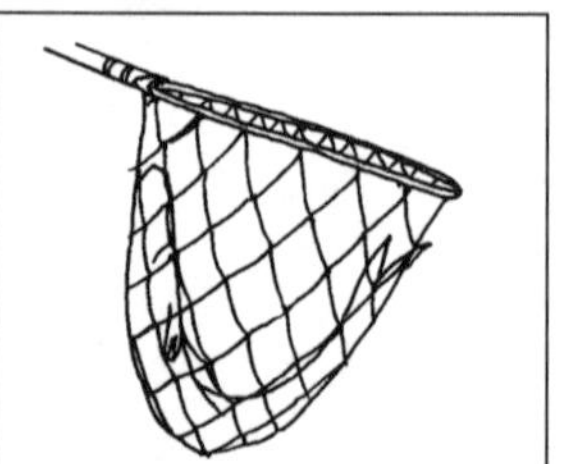
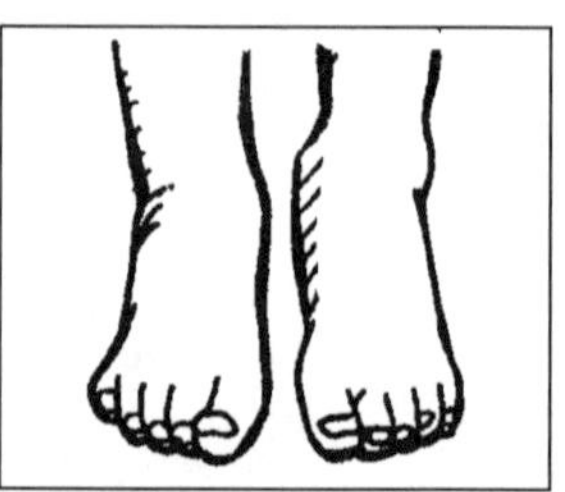

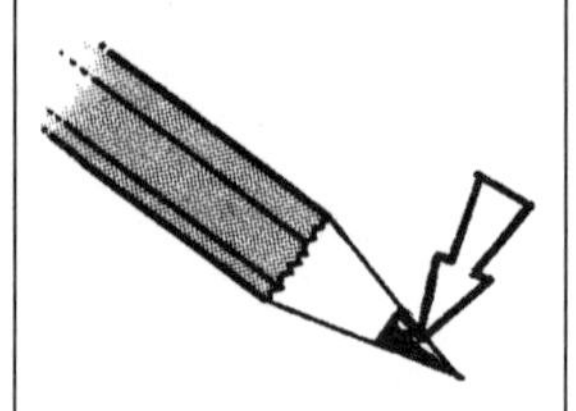

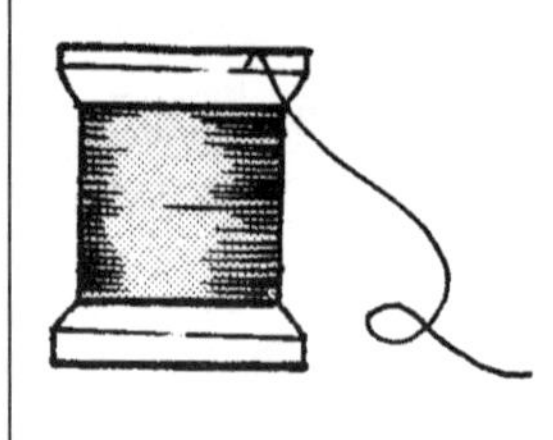

OO 

Read the passage aloud and tell children to say "boo" whenever they hear the /o͞o/ sound as in moo. Read the passage again and tell children to circle the letters that stand for the /o͞o/ sound. Mention that /ou/ in you also has the /o͞o/ sound.

If you get a nice present, you say, "Oo." If you want to scare someone, you might jump out from behind a curtain and say, "Boo!" Sticky stuff is goo. A pigeon coos. A cow says, "Moo." The wind says, "Woo." Can you say "woo," too?

Tell children to print the correct /o͞o/ word under each picture.

___ ___ ___

___ ___

___ ___ ___

___ ___ ___

___ ___ ___

___ ___ ___

Name: ______________________ Date: ____________ 8-215

ood, ool

Read the verse aloud and tell children to say /o͞o/ when they hear the /o͞od/ sound as in food. Read the verse again and tell children to circle the letters that stand for the /o͞od/ sound.

When I'm in a bad mood,

I never eat my food.

Read the verse aloud and tell children to pretend they're swimming when they hear the /o͞ol/ sound as in pool. Read the verse again and tell children to circle the letters that stand for the /o͞ol/ sound.

If the day was warm

Or the day was cool

Bobby Brooks

Wouldn't go to school.

He swam all day

In a swimming pool,

And grew up

to be a fool.

Read the following numbered words and tell children to circle oo beside the number of words that have the /o͞o/ sound as in boo: 1. school, 2. good, 3. pool, 4. wood, 5. moo, 6. too, 7. tool, 8. foot.

1. oo
2. oo
3. oo
4. oo
5. oo
6. oo
7. oo
8. oo

Name: ______________________ Date: ____________

oom, oon

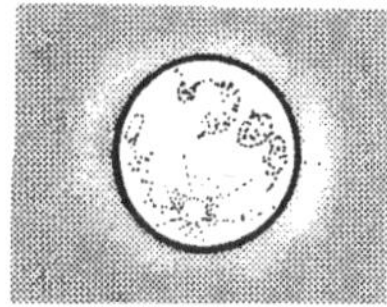

Read the verse aloud and ask children to tap out drum rhythms on their legs when they hear the /o͞om/ sound as in <u>boom</u>. *Read the verse again and tell children to circle the letters that stand for the /o͞om/ sound.*

Boom-lay, boom-lay,
Boom-lay, boom.
Tom has a drum
In his living room.

Read the verse aloud and tell children to put two fingers up like the hands on the clock pointing to noon when they hear the /o͞on/ sound as in <u>moon</u>. *Read the verse again and tell children to circle the letters that stand for the /o͞on/ sound.*

The man in the moon
Came out at noon.
"Go back," said Jack.
"You came too soon."

oop, oot

Read the verse aloud and tell children to move hips as if they were whirling a hoop when they hear the /o͞op/ sound as in <u>hoop</u>*. Read the verse again and tell children to circle the letters that stand for the /o͞op/ sound.*

Little Barbara Boop
Had a hula hoop.
All alone in a chicken coop,
She whirled and whirled
Her hula hoop.

Read the verse aloud and tell children to make a fierce, pirate face when they hear the /o͞ot/ sound as in <u>root</u>*. Read the verse again and tell children to circle the letters that stand for the /o͞ot/ sound.*

A pirate whose face
Was covered with soot*
Stole gold from a ship.
He buried his loot
Underneath an old
Tree root.

***Note:** <u>Root</u> and <u>soot</u> are correctly pronounced with /o͞o/ and /o͝o/ sounds.

Name: ________________________ Date: ____________

Long oo Review

Tell children to draw lines to connect the words to the pictures.

boo
boot
broom
coop
food
moo
mood
moon
noon
soon
spoon
stool
tool
toot
zoom

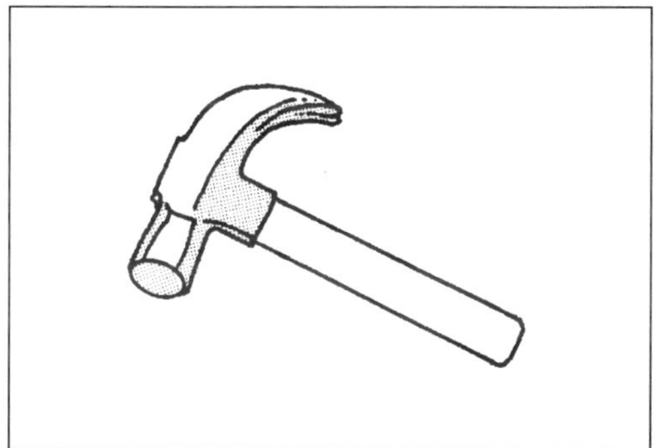

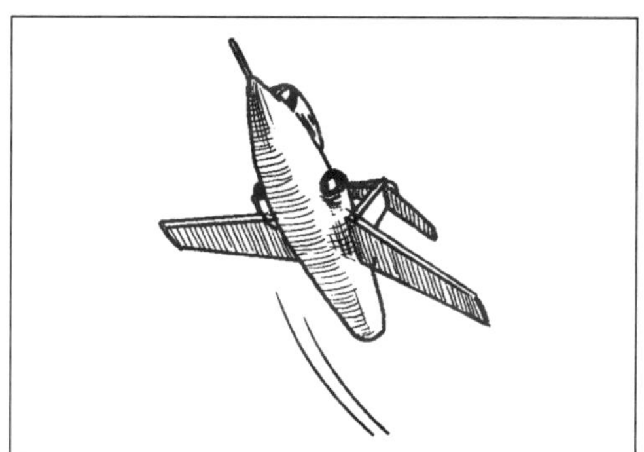

Name: ______________________ Date: __________ 8-219

Long oo Spelling Variations

Explain that sometimes different letters can stand for the /o͞o/ sound as in boo. Read the verse aloud and ask children to circle all the different letters in the verse that stand for the /o͞o/ sound.

I'll tell you a story
About Betty Blue,
A sweet little girl
Who maybe you knew.
She was sad when she lost
Her holiday shoe.
But as a smart little girl,
She knew what to do.
She bought another
To match the other.
And now she walks on two.

Tell children to circle the pictures whose names have the /o͞o/ sound as in boo.

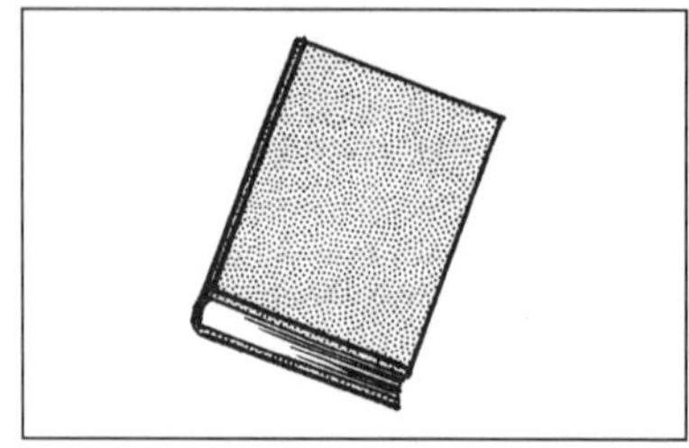

Name: ______________________ Date: ____________ 8-220

More Long oo Spelling Variations

Explain that different letters can stand for the /ōō/ sound as in moo. Read the verse aloud and ask children to say "moo" when they hear the /ōō/ sound. Read the verse again and tell children to circle the letters that stand for the /ōō/ sound.

The moon sang a tune
Until the new day came.
Little birds flew
In the blue, blue sky.
The little birds sang
Because they knew
Fat bugs hid in the
Morning dew.
Bugs for breakfast
And dinner, too,
When Mom would make
A big, bug stew.

Remind children that different letters can stand for the /ōō/ sound as in moo. Read the sentences aloud and ask children to say "moo" when they hear the /ōō/ sound. Read the sentences again and ask children to circle the different letters that stand for the /ōō/ sound.

1. Who are you?
2. Lou shook the book.
3. Are you in school?
4. Is it cool on the moon?
5. Do cows say "Moo"?
6. Do cats say "Moo," too?
7. Is wood good to eat?
8. Is that true?

Name: ______________________ Date: ____________ 8-221

Long oo Student Reading Selection

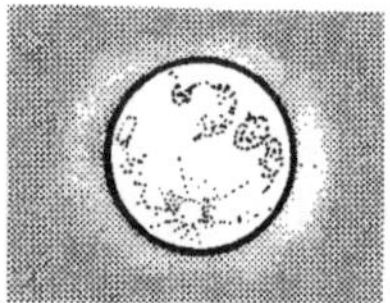

Review is, said, the, *and* was *as sight words. Explain that two-part words, like* daylight, daytime, *and* moonlight *can be sounded out in separate syllables or word parts. Now children can read the story by themselves.*

The Moon

The day was dark. Gloom was in the sky. So the moon came out at noon. "Go back," said Jack, "you came too soon." The moon said, "Oops, I came at noon." The cow said, "Moo, moonlight in daylight is odd." The sun got in a bad mood. The sun said, "Daytime is my time." The baboon said, "No room, no room for sun and moon." The drum said, "Boom, boom. The moon is a fool." The train said, "Toot, toot, the moon is a goof." The moon shone on the pool. Kids swam in the pool and said, "The moon at noon is cool." The owl said, "Hoot, hoot, I came at noon. The moon can, too."

Tell children to put the number of each word in the circle next to the correct picture.

1. boo	3. boot	5. spool
2. boom	4. cool	6. tool

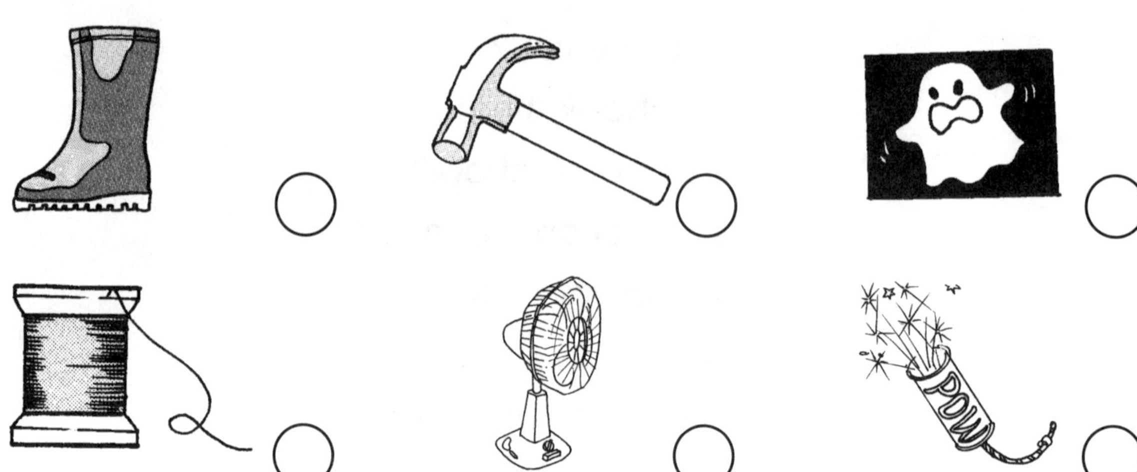

Name: ______________________ Date: ____________ 8-222

ood, oof 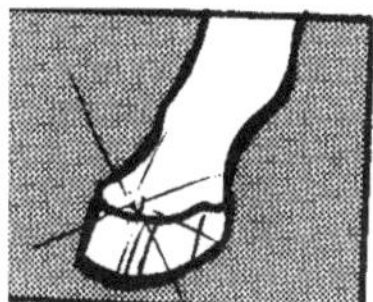

Read the verse aloud and tell children to pretend they are flying when they hear the /ŏŏd/ sound as in hood. *Read the verse again and tell children to circle the letters that stand for /ŏŏd/.*

There was a fairy
Who lived in a wood
With a silver wand
And a silver hood.
The children
Loved her
Because she was good.

Read the verse aloud and tell children to say "woof woof" when they hear the /ŏŏf/ sound as in hoof. *Read the verse again and tell children to circle the letters that stand for the /ŏŏf/ sound.*

A unicorn with a golden hoof*
Met an old, black crow
That sat on a roof
And a plain old dog
That said, "Woof woof."

***Note:** Hoof, roof, and woof are correctly pronounced with both the /o͞o/ and /ŏŏ/ sounds.

Name: ______________________________ Date: ______________ 8-223

ook 

Read the verse aloud and tell children to pretend they are shaking in fear when they hear the /ŏŏk/ sound as in book. *Read the verse again and tell children to circle the letters that stand for the /ŏŏk/ sound.*

There was a pirate
Named Captain Cook.
Instead of a hand,
He had a hook.
When he walked on the deck,
The pirates shook.
They hid in every
Corner and nook.
They shivered in fear
Whenever he took
A pen to write names
In his big black book.

Tell children to circle the pictures whose names have the /ŏŏ/ sound as in book.

boot

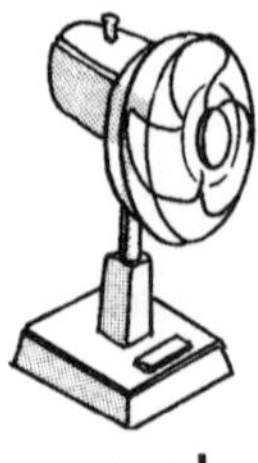

cool

wood

boom

hook

cook

Name: ______________________ Date: ____________ 8-224

Short oo Student Reading Selection

woof

Review said as a sight word. Then children can read the story by themselves.

Pam Can Read

"Look, look," said Mom. "Pam can read her book." "Good, good," said Dad. "Pam took a book, and she can read it." Mom said, "I will cook a good meal for Pam." Tod said, "I will hook a big fish for Pam." Bob said, "I will tap my foot for Pam." The tree said, "I will get wood for Pam." Rip said, "I will woof for Pam. Woof, woof, woof. Pam can read her book."

Read the numbered words aloud. Tell children to draw a straight line over oo when the word has the /o͞o/ sound as in boo and a curved line over oo when the word has the /o͝o/ sound as in book. 1. shook, 2. moo, 3. cool, 4. hoop, 5. wood, 6. stool, 7. fool, 8. pool, 9. cook, 10. too, 11. wool, 12. woof, 13. moon, 14. bloom, 15. hook.

1. oo
2. oo
3. oo
4. oo
5. oo
6. oo
7. oo
8. oo
9. oo
10. oo
11. oo
12. oo
13. oo
14. oo
15. oo

Section 9
Initial Consonant Blends

Let's think of things
We're thankful for
Like Thanksgiving turkey
And so much more.

Name: ______________________________ Date: ______________

bl 

Read the sentence aloud and ask children to blink their eyes when they hear the /bl/ sound as in blouse. *Read it again and ask children to circle the letters that stand for the /bl/ sound.*

Blackie Bloom loved to play blind man's bluff in the big blue room. He said, "Blind man's bluff is a blast."

Tell children to print the correct /bl/ words in the blanks.

black	blaze	blink	blocks	bloom	blouse	blow	blue

1. bl___ ___ ___.
2. I can bl___ ___ .
3. I can bl___ ___ ___ my
4. A crow is bl___ ___ ___.
5. Kids like to play with bl___ ___ ___s.
6. A big fire is a bl___ ___ ___.
7. The flag is red, white, and bl___ ___.
8. Mom's bl___ ___ ___ ___ is red.

Name: ______________________ Date: ____________ 9-226

br 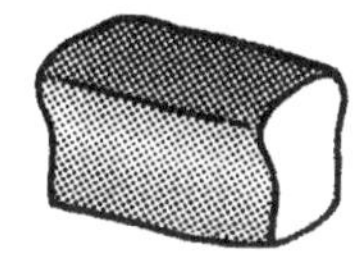

Read the verse aloud and tell children to circle the words that begin with the /br/ sound as in bread.

Brad brought a fishing pole,
And Brian brought a hook.
They caught dinner
In a little brook.
They broiled whitefish
Under a bridge,
And ate them with brown bread
From out of Grandma's fridge.

Tell children to draw a circle around the pictures that begin with br.

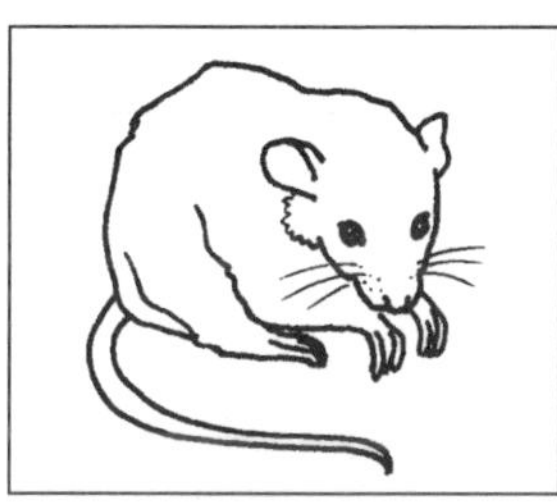

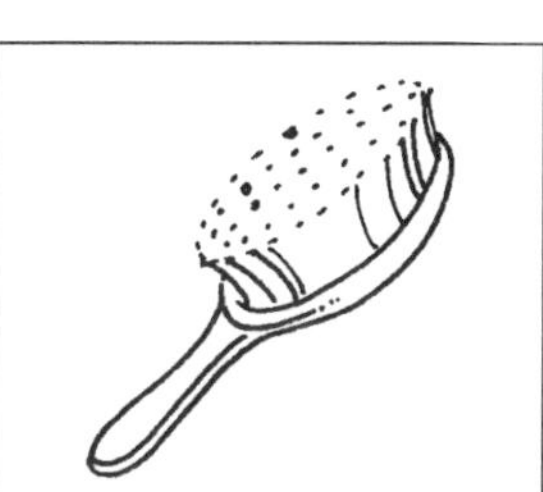

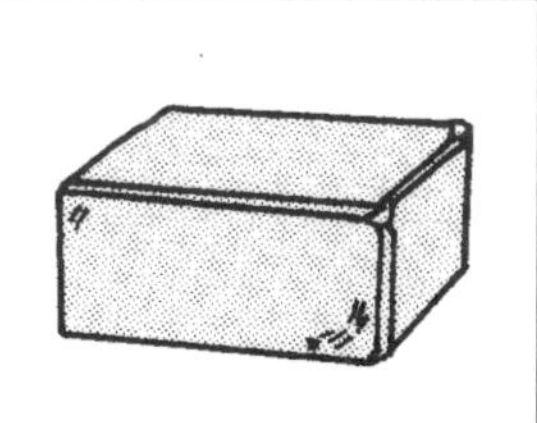
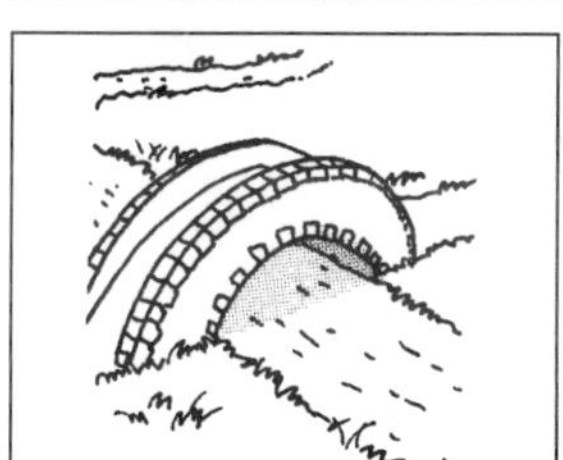

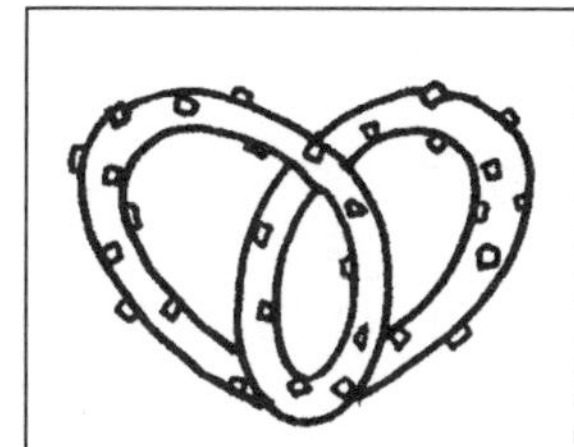
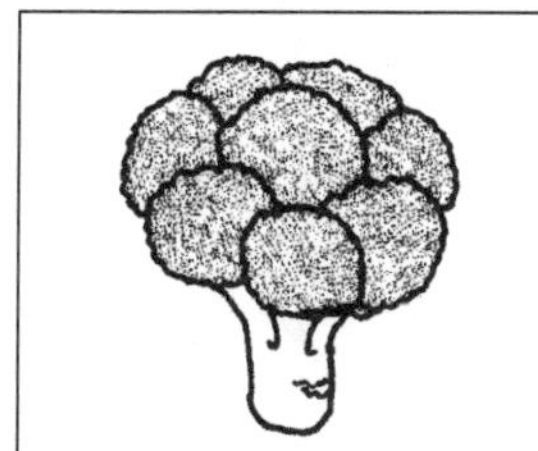

Name: ______________________ Date: ____________ 9-227

ch  clang

Read the story aloud and ask children to make a choo-choo train noise when they hear the /ch/ sound as in chair. Read the story again and ask children to circle the letters that stand for the /ch/ sound.

Chucky is chewing a chunky bone and I am eating chili. Mom is chatting on the phone with her old chum, Millie. Dad is watching champions play a boring game of chess, and Charlotte's sitting in a chair sewing on a dress. Chad is playing checkers and sitting on the floor, while Mrs. Chan from Charleston is knocking on the door.

Tell children to print ch under the words whose names begin with ch.

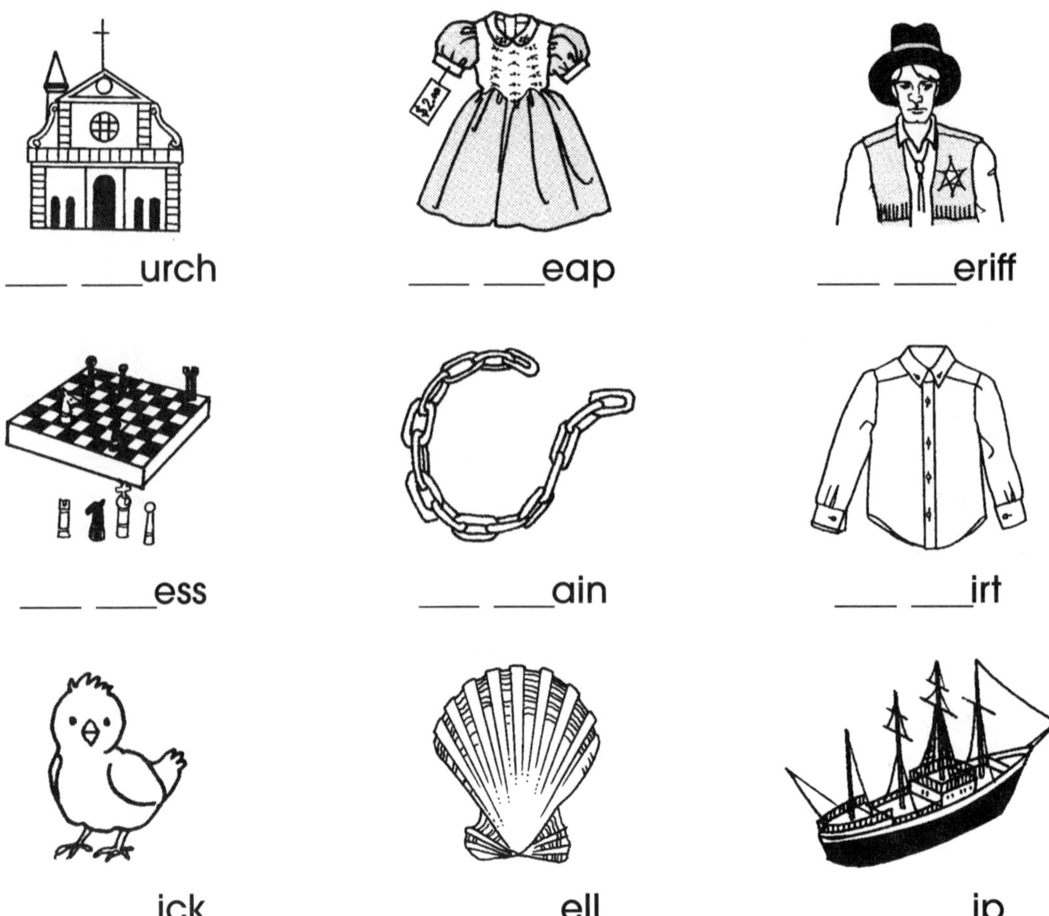

Name: ______________________________ Date: ______________

cl

clang

Read the verse aloud and tell children to make each of the sounds when they hear words beginning with the /cl/ sound. For example, the children can make a clopping noise when they hear the word clop, a clinking noise when they hear the word clink, etc. Wait a few seconds after reading each /cl/ word so that children have time to make an appropriate sound. Read the verse again and tell children to circle letters that stand for the /cl/ sound.

Noises

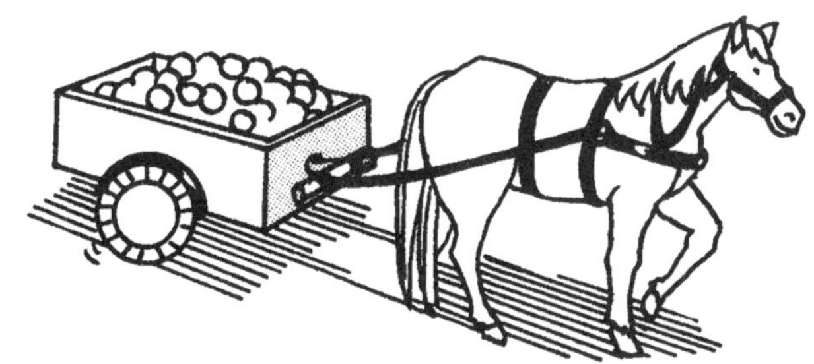

A horse might clop
Going down a street
While a penny clinks
When it falls at your feet.
People clap at the end of a play.
A clock says tick-tock every day.
A hen can cluck,
But never a duck
Who can only quack
As it swims in a pond.
A giant clops
As he clomps on the ground.
A fire engine goes clang, clang, clang,
While a firecracker goes bang, bang, bang.
What in the world
Goes clank, clank, clank?
The tin woodsman of Oz
Or maybe a tank.

Name: ______________________________ Date: ____________ 9-229

cr 

Read the verse aloud and tell children to make claw movements with their hands when they hear the /cr/ sound as in crab. Read the verse again and tell children to circle the letters that stand for the /cr/ sound.

A crocodile in a creek
Is a critter I'm afraid to meet.
But a baby creeping on the floor
Doesn't scare me, not at all.
A crab in a dish
Is a critter like a fish,
While peanut butter crunch
Is food I eat for lunch.

Tell children to put the correct cr words in the blanks. Read the sentences aloud if necessary.

crackers
crayon
cream
crib
cross
crown
crust

1. I like to eat ___ ___ ___ ___ ___ ___ ___ ___ and jam.
2. I like ice ___ ___ ___ ___ ___.
3. A baby sleeps in a ___ ___ ___ ___.
4. A king wears a ___ ___ ___ ___ ___.
5. I need a red ___ ___ ___ ___ ___ ___ to draw with.
6. The light is green. You may ___ ___ ___ ___ ___ the street.
7. Do you eat the ___ ___ ___ ___ ___ on your bread?

Name: ______________________ Date: __________ 9-230

dr

Read the verse aloud and tell children to pretend they are dragons when they hear the /dr/ sound as in dragon. *They can make a dragon face or sound or extend their hands like dragon claws. Read the verse again and ask children to circle the letters that stand for the /dr/ sound.*

I had a dream the other night
About a dragon that was black and white.
It really gave me quite a scare
Until I dreamed it wasn't there.
In the morning, in the light,
At the very end of night,
I drew a picture I could draw
Of the dragon that I saw.

Tell children to print /dr/ words in the correct spaces across the puzzle.

dragon
draw
dress
drew
drip
drum

			D					
			R					
			E					
			A					
			M					
			S					

Name: ______________________ Date: ____________ 9-231

fl 

Read the verse aloud and tell children to pretend they're flying when they hear the /fl/ sound as in fly and flag. Read the verse again and tell children to circle the letters that stand for the /fl/ sound.

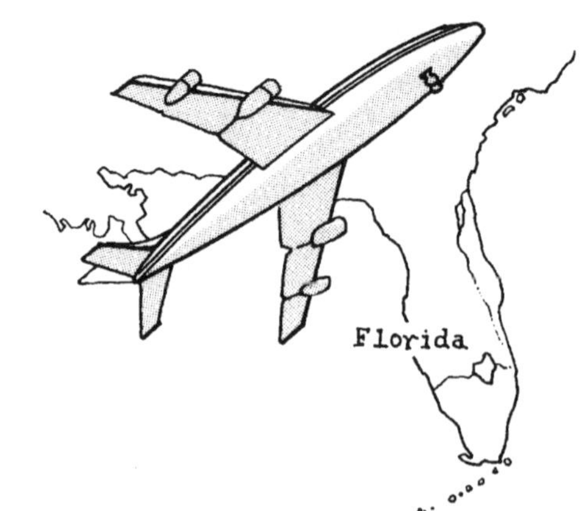

Mom and Dad and Flossie get
A flight to Florida in a jet.
This is the first time Flossie flew.
She had questions,
Wouldn't you?
"Why does a plane stay in the sky?
Do plane wings flap when they fly?
Are these clouds I'm looking at?
Can an airplane get a flat?"

Tell children to circle the word that goes in the blank.

1. This was the first time Flossie _____.
   drew grew flew
2. Flossie asked, "Can an airplane get a _____?"
   that flat chat
3. I see a _____ of sheep.
   flock clock knock
4. Flossie and her mom and dad got a _____.
   bright flight fright
5. Flossie doesn't understand how an airplane _____.
   flies tries cries
6. We make cake with _____.
   flower hour flour
7. Fire is _____.
   blame flame frame
8. Flossie asked if an airplane's wings _____ when they fly.
   clap slap flap

Read the letter aloud and tell children to pretend they are eating French fries when they hear the /fr/ sound as in French fries. Read the verse again and tell children to circle the letters that stand for the /fr/ sound.

Dear Uncle Fred,

Thank you for taking Francis and me to the French restaurant. My friend Francis and I loved the French fries, the fritters, the fried fish, the fresh berries, and the fruit frosty. It was the best frozen dessert we've ever had. Please send lots of love to Friskie from Francis and me.

Love,

Frieda

Tell children to draw a circle around the letters that begin the name of each picture.

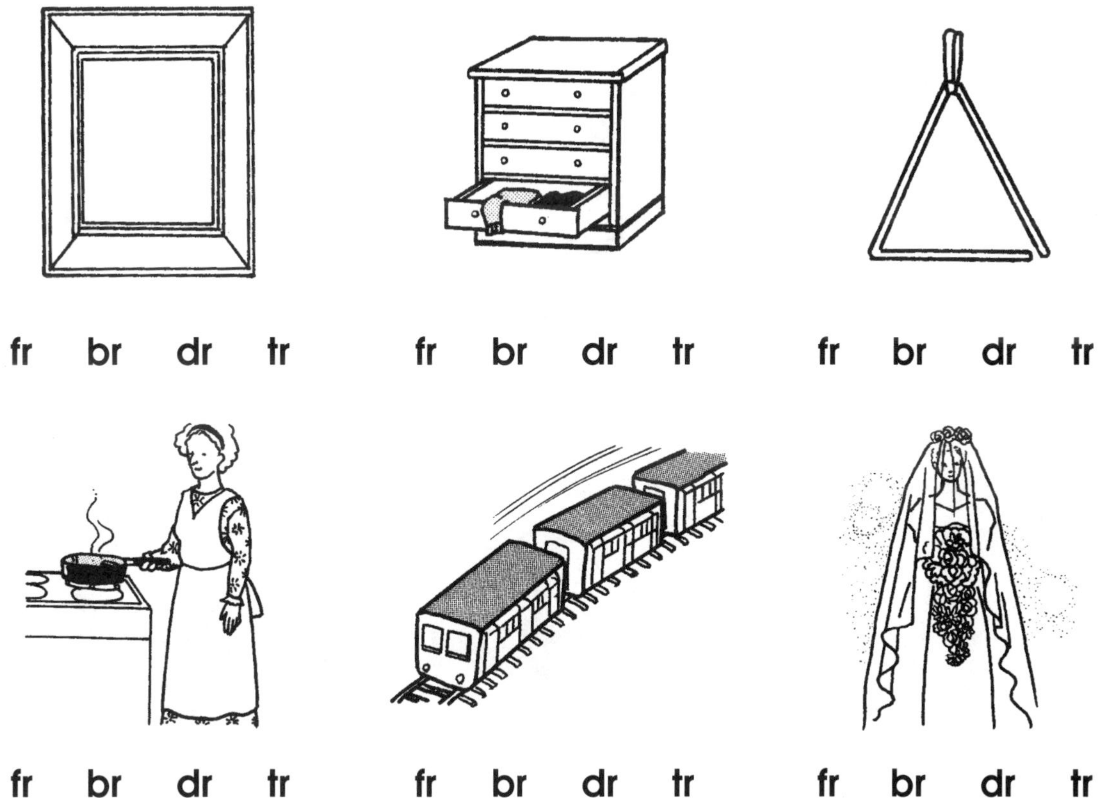

Name: ______________________ Date: ____________ 9-233

gl

Read the verse aloud and tell children to pretend they are ice skating when they hear the /gl/ sound as in glass. Read the verse again and tell children to circle the letters that stand for the /gl/ sound.

I love to skate when the ice is like glass
And the whole rink glitters when I pass.
I love to twirl
And glide and whirl.
I'm glad to be here in the rink tonight,
To see ice glowing in the light.

Tell children to circle the letters that begin the name of each picture.

block	flag	flat	glad	globe	plant

bl fl gl pl

bl fl gl pl

bl fl gl pl

bl fl gl pl

bl fl gl pl

bl fl gl pl

Name: ______________________________ Date: ______________

gr

Read the verse aloud and tell children to grin when they hear the /gr/ sound as in grin. Read the verse again and tell children to circle the letters that stand for the /gr/ sound.

Great-grandma was so very proud
When I passed to second grade.
She made green cookies for the class
And pitchers full of lemonade.
She frosted grapes with sugar grains
And hung them on the window panes.
She lifted me high above the grass,
Saying, "Greg is growing up so fast."

Tell children to print the correct /gr/ words in the blanks.

grade
grandfather
grandmother
grass
green
Greg
grin
grows
grunt

1. My mom's ___ ___ ___ ___ ___ ___ ___ ___ ___ ___ ___ is my great-grandmother.
2. I have a ___ ___ ___ ___ ___ coat.
3. A smile is a ___ ___ ___ ___ .
4. ___ ___ ___ ___ ___ ___ ___ ___ ___s in the yard.
5. I am in first ___ ___ ___ ___ ___.
6. Pigs ___ ___ ___ ___ ___.
7. My dad's ___ ___ ___ ___ ___ ___ ___ ___ ___ ___ ___ is my great-grandfather.
8. ___ ___ ___ ___ is a boy's name.

Name: ______________________ Date: ____________ 9-235

pl 

Read the story aloud and tell children to circle the words that begin with the /pl/ sound as in plum.

Mr. Platt said to Mrs. Platt, "Please plant plenty of plum tomatoes." Mrs. Platt said to Mr. Platt, "I don't like plum tomatoes. I'm planning to plant plenty of potatoes."

Read children the following numbered words and tell them to print the letters pl *beside the numbers of words that begin with the /pl/ sound as in* plum. *1. print, 2. pan, 3. plan, 4. pretty, 5. prince, 6. play, 7. pay, 8. pat, 9. bat, 10. place, 11. prize, 12. plum, 13. please, 14. plate, 15. panda, 16. plenty.*

1. ___ ___
2. ___ ___
3. ___ ___
4. ___ ___
5. ___ ___
6. ___ ___
7. ___ ___
8. ___ ___
9. ___ ___
10. ___ ___
11. ___ ___
12. ___ ___
13. ___ ___
14. ___ ___
15. ___ ___
16. ___ ___

Name: ______________________ Date: __________ 9-236

pr 

Read the verse aloud and tell children to circle the words that begin with the /pr/ sound as in prize.

The prince was strong.
The prince was proud.
Priscilla saw him
And she bowed.
His prize horse pranced
In the tall, green grass,
And Priscilla tossed
Primroses as he passed.

Tell children to print the letters pr *in the blanks under pictures that begin with the /pr/ sound as in* prize.

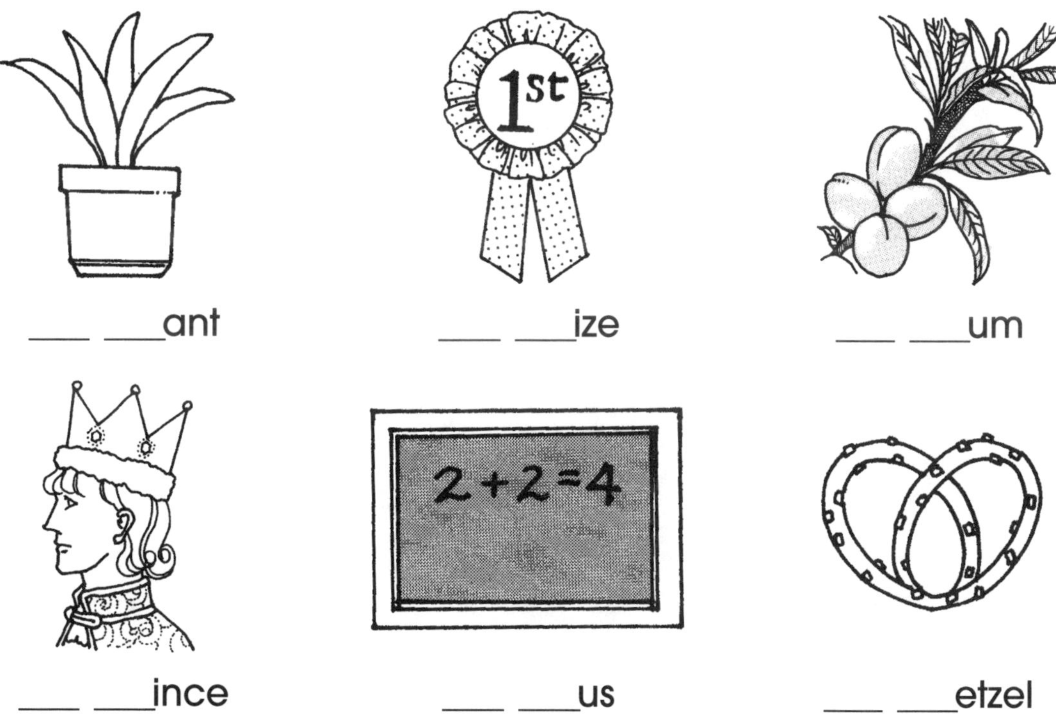

___ ___ant   ___ ___ize   ___ ___um

___ ___ince   ___ ___us   ___ ___etzel

Name: ______________________ Date: ____________ 9-237

sc, sk

Read the story aloud and tell children to skip when they hear the /sk/ sound as in skeleton and in scale. Read the story again and tell children to circle the letters that have the /sk/ sound.

A skeleton met a skunk. The skunk said to the skeleton, "You are very skinny." The skeleton said to the skunk, "I'm scared of you. I can scrub and scour for half an hour, and all my skill will not kill your smell." The skeleton scurried away.

Tell children to circle the first letters of the name of each picture.

scale	skis
skates	skunk
skeleton	slacks
skinny	slide

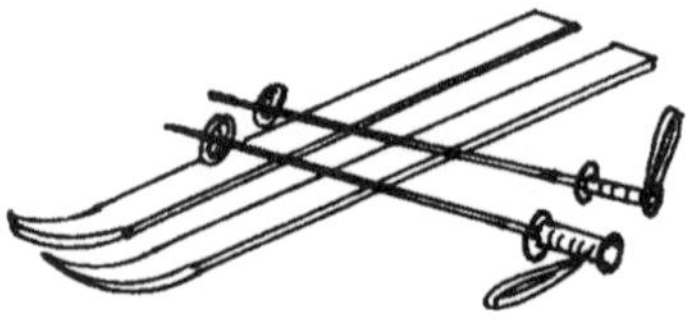

sc sk sl

sc sk sl

sc sk sl

sc sk sl

sc sk sl

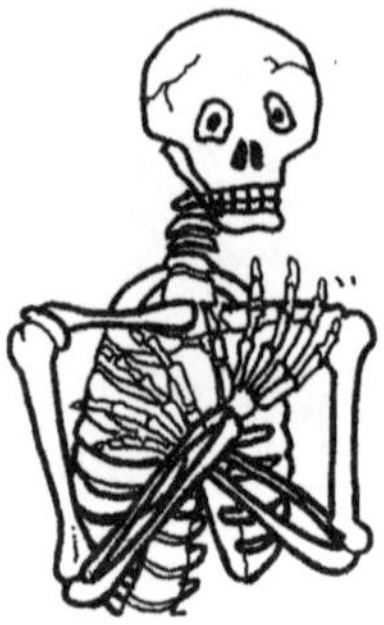

sc sk sl

sc sk sl

sc sk sl

Name: ______________________ Date: __________ 9-238

sh 

Read the verse aloud and tell children to say "shh" when they hear the /sh/ sound as in ship. Read the verse again and tell children to circle the letters that stand for the /sh/ sound.

Shirley and Sherry sailed on a ship.
Shirley and Sherry took a long trip
To a land of shepherds
Tending their sheep
And shouting boys who didn't sleep.
On to an island the shaky ship rolled
Where the shells on the shore
Were shining with gold.

Tell children to draw lines between words that begin or end with the same two letters. If they draw lines correctly, they will make a picture.

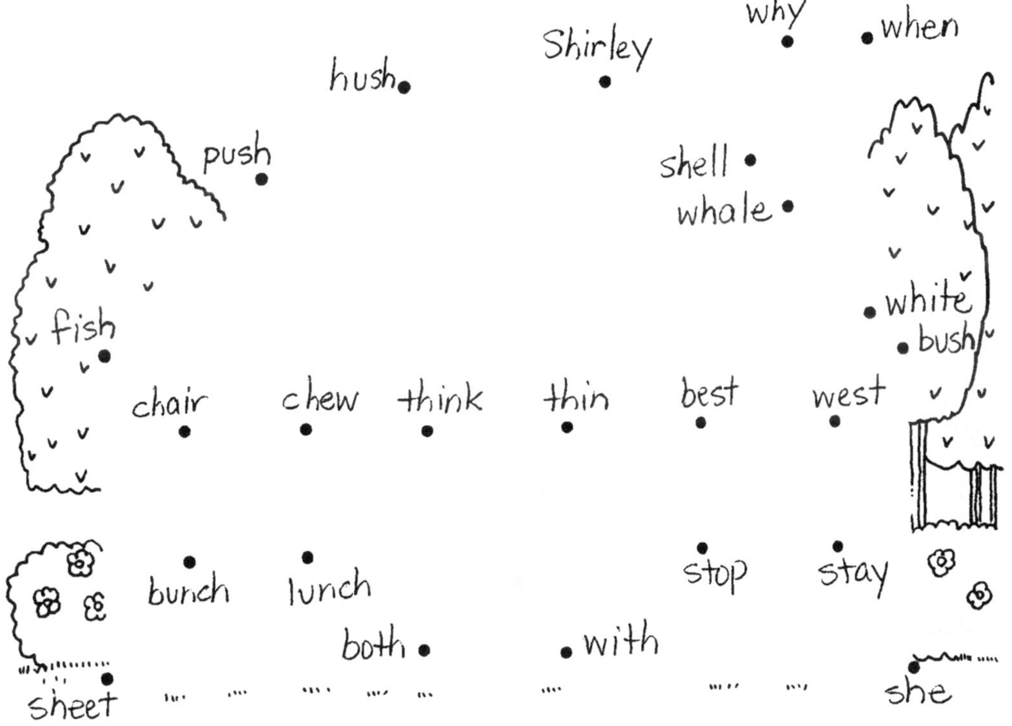

sl 

Read the verse aloud and tell children to slide on the floor when they hear the /sl/ sound as in sled. Read the verse again and tell children to circle the letters that stand for the /sl/ sound.

Sally Slade had a sled
That she painted white and red.
She really loved to slip and slide
Down a slope all white and wide.
How she loved to slosh and rush
In the snow and through the slush.

Tell children to put the number of the correct word in the circle next to each picture.

1. slam
2. slap
3. slide
4. slim
5. slip

sm, sn

Tell children to pretend they are smelling something good to eat when they hear the /sm/ sound as in smock. Read the verse again and tell children to circle the letters that stand for the /sm/ sound. Tell children there are only three /sm/ words in the verse.

Samantha wore an orange smock
To protect her pretty frock
From every smear and every smudge
From finger paints or chocolate fudge.

Tell children to print sm or sn in the blanks that begin each word

___ ___ack

___ ___all

___ ___oke

___ ___ake

___ ___ock

___ ___ell

Name: ______________________ Date: ____________

sn

Read the story aloud and tell children to snap and snarl like Sneakers in the story when they hear the /sn/ sound as in snake. Read the story again and tell children to circle the letters that have the /sn/ sound.

Sneakers saw a narrow fellow. He wasn't brown and he wasn't yellow. Sneakers sniffed and Sneakers snapped. Then he snarled at the grass when a snake tried to pass. My dad lay down to snatch a nap. He was snoring when I tapped. He came running when I told him. But when finally I showed him, he said, "Sneakers, move your snout and let that harmless snake come out."

Tell the class that eight children have each lost one mitten. Students must help the children find their missing mittens by matching beginning and ending parts of sm and sn words. They must draw lines between the mittens that belong together.

Name: ______________________ Date: ____________ 9-242

sp 

Read the verse aloud and tell children to lift their heads high as if they are looking at stars when they hear the /sp/ sound as in spoon. Read the verse again and tell children to circle the letters that stand for the /sp/ sound.

What Are They?

Tiny specks that sparkle bright,
We can see them every night.
Sometimes like a spear of light,
One falls speeding out of sight.*
One group is like a silver spoon,*
And one a highway to the moon.*
Some have names I cannot spell,
But my teacher taught me well.
Every spark in endless space
Is a world in its own place.

*a comet, Big Dipper, Milky Way

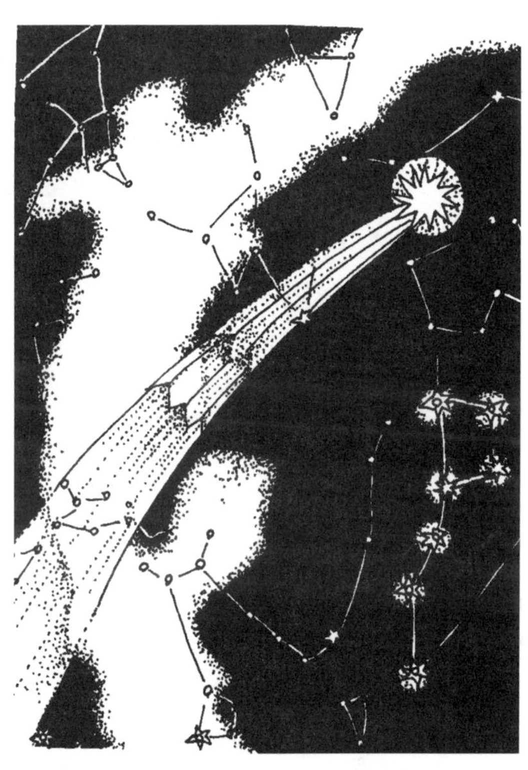

Tell children to circle the pictures whose names begin with the /sp/ sound.

spill slacks

skates spoon

spot

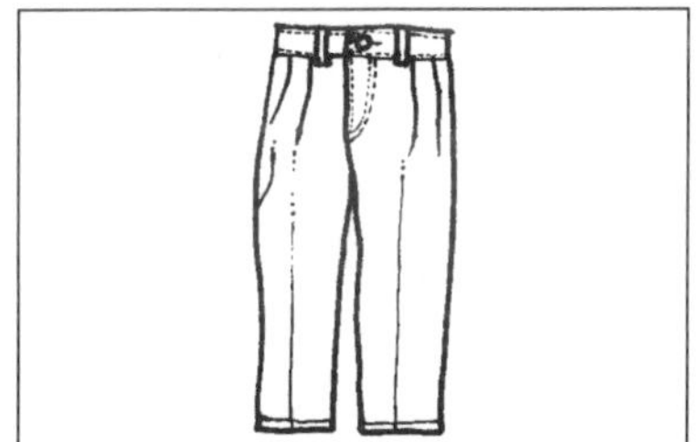

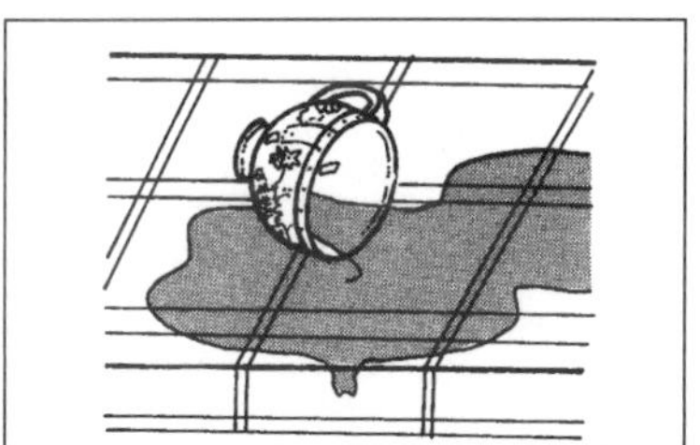

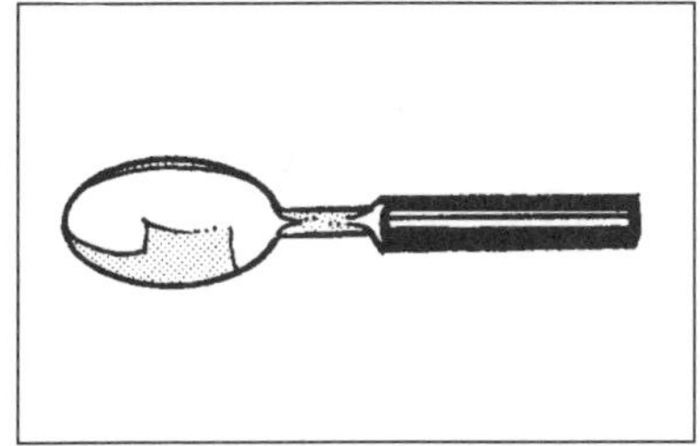

Name: ______________________________ Date: ______________ 9-243

squ

Have children brainstorm and tell you squ words they know. Explain unfamiliar words in the story. Mention that ua in squa words has the sound of /ô/ as in saw. Then read the story aloud and tell children to squat when they hear the /skw/ sound as in squash. Read the story again and tell children to circle the letters that stand for the /skw/ sound.

A squiggle in a curly line. It never is a square. Whales come out and sometimes spout or squirt into the air. Can a person squabble with a friend who isn't there? When you sit, you do not squat. Tell me, were you ever taught how to cook a summer squash? Which can squeak, a squirrel or mouse? Which can blow away a house, a cyclone or a summer squall?

Tell children to draw lines between the words and their pictures.

square

squash

squat

squeak

squiggle

squirrel

squirt

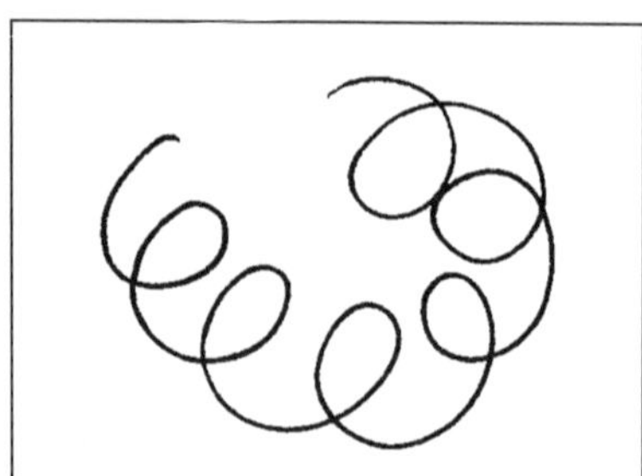

Name: ______________________ Date: ____________

st

Read the story aloud and tell children to pretend they are climbing stairs when they hear the /st/ sound as in stairs. Read the verse again and tell children to circle letters that stand for the /st/ sound.

Steps on the Stairs

Why is it tonight I cannot sleep? Is it the sound of a stranger's feet? I hear steps upon the stairs and I wonder who is there. Has a robber come to steal lots of stuff from Sunday's meal? Has a burglar from Ontario come to steal our brand new stereo? I wouldn't worry if I knew. I'd start sleeping, wouldn't you? Then Stumpy stole into my bed and stuck his nose against my head. It was Stumpy on the stairs, and so I stopped being scared.

Tell children to put the correct letters in the blanks.

sl	sm	sp	st

1. : ___ ___airs

2. hit: ___ ___ap

3. hit: ___ ___ack

4. fat: ___ ___out

5. talk: ___ ___eak

6. pants: ___ ___acks

7. : ___ ___ove

8. sniff: ___ ___ell

Name: ________________________________ Date: ______________ 9-245

sw

Read the story aloud and ask children to pretend they are swimming when they hear the /sw/ sound as in swing and swim. Read the verse again and ask children to circle letters that stand for the /sw/ sound. Next, help children learn the more unfamiliar /sw/ words. For example, ask children to demonstrate swooping and swirling. Ask children to mop their foreheads when you say, "It's a swell day, but it's sweltering."

S and W

Of all the s and w words, how many have you used or heard? Sweden is a country. A swallow is a bird. People sweat when they are hot and put on sweaters when they're not. Have you ever swept a floor? Have you ever slammed a door? Did you ever swat a fly, buzzing low and swirling by? In swimming, are you swift or slow? If a school is swank, would you like to go? Do s and w together begin a word about hot weather? I know the answers. You will, too. Just study s and w.

Tell children to put the number of the correct word in the circle next to each picture.

1. swan 2. sweat 3. sweep 4. sweet 5. swim 6. swing

Name: ______________________ Date: ____________ 9-246

th

Read the verse aloud and ask children to circle letters that stand for the /th/ sound as in thin.

Let's think of things
We're thankful for
Like Thanksgiving turkey
And so much more.

Read the verse aloud and ask children to circle letters that stand for the /th/ sound as in they.

This and these are near,
That and those are far
Like the snow on top of a mountain
Or the light of the evening star.
They are in the distance.
They are over there,
And we cannot touch them
Through the endless air.

Read the numbered words aloud and tell children to circle the number if the word they hear begins with the /th/ sound as in thin. *Tell children to put an X through the number if the word they hear begins with the /th/ sound as in* they: *1. thanks, 2. thin, 3. then, 4. the, 5. thunder, 6. thirteen, 7. thirty, 8. though, 9. themselves, 10. think.*

1	6
2	7
3	8
4	9
5	10

Name: ______________________ Date: __________ 9-247

tr

Read the verse aloud and ask children to make train-whistle noises when they hear the /tr/ sound as in train. Read the verse again and tell children to circle the letters that stand for the /tr/ sound.

Let's take a trip on the trolley
To the grand old circus train.
There's a bear
On a red-trimmed bicycle
And high on a tractor-tricycle
Is a trumpet player
With orange hair.
While under the trees
Are the well-trained bees
And the daring young man
On the flying trapeze.
A parrot is singing
"Tra-la la-la-la,"
While a trombone is playing
"Be-bah, bah-bah-bah."

Tell children to circle the words that begin with the /tr/ sound. Read the sentences aloud if necessary.

1. An elephant has a trunk.
2. In restaurants we throw out the trash, but not the tray.
3. A train runs on a track.
4. When you tremble, you are scared.
5. You trick or treat on Halloween.
6. To trade is to swap.

tw

Read the verse aloud and tell children to sing "tweet tweet" when they hear the /tw/ sound as in tweet. Read the verse again and ask children to circle the letters that stand for the /tw/ sound.

Twenty blackbirds sitting in a tree,
Singing "Tweet-tweet-tweet" to me.
When Dad went to sit in the family car
And twanged a tune on his guitar,
The blackbirds twittered from afar.

Tell children to put the number of the correct word in the circle next to each picture.

1. twang
2. twelve
3. twenty
4. twig
5. twins
6. twist

Name: ______________________________ Date: ____________ 9-249

wh

Read the verse aloud and tell children to say "whoo" when they hear the /hw/ sound as in whale. *Read the verse again and tell children to circle the letters that stand for the /hw/ sound.*

In the whooshing waves
And the whirling foam,
A small white whale
Is far from home.
He whispers to the
Wailing wind,
"Whoo, whoo, whoo."
And a stranger whale answers,
"Who are you?"
The lost whale whispers,
"I'm a white whale, too."

Tell children to circle the /hw/ word that goes in the blank.

1. _____ is Jack? (When Where)
2. _____ time is it? (When What)
3. _____ is Bill's hat? (Which Why)
4. I can _____. (whale whistle)
5. Ann has a _____ dress. (whiff white)
6. My bike has two _____. (wheels whooshes)
7. To hit is to _____ . (whistle whack)
8. _____ did Mom go? (When White)
9. _____ are you mad? (Where Why)
10. Tom ate the _____ cake. (whole whale)

Section 10

Final Consonant Blends

It's a fact
That Bobby Bact
Never knows how to act.
He told a clown,
"You have big feet."
He asked a cow
If she's good to eat.

Name: ______________________________ Date: ____________ 10-250

atch, itch, utch

Read the story aloud and tell children to make wicked-witch faces when they hear the /tch/ sound as in match, witch, and crutch. Read the story again and tell children to circle the letters that stand for /tch/.

Dad came home and turned the latch. The lights were out. He lit a match. The lonely room was black as pitch, like the old house of a witch. Then he saw a patch of light, little candles in the night. Not so many, not so much—a birthday cake upon the hutch. Then he heard a happy shout, and Mama and the kids jumped out. "We were worried you'd get wise. Happy birthday, Dad. SURPRISE!"

Tell children to print the correct letters in the blanks.

catch	crutch	ditch	hatch
match	patch	stitch	watch

___ ___ tch   ___ ___ tch   ___ ___ ___ tch   ___ ___ tch

___ ___ tch   ___ ___ tch   ___ ___ ___ tch   ___ ___ tch

Name: ______________________ Date: ____________

Read the story aloud and tell children to pretend they are eating a peach when they hear the /ēch/ sound as in peach. Read the story again and tell children to circle the letters that stand for the /ēch/ sound.

Mary and Tommy went to the beach. Tom had a sandwich and Mary, a peach. They shared food with each other like a good sister and a good brother.

Tell children to put the each and oach /ōch/ words in the correct spaces in the grid.

ACROSS: beach, coach, reach, each

DOWN: broach (to introduce), peach, roach, teach

Name: ______________________ Date: __________ 10-252

unch 

Read the verse aloud and tell children to say "crunch-crunch" when they hear the /ŭnch/ sound as in lunch. Read the verse again and tell children to circle the letters that stand for the /ŭnch/ sound.

We went to lunch.
We sat in a bunch,
And ate jam sandwiches
With peanut butter crunch.
Munch, munch!

Ask children to put words ending with anch, ench, inch, and unch in the blanks. Write these endings on the board.

1. I have a ___ ___ ___ ___ ___ of flowers.
2. Mom bought a ___ ___ ___ ___ ___ of carrots.
3. I eat peanut butter sandwiches for ___ ___ ___ ___ ___.
4. There are 12 ___ ___ ___ ___es in a foot.
5. I have a ___ ___ ___ ___ ___ing bag.
6. Potato chips ___ ___ ___ ___ ___ ___ when we eat them.
7. My uncle lives on a ___ ___ ___ ___ ___.
8. I am sitting on a park ___ ___ ___ ___ ___.
9. I ___ ___ ___ ___ ___ed my finger in the door.
10. Can you ___ ___ ___ ___ ___ ___ your fists?

bench	clench	inch	pinch	ranch
bunch	crunch	lunch	punch	

Name: ______________________ Date: ____________ 10-253

act

Discuss the meaning of the word tact*. Ask children to give examples of tact and the absence of tact. Then read the verse and ask children to circle the letters that stand for the /ăct/ sound.*

It's a fact
That Bobby Bact
Never knows how to act.
Everyday, he'll always say
Something wrong in every way.
He told a clown,
"You have big feet."
He asked a cow
If she's good to eat.
It's a fact, Bobby Bact
Doesn't have any tact.

Read the following numbered words to children. Ask them to circle the letters they hear at the end of each word: 1. back, 2. act, 3. black, 4. tack, 5. tact, 6. Jack, 7. fact, 8. pact, 9. pack, 10. track, 11. subtract, 12. exact.

1.	ack	act	7.	ack	act
2.	ack	act	8.	ack	act
3.	ack	act	9.	ack	act
4.	ack	act	10.	ack	act
5.	ack	act	11.	ack	act
6.	ack	act	12.	ack	act

Name: ______________________ Date: ____________ 10-254

ift

Read the verse aloud and tell children to whisper "Thank you" when they hear the /ĭft/ sound as in gift. Read the verse again and tell children to circle the letters that stand for the /ft/ sound.

Christmas morning outside the door
Was something I never saw before—
A great big gift
In a white snowdrift.
Rover sniffed it.
I couldn't lift it.
Dad, himself, came to see.
He lifted it under the Christmas tree.
A great big bike in a box for me,
My very best Christmas gift—
Hiding in a big snowdrift.

Tell children to circle the pictures whose names end in ft.

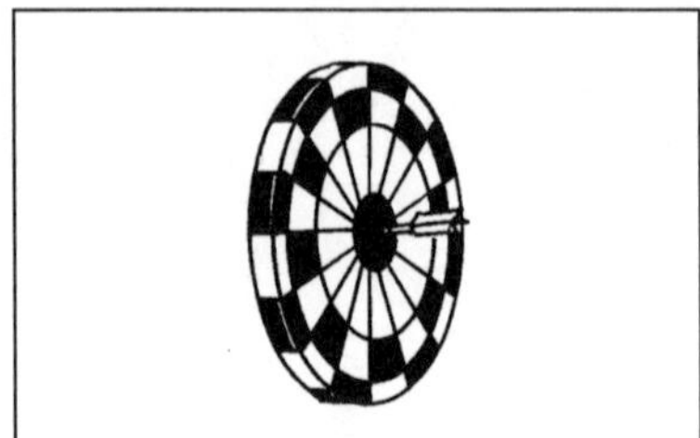

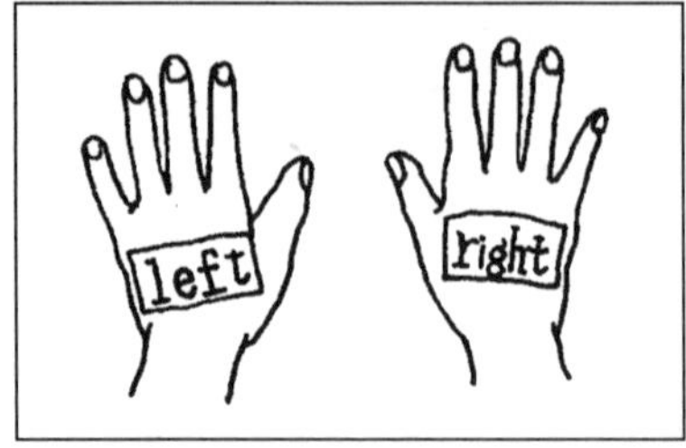

ild

Read the verse aloud and tell children to make an angry face when they hear the /īld/ sound as in child. Mention to them they studied the /ī/ sound in words like mile and pile. Rile, meaning to annoy or make angry, is in the same word group. Read the verse again and tell children to circle all the letters that stand for the /īld/ sound.

Dad said to Mom,
"Now, don't get riled.
Ronnie's just a little child.
Sometimes he gets a little wild.
If he were always sweet and mild,
Insofar as I can tell,
He wouldn't be completely well."

Tell children to print the correct /ī/ words under each picture.

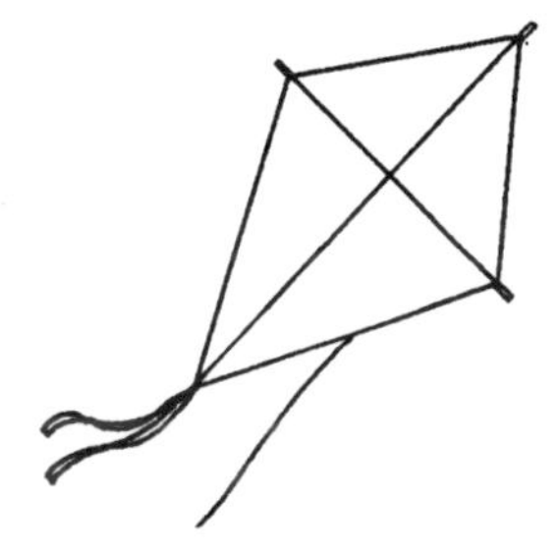

white ___ ___ ___ ___

five ___ ___ ___ ___

___ ___ ___ ___ pines

dice in ___ ___ ___ ___

___ ___ ___ ___ child

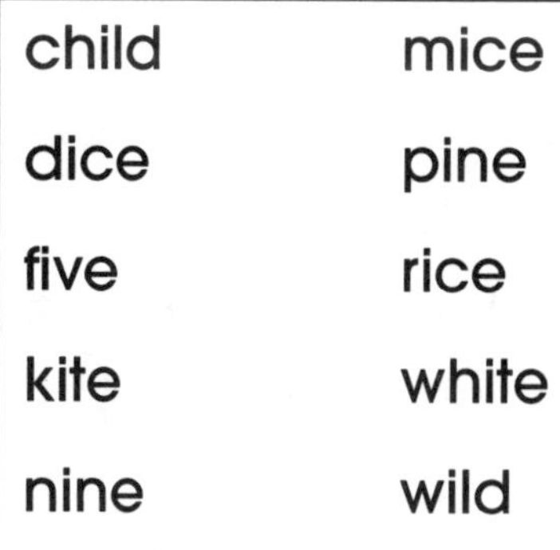

child	mice
dice	pine
five	rice
kite	white
nine	wild

Name: ______________________ Date: __________ 10-256

old

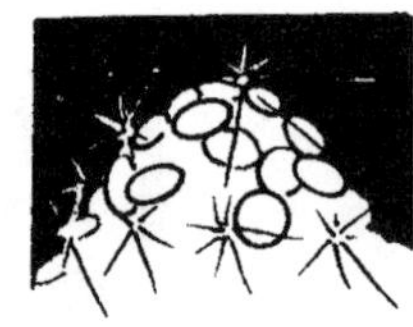

Read the verse aloud and tell children to pretend to cry when they hear the /ōld/ sound as in gold. Read the verse again and tell children to circle the letters that stand for the /ōld/ sound.

I'll tell you a story that I heard told,
About King Midas from days of old.
Whatever he touched turned into gold.
He touched a flower; it turned to gold.
It could be bought, it could be sold,
But it was hard, and it was cold.
He touched his daughter. She turned to gold,
Glittering gold without the charm
Of the little girl he held in his arms.
He cried, "Oh nothing could be worse.
Rid me, rid me of this curse.
I am tired, and I am old.
I love my daughter more than gold."

Tell children that King Midas once wished that everything he touched would turn to gold. But he was unhappy when his wish came true. Ask children what bad things might happen if the following wishes came true.

1. I wish I had all the money in the world.
2. I wish I could control the weather.
3. I wish I had a robot to clean my room.
4. I wish my dog could talk.
5. I wish I could live forever.
6. I wish I had a magic carpet that would take me anyplace in the world.

Name: ______________________ Date: ____________ 10-257

elt, olt

Read the verse aloud and tell children to circle the letters that have the /ĕlt/ sound as in belt *and the /ōlt/ sound as in* colt.

"Winter will never end," I felt.
"The ice and snow will never melt."
For a second I sadly knelt,
Just to tighten up my belt.
Then I felt a little jolt
Like a light electric volt.
Underneath the ice and snow,
Grass had begun to grow.

Tell children to circle the words in each row that end with the same three letters as the word in the picture.

1. belt	melt	gilt	knelt	felt
2. colt	sold	bolt	cold	jolt
3. wilt	spilt	belt	malt	Milt
4. salt	pelt	halt	Walt	fault

Name: ______________________________ Date: ____________ 10-258

amp 

Read the verse aloud and tell children to pretend they are swimming when they hear the /ămp/ sound as in lamp. Read the verse again and tell children to circle the letters that stand for the /ămp/ sound.

Susie went to summer camp.
She wrote to her mom
When she found a stamp.
"In a water race, I was champ.
But when I was swimming, I got a cramp.
I like to tramp in the woods at camp,
But at night my cabin is cold and damp.
I have a wood table and kerosene lamp.
Instead of stairs, we walk up a ramp.
I like it here and want to stay,
But I miss my room in the very worst way."

Tell children to circle the correct word to finish each sentence.

1. In the water, Susie got a _____. lamp champ cramp
2. Susie thinks _____ is fun. camp damp lamp
3. Susie's cabin has a _____. damp clamp ramp
4. Susie needs a _____ for her letter. lamp stamp champ
5. Susie likes to_____ in the woods at camp.
   ramp damp tramp
6. Susie has a _____ in her cabin. camp damp lamp
7. Susie's cabin is cold and _____. champ damp ramp
8. In a race, Susie was _____. champ lamp ramp

Name: ______________________________ Date: ____________ 10-259

ump

hump

Read the verse aloud and tell children to put the missing letters in the blanks. Also tell them to fill in the missing letters under the pictures.

b	cl	d	h	j	l	m	p	pl	r	st

1. If your basement floods, you need a ___ump.
2. How high can you ___ump . . .
3. Without falling on your ___ump?
4. If you fall, you'll get a ___ump.
5. Sammy Jones has the ___umps.
6. A desert camel has two ___umps.
7. If you're fat, folks say you're ___ ___ump.
8. A bunch of bushes is a ___ ___ump.
9. Cut down a tree, and there's a ___ ___ump.
10. Old cars go to the city ___ump.

___ump

___ump

___ump

Name: ______________________________ Date: ____________ 10-260

and

Read the verse aloud and tell children to raise their hands when they hear the /ănd/ sound as in hand. *Read the verse again and tell children to circle the letters that stand for the /ănd/ sound.*

Billy Band and Betty Rand
Are building castles in the sand.
They make a wall and a tower,
And let them stand for an hour.
They are king and queen of the land,
But their kingdom's made of sand.

Tell the children to complete the sentences with words ending in and *or* end.

1. I will l___ ___ ___ Ben a book.
2. Pam puts s___ ___ ___ in a pail.
3. Nan plays a sax in the b___ ___ ___.
4. Ann will m___ ___ ___ her dress.
5. Pat has a pail in her h___ ___ ___.
6. Bob will st___ ___ ___ in the sand.
7. I will s___ ___ ___ a [letter] to Ben.
8. I am at the ___ ___ ___ of the line.
9. Jan ___ ___ ___ Bob have fun in the sand.
10. I can b___ ___ ___ the wire.

and
band
bend
end
hand
land
lend
mend
sand
send
stand

Name: ______________________________ Date: ____________ 10-261

end 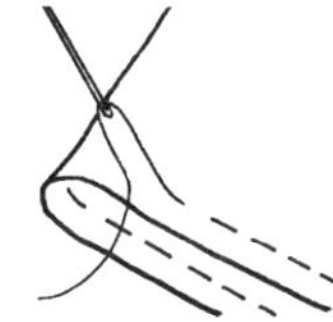

Read the verse aloud and ask children to bend their fingers when they hear the /ĕnd/ sound as in <u>mend</u>*. Read the verse again and ask children to circle the letters that stand for the /ĕnd/ sound.*

Tom said,

"Will you send it?"

Bob said,

"I have to mend it.

Then you can spend it.

It was nice of you to lend it.

What is it?"

(Answer: A dollar bill)

Tell children to circle the correct ending of the name of each picture.

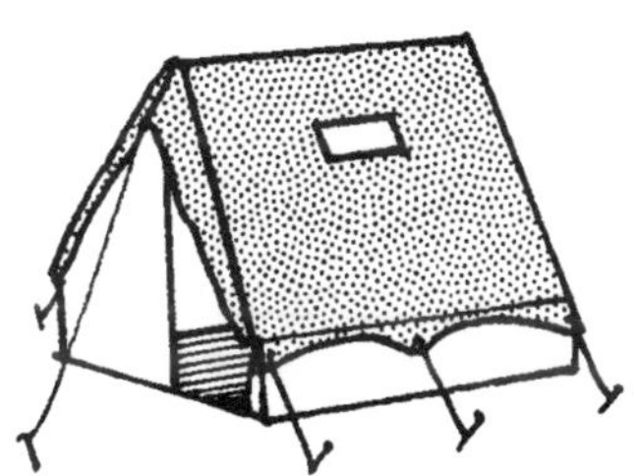

and ant end ent

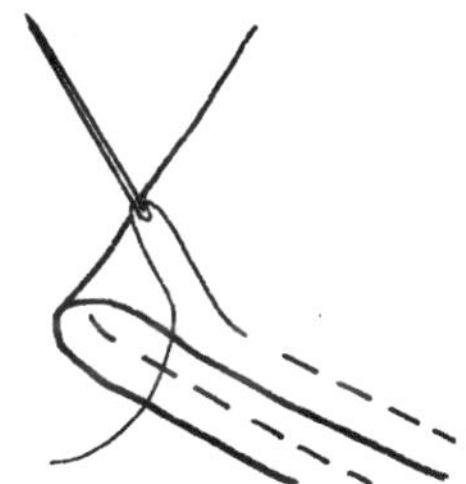

and ant end ent

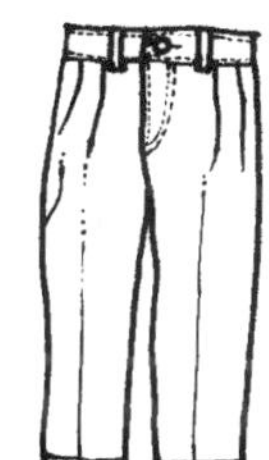

ands ants ends ents

and ant end ent

and ant end ent

bend
mend
pants
sand
tent

ind 

Read the verse aloud and tell children to look around as if they are lost when they hear the /īnd/ sound as in rind. Read the verse again and tell children to circle the letters that stand for the /īnd/ sound.

Tom lost his mom in a grocery store
Where he had never been before.
The manager was very kind.
Tom said,
"Please help me find her.
And if you do, I'm telling you
That I will always mind her."
The aisles are straight,
But sometimes wind,
And Tom was right behind her!

Tell children to circle **yes** *if the sentence under the picture is correct and* **no** *if it is wrong.*

Tom is behind his mom. **YES NO**

Tom finds pup on his bed. **YES NO**

He binds Tom's hand. **YES NO**

Tom winds a top. **YES NO**

Name: ______________________ Date: ____________ 10-263

ound

Read the story aloud and tell children to jump when they hear the /ound/ sound as in hound. Read the verse again and tell children to circle the letters that stand for the /ound/ sound.

Johnny found a puppy rolling on the ground. It was a little puppy that didn't make a sound. His ears were black. His tail was white. He was completely round. Johnny ran and told his mother, "Look at what I've found." Mom said, "Oh no. I mean it. No! You cannot keep that hound. I'll get the car from the garage and take him to the pound." But Johnny cried, "Oh, Mommy, no. You can't because I love him so." The pup was quiet as a mouse, and Mom said, "Bring him in the house!"

Tell children to write rhyming words under each word below.

1. **hound**

   ____

   ____

   ____

2. **house**

   ____

   ____

   ____

3. **cow**

   ____

   ____

   ____

4. **bow**

   ____

   ____

   ____

5. **out**

   ____

   ____

   ____

6. **not**

   ____

   ____

   ____

ang, ing, ung

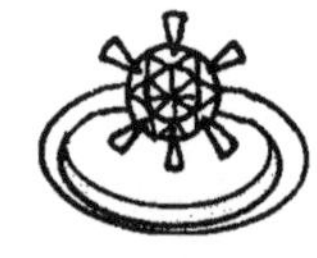

Read the story aloud and tell children to sing when they hear the /ng/ sound as in ring and sing. Read the story again and tell children to circle the letters that stand for the /ng/ sound.

Betty Lee Bing couldn't sing. When she tried, the children cried, "Betty Lee sings off key." Betty moaned, "It's always me. Any song, I sing wrong." Then the teacher said to Betty Lee, "Won't you sing along with me?" She and Betty sang and sang. The children left. The school bell rang. Then the teacher said, "You're singing now." "Yes," sang Betty, "I know how." When Betty had sung for an hour, she sang like a bird on a flower.

Tell children they are going to make a star quilt by coloring /ăng/ words red, /ĭng/ words green, /ông/ words blue, and /ŭng/ words purple.

bang	song	sang	sing
hung	ring	long	lung
bong	rung	hang	wing

Name: ______________________ Date: ____________ 10-265

ank, ink, unk

Read the verse aloud and ask children to wink when they hear words ending in the /nk/ sound as in sink. Tell children they will hear words ending in ănk and ĭnk. Read the verse again and ask children to circle the letters that stand for the /nk/ sound.

Hank sat on the river bank

As his sailboats slowly sank.

Some were yellow. Some were pink,

And he didn't really think

His paper boats would ever sink.

But the fun was making a paper boat

Even though it didn't float.

Tell children to put a, i, or u in the blanks under the pictures.

j____nk s____nk b____nk

b____nk ____nk H____nk

Name: ______________________ Date: ____________ 10-266

ant, ent

Read the verse aloud and ask children to circle all words that have the /ănt/ sound as in plant *and the /ĕnt/ sound as in* tent.

Mandy is gone. Where did she go?
Her mother really wants to know.
She went to a tent
In the desert sand.
She found a flower
In fairyland.
She went to a slant
In the road that bent
In no direction,
And then she went.
She took her allowance
She hadn't spent.
She wrote a note
With a pen I'd lent.
"I'm going to find a magic plant.
But don't be worried
'Cause if I can't,
I'll be back in half an hour,
Just in time to take a shower
And have dinner with you and Dad.
So, Mamma, please, don't be mad."

Name: ______________________ Date: __________ 10-267

ash 

Read the verse aloud and tell children to pretend they are batting balls when they hear the /ăsh/ sound as in bash and cash. Read the verse again and tell children to circle the letters that stand for the /ăsh/ sound.

Johnny Nash pitched a ball
That Billy smashed.
In a flash
Annie Cash made a dash
To catch the ball
That Billy bashed.

Tell children to write the number of the correct /ăsh/ word in the circle next to each picture.

1. ash	2. dash	3. flash	4. mash	5. rash	6. sash

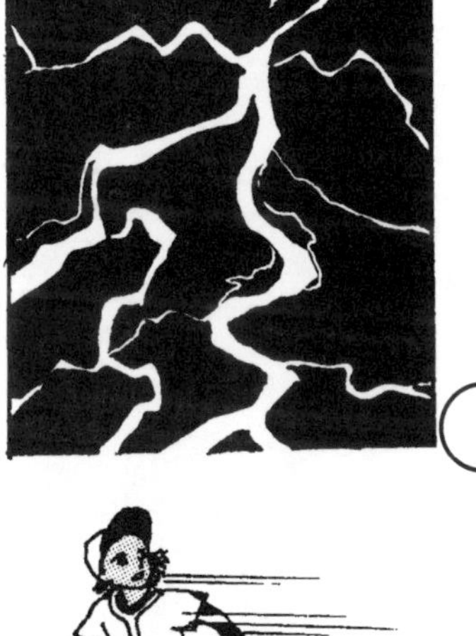

Name: ______________________ Date: ____________ 10-268

ish

Read the verse aloud and tell children to circle letters that have the /ĭsh/ sound as in fish.

How I wish
That every fish
In the pond
Was in my dish.

Tell children to put the letters of the correct definition next to the /sh/ words on the left.

___	1. cash	A. Gee or gee whiz
___	2. crash	B. Money
___	3. dash	C. Shh
___	4. hash	D. We eat on this.
___	5. flesh	E. A boy's name
___	6. dish	F. Cars can _____
___	7. fish	G. Wet snow
___	8. wish	H. Run fast
___	9. gosh	I. This is on our bones.
___	10. Josh	J. Corned beef _____
___	11. hush	K. Hope
___	12. slush	L. It lives in water.

ush

Read the verse aloud and tell children to say "shush" when they hear the /ŭsh/ sound as in hush. Read the verse again and tell children to circle the letters that stand for the /ŭsh/ sound.

The wind in a rush
Turned snow into slush
And mud into mush.
So I told the wind, "Hush!
What's the big rush?"

Tell children that u sometimes has the sound of /u/ in rush and cut, and sometimes the sound of /oo/ as in push and book. Tell children to circle the words next to the picture that have the same vowel sound as the word in the picture.

push	rush	book	wood
nut	cut	put	mud
good	duck	hood	us

bush

rush	mush	cook	full
took	luck	tub	bug
must	dust	cook	gum

hush

Name: ______________________________ Date: ____________ 10-270

ask

Read the verse aloud and tell children to place their hands over their faces as if they are wearing masks when they hear the /ăsk/ sound as in mask*. Read the verse again and tell children to circle the letters that have the /ăsk/ sound.*

Four trick-or-treaters
Went to the ladies up the lane.
Giving candy can be a task.
So Mrs. Haskin and Mrs. Baskin
Didn't have the time to ask,
"Who's behind the witch's mask?
Who's the ghost in a sheet
With winter boots upon his feet?"

Tell children to circle the letters that end each word.

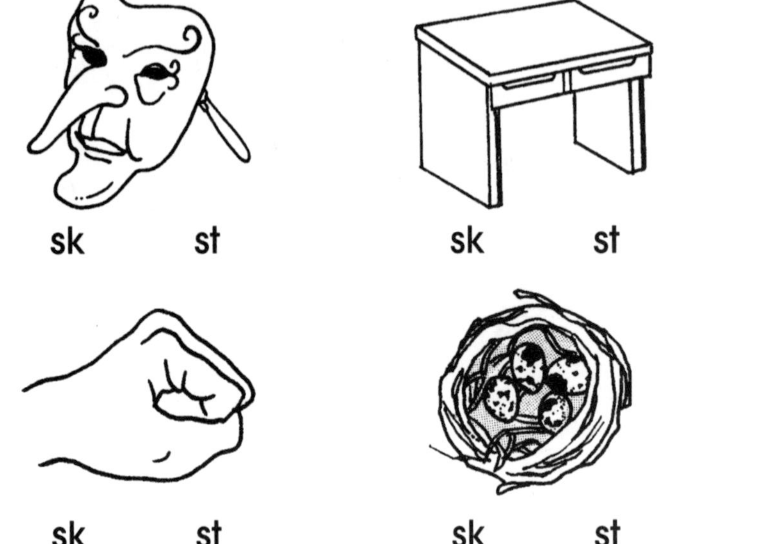

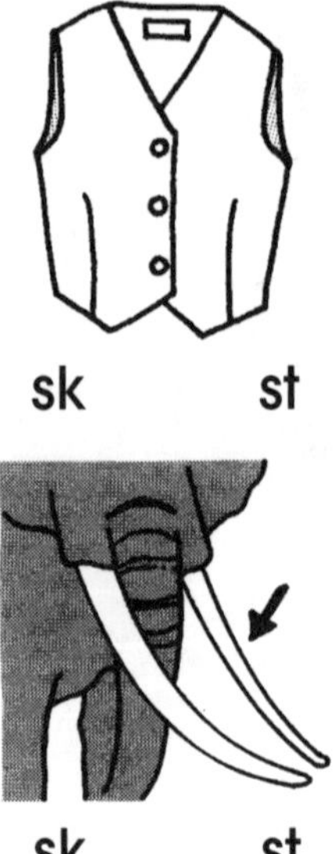

sk st   sk st   sk st

sk st   sk st   sk st

Name: ______________________________ Date: ______________ 10-271

ast 

Read the verse aloud and tell children to pretend their arms are in casts as they hear the /ăst/ sound as in cast. Read the verse again and tell children to circle the letters that stand for the /ăst/ sound.

Molly's arm was in a cast,
And Molly always finished last.
She couldn't do her work as fast
As other kids in the class.
Her teacher thought she might not pass.
But all of that is in the past.
Her arm's no longer in a cast,
And Molly doesn't finish last.

Read the following list of numbered words aloud. Ask children to circle the last three letters of the words as you read them: 1. task, 2. west, 3. pest, 4. past, 5. cast, 6. cask, 7. mask, 8. mast, 9. fast, 10. fest, 11. last, 12. best.

1. ask ast est
2. ask ast est
3. ask ast est
4. ask ast est
5. ask ast est
6. ask ast est
7. ask ast est
8. ask ast est
9. ask ast est
10. ask ast est
11. ask ast est
12. ask ast est

Name: ______________________ Date: __________ 10-272

est 

Read the verse aloud and tell children to stamp their feet when they hear the /ĕst/ sound as in vest. *Read the verse again and tell children to circle the letters that stand for the /ĕst/ sound.*

Old Mr. West

Took off his vest

And found a bird's nest.

"Out of my vest,"

Shouted Mr. West.

"Out of my vest,

You pest."

Tell children to select a word from the list that describes each picture. They are to write the word on the blanks.

best	chest	forest	rest	tallest	test	west

_ _ _ _ _   _ _ _ _ / _ _ _ _   _ _ _ _

_ _ _ _   _ _ _ _ _ _   Ann is _ _ _ _ _ _ _

Name: ______________________ Date: __________

oast

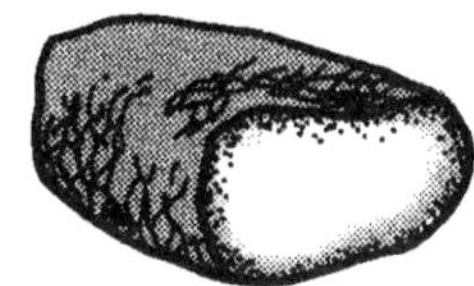

Read the verse aloud and tell children to pretend they are riding a roller coaster when they hear the /ōst/ sound as in roast. Read the verse aloud again and tell children to circle the letters that stand for the /ōst/ sound. Mention that in this verse /ōst/ is spelled once as ost and the other times as oast.

Bobby Oaster
Was a boaster.
When he rode
The roller coaster,
He liked to boast,
"I am the most
Fearless boy
From coast to coast."

Tell children to put the number of the correct word in each sentence.

1. boast
2. coast
3. host
4. most
5. roast
6. toast

a. Bob has the _____ pie.

b. Bob Oaster likes to _____.

c. _____ beef is meat.

d. Land by the sea is the _____.

e. _____ is bread.

Name: ______________________ Date: __________ 10-274

ost 

Explain to children that the h in ghost is silent. Also explain that the o in ost sometimes has the sound of /ō/ as in most and sometimes the /ô/ sound as in lost. Read the sentences aloud and then repeat the underlined word clearly. Ask children to circle the words that have the /ō/ sound and put a box around the words that have the /ô/ sound.

1. There is a picture of a ghost on this page.
2. I walked in the woods and got lost.
3. When you invite people to your house, you are the host.
4. I saved almost $15.00.
5. There is frost on the windowpane.
6. How much does a loaf of bread cost?
7. There is a telephone post behind my house.
8. The package came parcel post.
9. Tom has two marbles. Pete has four. Ed has six. Ed has the most.
10. Mom has to defrost the refrigerator.

Tell children to circle the pictures of words whose names have the /ō/ sound and cross out pictures whose names have the /ô/ sound.

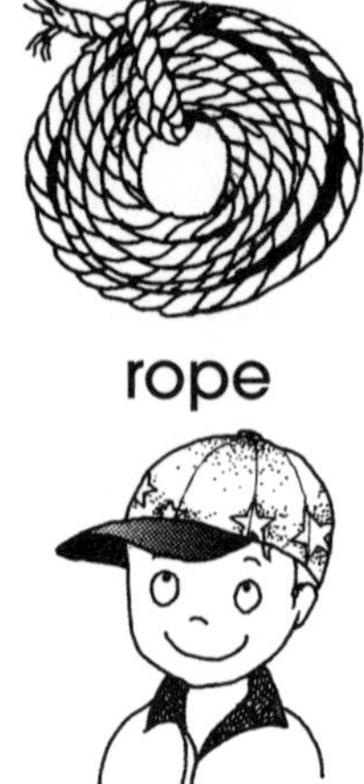

rope

goat

claw

Paul

nose

toe

Name: ______________________ Date: ____________ 10-275

ust

Read the verse aloud and ask children to make ghost noises when they hear the /ŭst/ sound as in dust. *Read the verse again and ask children to circle the letters that stand for the /ŭst/ sound.*

The haunted house upon the hill
Is very quiet, very still.
All the walls are gray with dust.
The water pipes are brown with rust.
A gust of wind thrust open the door.
A sad little ghost sat on the floor.
I asked why he lived in the dark
and the dust.
He answered softly,
"Because I must."

Tell children to print the correct /ŭst/ word in each blank

crust
dust
gust
just
must
rust
trust

1. Mom made a pie ___ ___ ___ ___ ___.
2. Mom has to ___ ___ ___ ___.
3. Bob is ___ ___ ___ ___six years old.
4. I ___ ___ ___ ___go home.
5. A ___ ___ ___ ___of wind blew.
6. I ___ ___ ___ ___ ___ my dad.
7. It is wet. The pipe will ___ ___ ___ ___.

Name: ______________________ Date: __________ 10-276

th 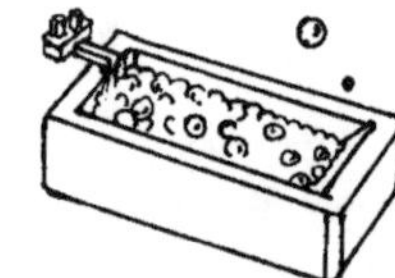

Read the verse aloud and tell children to circle the final letters that have the /th/ sound as in bath.

Mrs. Rath took a bath
While her son did his math.
Ruth Rath didn't do math.
She said she had a sore tooth.
But if you want to know the truth,
Ruth Rath hated math.

Tell children to draw lines between the /th/ words and the pictures.

1. 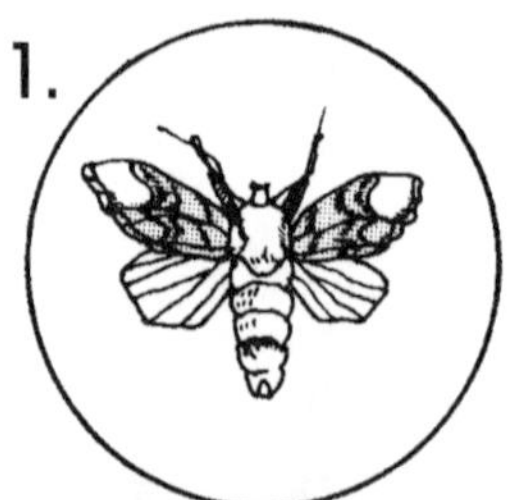
2. 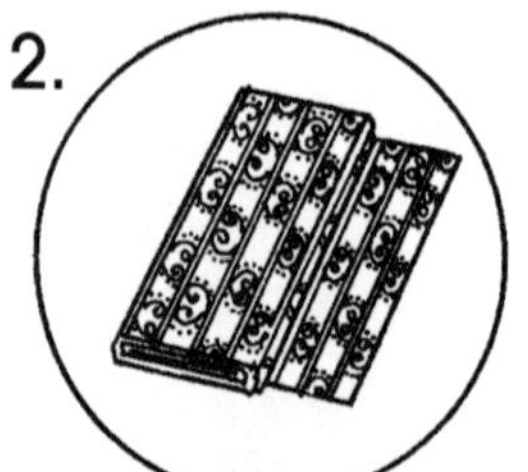
3. 
4. 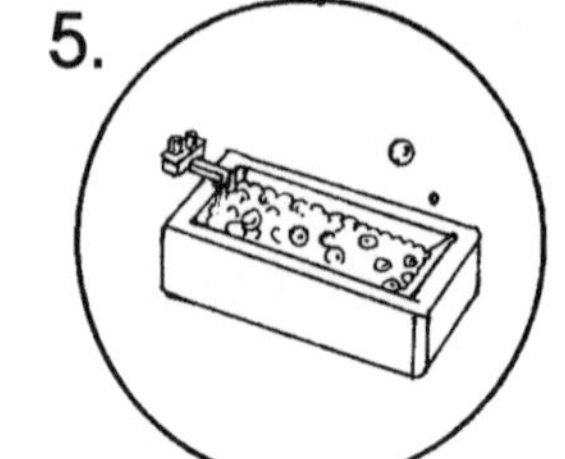
5. 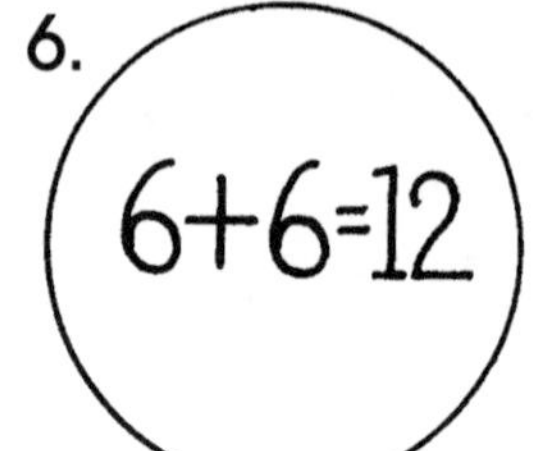

6.
7. 

A. Bath 
B. Ruth Rath and dog
C. Broth
D. Cloth
E. Math
F. Moth
G. Ruth Rath 

Answer Key

Section 1: Initial Consonants

1-1.	Bb:	Children should circle pictures of birthday cake, bean shooter, bed, balloon. The bad things are biting the cake, blowing beans, banging bed, popping balloons.
1-2.	Cc /k/:	Children should color 1, 4, 5, 6, 9, 10, 13, 14.
1-3.	Cc /s/:	Children should put X through pictures of circus, city.
1-4.	Dd:	Children should print *D* in corner of deer, dart, dollar, doll.
1-5.	Ff:	Children should circle all lowercase and capital *F*'s.
1-6.	Gg /g/:	Uppercase and lowercase G's under girl, goat, gift, gate, goose.
1-7.	Gg /j/:	Children should color 1, 5, 6, 8, 9, 11, 15.
1-8.	Hh:	Children should color hill, hen, house, hand, hippo.
1-9.	Jj:	Children should circle j (jar), j (jogging), h (hopping), b (boat), j (jailed), j (jumping).
1-10.	Kk:	Children should color kangaroo, king, kitten, key.
1-11.	Ll:	Answers will vary. Identifications based on imagination.
1-12.	Mm:	Children should circle girl meeting man from Mars, Mary meets a monkey in a mask.
1-13.	Nn:	Children should circle nails, napkins, noodles, nest, neck, nap.
1-14.	m,n:	(*row 1*) m, n, n; (*row 2*) n, m, m; (*row 3*) m, n, n; (*row 4*) n, n, m
1-15.	m,n:	(*Top*) 1. m, 2. m, 3. n, 4. m, 5. n, 6. n, 7. m, 8. n, 9. n, 10. n, 11. m, 12. m, 13. n, 14. n, 15. m, 16. n, 17. m, 18. m, 19. n (*Bottom*) n, m, n, n
1-16.	Pp:	Children should circle pig, pan, mop, top.
1-17.	Qu,qu:	Children should draw lines to connect quiet, quick, quack, queen—and back to quiet.

1-18.	Rr:	Children should print *r* under rat, rug, rabbit, ring.
1-19.	Ss:	Children should circle (*across*) s, s, f, s, f, c, c, s, c.
1-20.	Tt:	Children should print *Tt* under tie, tam, top.
1-21.	Vv:	Children should circle van, vine, violin, vest, vase.
1-22.	Ww:	Children should print *w* beside web, boy winking, dog wagging tail, boy waving.
1-23.	Yy:	Children should circle bubble with yummy, yard, yo-yo, person yawning.
1-24.	Zz:	Children should blacken circles beside zoo, zap, zebra, zipper, zoom, zigzag road.
1-25.	b,d,p:	Children should print (*across*) a *b* on bike, *b* on bulb, *b* on bee, *p* on pin, *p* on pig, *d* on dog, *d* on deer, *b* on bird, *b* on butterfly, *p* on pencil, *b* on bat, *p* on pan, *d* on doughnuts, *b* on box (*p* also okay if children think of present), *d* on dollar (*b* also okay if children think of bill).
1-26.	b,d,p:	Children should circle (*across)* cap on map, bib, cob, dad, cap, rib, pup, sub, mop, top, cop, sob.
1-27.	b,p,d,t:	Children should circle (*across*) b, p, b, p, p, b, d, t, t, d , t, d.
1-28.	b,p,d,t:	(*across*) b (for sob), p, p, b, b, p, d (for dad), t, d (for pod), d (for mad), t (for hat)
1-29.	f,v:	1. v, 2. f, 3. f, 4. v, 5. f, 6. v, 7. f, 8. v, 9. f, 10. v, 11. f, 12. v, 13. f, 14. v, 15. f, 16. v

Section 2: Short Vowels and Final Consonants

2-30.	ab:	Children should draw lines between Lab and picture 4, Bab and picture 2, Cab and picture 5, Gab and picture 3, Dr. Fab and picture 1.
2-31.	ack:	Children should circle Jack, Zack, Dack.
2-32.	ad:	Children should print Dad, mad, sad, bad, pad, Tad.
2-33.	ag:	Children should put X on cab, tack, sad.
2-34.	al:	Children should color balloons with pal/Val, Al/Sal.
2-35.	am:	Children should print tam, ham, am Pam, jam, am Sam.
2-36.	an:	Children should circle no, yes, yes, no, yes, yes.
2-37.	ap:	Children should circle no, yes, yes, no, yes, no.

2-38. Class:

G	B	A	S	S	C
A	M	A	L	N	A
S	A	P	A	S	S
B	S	A	S	S	S
A	S	C	S	G	M
N	O	A	S	S	S

2-39.	at:	Children should circle hat, cat, mat, bat, rat, fat.
2-40.	ax:	Children should print wax, fax, Max, sax, ax.
2-41.	Scat Cat:	Children should circle pictures of ant, ham, apple, cat.
2-42.	An Ant Can't	Children should circle gas, fan, can, wag, hat, tan.
2-43.	Bad Cat:	1. yes, 2. no, 3. no, 4. yes, 5. no, 6. yes, 7. no, 8. no, 9. yes, 10. no
2-44.	ib:	Missing letter: f. Children should put X next to rib/bib, Tib/bib, map/cap.
2-45.	ick:	Children should circle no, yes, no, yes, yes, no.
2-46.	id:	Children should color hid/did, rib/fib, Tib/bib, lid/did, hid/lid.
2-47.	if, iff:	1. yes, 2. yes, 3. no, 4. no, 5. yes
2-48.	ig:	Children should circle jig, fig, wig, big, rig, dig.
2-49.	ill:	Answers will vary.
2-50.	im:	Children should print swim, brim, him, slim, dim.
2-51.	in:	Children should print t, f, p, b, R, ch.
2-52.	ip:	Children can circle girl with hand on hip, girl with finger on lip, boy with finger on tip of nose, girl moving through group of dancers, girls dipping.
2-53.	is, iss:	1. hiss, 2. kiss, 3. Miss, 4. hiss, Sis, 5. Sis, kiss
2-54.	it:	2, 4, 7, 6
2-55.	ix:	Children should draw a hook through fix, six, tricks, mix, bricks, picks.
2-56.	Kit Cat and the Catnip:	1. ill, 2. lit, 3. sack, 4. sips, 5. lid, 6. licks, 7. hit, 8. fits, 9. hid, 10. bib

2-57. Nip and Pip: Answers will vary. Here are some possibilities: 1. lick, nick, pick; 2. rid, hid, did; 3. fig, big, dig; 4. pill, fill, till; 5. whim, dim, him; 6. bin, din, win; 7. sip, rip, nip; 8. miss, kiss, sis.

2-58. ob: Lines should be drawn between man working in factory and job, between little girl eating corn on the cob and cob, between mob of people and mob, between robber and rob, between little girl crying and sob, between boy and Bob.

2-59. ock: 6, 1, 4, 5, 3, 2

2-60. od, odd: 1. b, 2. d, 3. b, 4. d, 5. d, 6. b, 7. d, 8. b, 9. b, 10. b, 11. d, 12. b

2-61. og: Children should circle dog, hog, log, dog, log.

2-62. om, on: Children should circle m, n, n, m.

2-63. op: Children should circle mop, knob, sob, top, rob, pop.

2-64. oss: Children should lightly fill in bubbles for Ross, moss, boss, toss. Word spelled: loss.

2-65. ot: Children should draw a line from the picture of a dot to d, from pot to p, from cot to c, from sun to h (hot), from baby to t (tot), from ink blot to bl.

2-66. ox: Children should print Mox, box, ox, frocks, rocks, socks, clocks, box, Mox.

2-67. oz:

<table>
<tr><td>s</td><td>o</td><td>x</td><td>z</td><td>l</td><td>p</td><td>x</td><td>o</td><td>z</td></tr>
<tr><td>i</td><td>d</td><td>t</td><td>o</td><td>b</td><td>e</td><td>t</td><td>o</td><td>t</td></tr>
<tr><td>z</td><td>z</td><td>o</td><td>o</td><td>m</td><td>j</td><td>o</td><td>d</td><td>d</td></tr>
<tr><td>e</td><td>l</td><td>n</td><td>g</td><td>b</td><td>d</td><td>o</td><td>x</td><td>o</td></tr>
<tr><td>m</td><td>g</td><td>u</td><td>o</td><td>e</td><td>z</td><td>i</td><td>p</td><td>n</td></tr>
<tr><td>x</td><td>z</td><td>t</td><td>h</td><td>i</td><td>z</td><td>e</td><td>r</td><td>o</td></tr>
<tr><td>b</td><td>d</td><td>l</td><td>o</td><td>z</td><td>m</td><td>d</td><td>g</td><td>o</td></tr>
<tr><td>o</td><td>g</td><td>c</td><td>x</td><td>d</td><td>h</td><td>s</td><td>i</td><td>p</td></tr>
<tr><td>x</td><td>o</td><td>k</td><td>x</td><td>m</td><td>o</td><td>z</td><td>d</td><td>p</td></tr>
</table>

2-68. Don and Lon: Children should circle cab, cap, top, hop, map, sock.

2-69. Tod Can Hop: Children should underline Tod can hop, Pot in sock, Stop, Top on Pop, Dog on hog, Mom and mop.

2-70. Tick-Tock: No answers needed.

2-71. ub: Children should color pictures of cub, tub, cub, sub, rub.

2-72. uck: 1. Buck, 2. Puck, 3. Cluck, 4. truck, 5. duck, 6. stuck, 7. tucks

2-73. ud: 1. d, 2. b, 3. p, 4. d, 5. d, 6. p, 7. b, 8. b, 9. p

2-74. uff: Children should color bubbles with buff/puff, stuff/muff, if/sniff, huff/cuff, fluff/stuff.

2-75. ug: Children should circle jug, hug, rug, bug, mug, tug.

2-76. uh: Children can answer "uh huh" or "uh uh" to questions 1–5. "Huh?" is the probable response to question 6.

2-77. ull: Children might print *f* for full; *p* for pull; *d* for dull; *h* for hull; *l* for lull. *(Lower page)* 1. gull, 2. hull, 3. full, 4. dull, 5. pull, 6. bull.

2-78. um: Children should blacken circles next to 1, 4, 6, 10, 12.

2-79. un: Children should circle yes, yes, no, yes, yes, no.

2-80. up: Children should print cup, pup, sup, up. Children should circle Pop, cop, sub, cub.

2-81. us, uss: Children should print s next to 1, 2, 3, 5, 7, 8, 13, 14, 15.

2-82. ut: Children should circle nut, bat, cot, hut, shut, rat, cut, mutt.

2-83. uz: Children might draw a bee or a doorbell for *buzz*, and a baby chick, a peach, or white dandelion fluff for *fuzz*.

2-84. Bud and Mum: 1. cub, 2. buck, 3. bud, 4. bug, 5. mum, 6. puff

2-85. Buck's Luck: Children should draw a line from mug, jug, cup, bug, sun.

2-86. eck: Children should print peck, neck, Mrs. Beck, wreck, deck.

2-87. ed: 1. Ed, 2. fed, 3. bed, 4. red, 5. led, 6. Ted, Ed, 7. Ed

2-88. eg, egg: 1. Meg (or Peg), 2. Meg (or Peg), 3. Leg, 4. Egg, 5. Beg

2-89. ell: Children should color circles next to bell, el, fell, well, tell, sell, Mel, swell, jell, Nell.

2-90. em: 1. n, 2. n, 3. n, 4. m, 5. n, 6. n, 7. n, 8. m, 9. n, 10. n, 11. n, 12. m, 13. m, 14. n, 15. n

2-91. en: Children should circle hen, hem, ham, men, Ken, Dan, pen, ten.

2-92. es, ess: Children should print a, e, e, e.

2-93. et: Children should print a, a, e (for pet), e, e, a.

2-94. ă, ĕ: Children should circle bed, jam, hat, ham, leg, man, pan, pet, ten, bat, bag, Ken.

2-95. Jeff Has a Net: 1. d, 2. b, 3. b, 4. d, 5. b, 6. d, 7. p, 8. d, 9. p

2-96. Mel in the Well: Children should circle pen, hat, bag, ten, bed, bat.

2-97. A Dog Is a Pal: Children should circle Het bats, Big man, Black pan, Bad kid, Meg, big bag.

Section 3: Long Vowels and Final Silent *e*

3-98. ace: Children should circle race, Grace, ace, face, lace.

3-99. ade: Children should darken circles next to ade, made, glade, wade, jade, fade.

3-100. age:

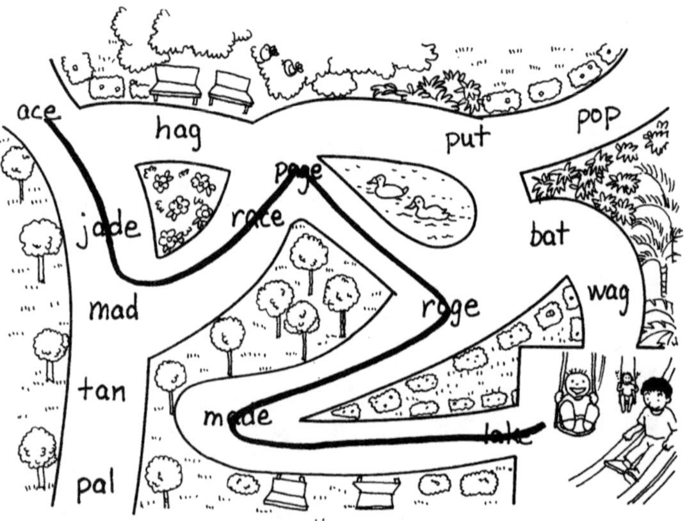

3-101. ake: Children should circle bake, fake, lake, rake, make, take.

3-102. ale: Children should draw a line between ghost and pale, between the boy and Dale or male, between father reading and tale, between department store scene and sale.

3-103. ame: Children should print c, g, s, l.

3-104. ane: Children should color kites with came/dame/fame; same/lame/game; cane/Dane/Jane.

3-105. ape: Children should circle no, no, yes, no, yes, yes.

3-106. ase: Children should circle the following words in the story: place, case, case, anyplace, lace, lace, vase, ace, ace, ace, anyplace, face, race, base.

3-107. ate: Children should circle yes, no, no, yes.

3-108. ave: Children should circle shave, Dave, cave, rave, gave, case.

3.109. aze: Children should circle gaze, haze, maze, daze, blaze.

3-110. Jake: 1. D, 2. D, 3. D, 4. D, 5. S, 6. D, 7. D, 8. D

3-111. ice: 1. nice, 2. Mice, 3. Dice, 4. Rice

Children should print under pictures mice, dice, slice, price.

3-112. ide: Children have bingo if they draw a line through ride, tide, wide, hide.

3-113. ife: Children should circle the following words in the verse: mice, mice, wife, knife, life, mice.

3-114. ike: Children should circle no, no, no, yes.

3-115. ile: Children should circle Nile, rake, win, Mike, hid, dime, dill, Dick. Sentences will vary.

3-116. ime: 1. M, 2. N, 3. N, 4. M, 5. N, 6. N, 7. N, 8. M, 9. M, 10. N, 11. N, 12. M, 13. M, 14. N, 15. N, 16. M

3-117. ine: Children should print the following letters in the verse: f, d, l, p, m, sh, t. The listed words in the grid are shine, dine (or mine or line), mine (or dine or line), line (or dine or mine), pines.

3-118. ite: Children should print the following words: kite, vine, mice, ride, knife, smile.

3-119. ive: Children should circle bite, alive, hide, knives, five, dime.

3-120. Mike Likes:

3-121. oke: 1. globe; 2. rode; 3. mole, pole, role, whole; 4. broke, joke, poke, woke; 5. dome, Rome; 6. bone, cone

3-122. ole: Children have bingo if they draw a line through hole, rose, rode, mole, pole.

3-123. ome: Children should print the following words: robe, rob, home, broke, cock, rod, code, pole, stone. Children should circle the following words from the list: broke, code, home, pole, robe, stone.

3-124. one: 1. n, 2. n, 3. n, 4. n, 5. m, 6. m, 7. n, 8. n

3-125. ope: Children should circle rope, stone, hose, note, rose, nose.

3-126. ose: Children should put the symbols for the following: short, long, short, long, short, long.

3-127. The Note: Children should circle note, robe, tone, rode, tube, mule, use, cute.

3-128. u: Children should print the following letters in the verse: t, c, r, r, m, t. Children should print the following letters: t, c, h, m, t, c.

3-129. a,e,i,o,u: 1. ate, 2. rate, 3. Kate, 4. cane, 5. Dane, 6. fate, 7. fade, 8. gale, 9. hate, 10. made, 11. pane, 12. same, 13. cape, 14. Jane, 15. pine, 16. hide, 17. dime, 18. bite, 19. ripe, 20. dine, 21. fine, 22. ride, 23. hope, 24. rode, 25. note, 26. robe, 27. code, 28. Pete, 29. cute, 30. tube

3-130. a,e,i,o,u: *a*—căn, sāme, căt, ăt, căp, cāne, hăt, cāpe, păn, Kāte, pāne, hāte, Săm, āte; *o*—mŏp, hŏp, cōde, rŏd, nōte, rōbe, cōne, mōpe, cŏd, hōpe, cŏn, rōde, nŏt, rŏb; *i*—rīde, pĭn, hĭd, fīne, bĭt, dĭm, hīde, rīpe, rĭp, rĭd, bīte, fĭn, dīme, pīne; *e, u*—cūte, pĕt, cŭb, cūbe, dŭd, mēte, cŭt, jŭt, dūde, sŭn, Pēte, jūte, mĕt.

Section 4: Final Long Vowels

4-131. e, ee: Children should circle the pictures of bee, tree, bird's beak, beads.

4-132. o: Children should circle go, picture of bone, loaf, so, picture of coat, load, rose, pole, hole, rope, hose, road, hose, picture of boat, low, road, ho ho, picture of cone, note, Rome, home, picture of nose, mow, dome.

4-133.	o, oa:	Children should print a large O on pictures of coat, bone, boat, cone, toe.

Section 5: Long Vowel Teams

5-134.	aid:	1. paid; 2. afraid, raid; 3. mermaid; 4. laid; 5. braids
5-135.	ail:	railfish, sailfish, jailfish, tail, pailfish, nailfish
5-136.	ail, ale:	1. pale, 2. mail, 3. male, 4. rail, 5. sale, 6. tail, 7. whale, 8. nail, 9. snail, 10. sail
5-137.	ain:	chain, pain, plain, rain, train
5-138.	Knock, Knock:	Reading activity; no answers needed.
5-139.	ay:	Children should circle gay, Jay, pay, day, may, stay.
5-140.	ea:	Children should circle pictures of bee, tea, tree, leaf, ice cream, peas.
5-141.	ead:	Children should circle pictures of tree, bean, read.
5-142.	eak:	1. beak, 2. peak, 3. weak, 4. speak
5-143.	eal:	Children should circle leaves with the following words: read/lead, beg/leg, steal/real, meat/neat.
5-144.	eam:	Children should circle Bream, dream, team, bleachers, screams, screeches, beam, cream, dream, team.
5-145.	ean:	Children should draw lines between team and 3 children, dream and child dreaming, bean and open string bean, scream and baby screaming, Dean and boy, mean and angry face, Jean and girl, clean and child sweeping.
5-146.	eat:	Children should choose balloons with lead/bead, mean/dream, lead/lean.
5-147.	Which Word Doesn't Belong?:	(*Top section*) 1. seat, 2. nail, 3. read, 4. bean, 5. deal, 6. jail, 7. Jake, 8. real, 9. seal, 10. Jean; (*Bottom section*) Children should circle pictures of tea, meat, read, Pete, seat, bee, seal, weed.
5-148.	A Real Meal:	Children should circle pea, tea, cream, bean, meat.
5-149.	eed:	Children should color pictures of mother feeding baby, team, weed, peak.
5-150.	eek:	Children should circle peak, leak, week.

5-151.	eel:	Children should draw lines through tea, bean, sea and through heat, bean, Pete.
5-152.	een:	1. thirteen; 2. queen, Halloween; 3. green; 4. seventeen; 5. screen; 6. between
5-153.	eep:	1. B, 2. sl, 3. d, 4. P, 5. sw, 6. st
5-154.	eet:	

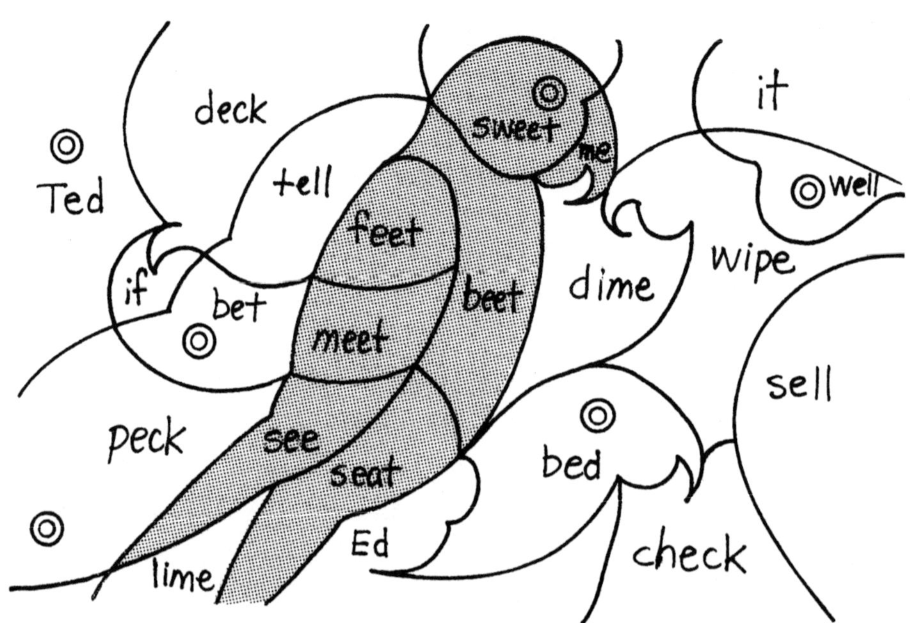

5-155.	The Bad Jeep:	Children should circle bead, he, meet, bee, need, Pete, meat, teen, wheel, feel.
5-156.	ie:	Children should circle pictures of pie, tie, cry, fly, sky.
5-157.	oa:	roam, foam, Joan, loan, toad, road, load, oak, soap, loaf, goal, coal, bat, float, goat, coat
5-158.	oat:	Children should circle pictures of goat, Mr. Cole, home, loaf, go, phone.
5-159.	Have You Ever Seen __?:	Reading activity; answers not needed.
5-160.	Long Vowel Team Review:	seat, goat, rain, feed, bean, pail, coat, toad, meat
5-161.	ow:	1. joke; 2. pole; 3. boat, float; 4. slow; 5. hole; 6. bone; 7. bow
5-162.	ow:	Children should circle nose, row, slow, coat.
5-163.	oe, ow:	Children should circle toes, row, hoe, go, no, slow, Joe

Section 6: Diphthongs

6-164.	aw:	Children should print saw, paw, law, claw, jaw, draw.
6-165.	Practice with More Difficult /ô/ Words:	Children should copy words in list into blanks.
6-166.	awn:	1. lawn; 2. saw; 4. bought; 5. caught; 6. Paul, caught; 7. walk; 8. talk; 10. thought, hauling
6-167.	Can You Draw?	Children should draw four pictures of their choice from the story.
6-168.	oil:	1. oil, 2. spoil, 3. boil, 4. toil, 5. foil, 6. soil, 7. coil
6-169.	oin:	1. join, loin; 2. toy, Roy; 3. oil, foil; 4. joint
6-170.	oy:	1. boil, 2. toy, 3. join, 4. Roy, 5. coin, 6. soil, 7. boy, 8. toil, 9. coin, 10. point, 11. foil, 12. oil
6-171.	I Can. I Can't:	Reading activity. No answers needed.
6-172.	out:	4, 1, 2, 3
6-173.	ow:	bow, wow, sow, meow
6-174.	own:	YES, YES, NO, NO
6-175.	Chow Time:	5, 1, 6, 3, 4, 2
6-176.	Diphthong Review:	1. saw, talk; 2. boil, oil; 3. join, joy, point; 4. soil, soy, boil; 5. out, how, shout; 6. wow, gown, town

Section 7: r-Controlled Vowels

7-177.	ar:	Answers may vary, but all suggested letters should be used: bar, car, far, card, star, hard, jar, tar.
7-178.	ard:	1. far, 2. jar, 3. Tar, 4. yard, 5. scar, 6. bars, 7. hard, 8. Pard
7-179.	ark:	rk (bark), ck (tack), ck (back), rt (cart), rd (card), ck (black), rk (spark), rk (shark), ck (track)
7-180.	arm, arn:	n (barn), m (arm), b (Barb), d (card), n (yarn), m (charm)
7-181.	arp:	ars (bars), ark (park), ark (shark), arp (harp), ard (card)
7-182.	art:	Children should darken circles next to Art in park, Shark in cart, Dart in art, Part of Art.

7-183. Hidden Pictures:

7-184.	Bark at the Stars:	car, part, barn, farm, hard
7-185.	or:	No answers needed.
7-186.	ork:	park, pork, stork, lark, cork, dark
7-187.	orm, orn:	Children should darken circles next to Corn with a thorn; A storm in a dorm; Torn pants; Corn in a dorm; A bike with a horn; She has torn the hat.

7-188. ort: fort, davenport, sport, port, short

7-189. Dad's sunshine: corn, horn, sport, fork

7-190. er: 1.H, 2. E, 3. B, 4. G, 5. F, 6. C, 7. D, 8. A

7-191. irt: sir, third, bird, dirt on a shirt, fir, stir

7-192. ur, urn, urp: burn, curl, fur, burp, slurp, burr

Children should draw lines between cat and purr, arm in cast and hurt, saluting soldier and sir. Other words are simply names and pictures.

7-193. The Mermaid: purr, skirt, bird, girl, burr, hurt, sir, fir

7-194. air:

		C				
		H	A	I	R	
	F	A	I	R	(or PAIR)	
P	A	I	R	(or FAIR)		
A	I	R				
		S	T	A	I	R

7-195. air, are, ear, ere: No answers needed.

7-196. ear: 1. tear, 2. ear, 3. fear, 4. near, 5. hear, 6. rear

7-197. earl: 2, 4, 3, 5, 1

7-198. oar: oar, air, ear, ear, oar, air

7-199. are: 1. bare, 2. wares, 3. fare, 4. hare, 5. rare, 6. pare, 7. mare, 8. care, 9. stare

7-200. ire: Children should draw a line diagonally through hire, fire, wire, tire.

7-201. ore: Children should circle these words: 1. core, 2. more, 3. door, 6. roar, 7. store, 8. wore, 10. tore, 11. floor, 12. Your.

7-202. arry, erry: Children should circle berry, merry, carry, Mary, Gary, ferry, very, cherry, Larry, Harry, honey, bunny, money.

7-203. arch, irch, urch: 1. B, 2. F, 3. G, 4. A , 5. C, 6. D, 7. E

7-204. war, wor: world, wart, warn, worm, war, word, warm, work, worth

Section 8: Irregular Vowel and Vowel Consonant Combinations

8-205.	able:	6, 4, 1, 5, 3
8-206.	alk:	Children should draw a line through words in top row—ball, paw, talk, yawn, hawk, tall.
8-207.	all:	small ball, tall, ball, call, mall, fall
8-208.	ight:	Children should circle knight, Dwight, night, fight, light, fright, right, fight, night, tight, delight.
8-209.	ould:	

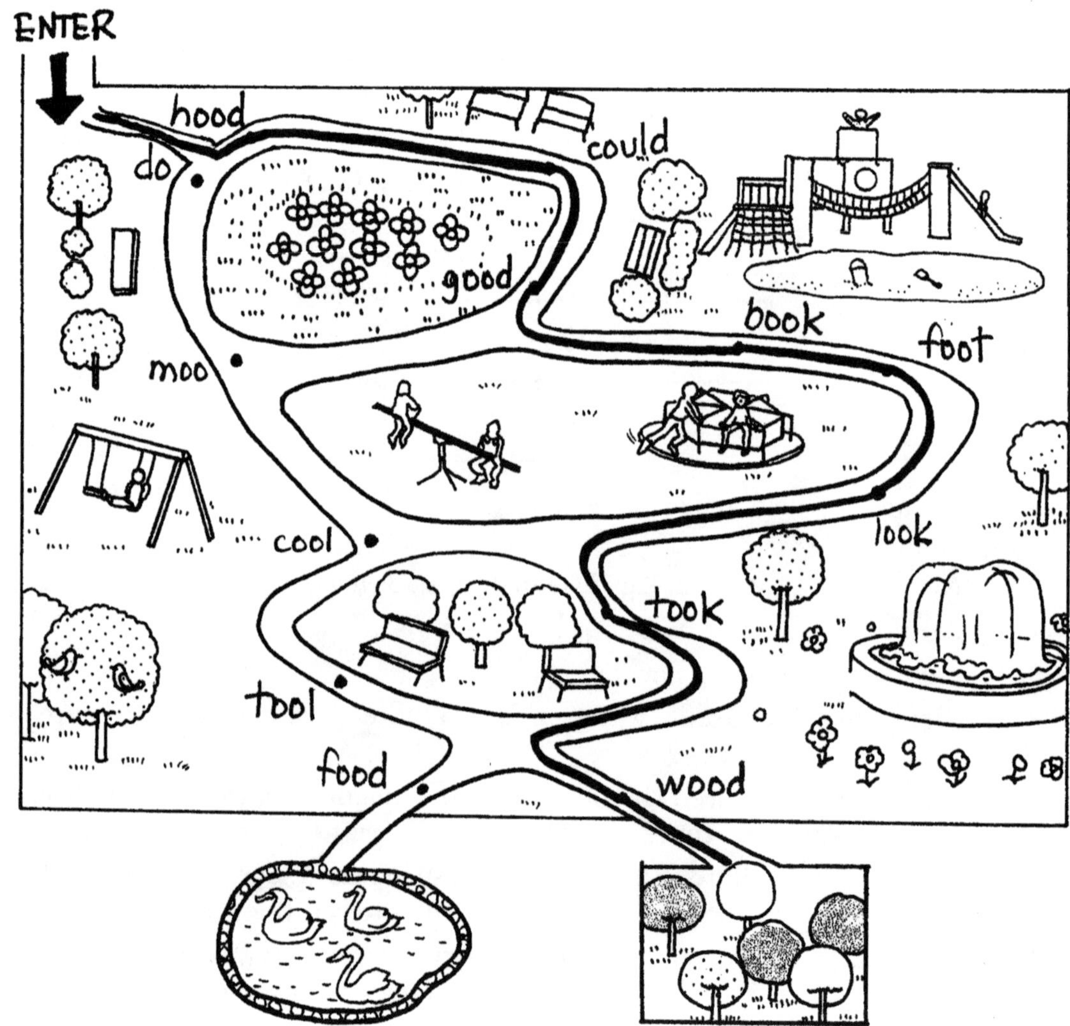

8-210. y: Dad in tie, big sky, Mike's bike, pie in sky, ice mice, fry rice

8-211. Long *i* Review:

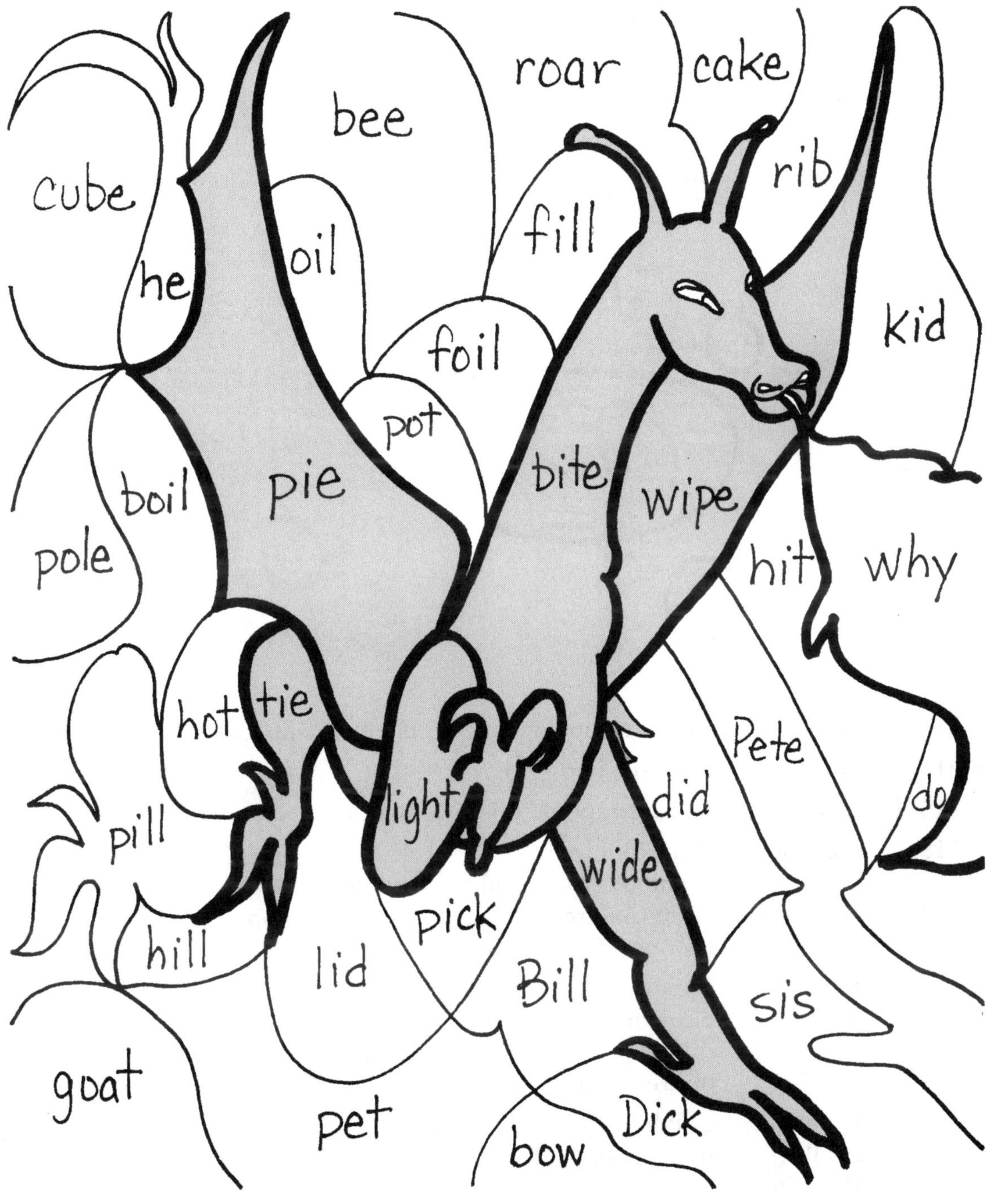

8-212. **Long Vowel Review:**

8-213.	**ead:**	Children should circle head, net, bread, lead, web, thread, ten.
8-214.	**oo:**	moo, oo, boo, goo, coo, woo
8-215.	**ood, ool:**	Children should circle *oo* beside numbers 1, 3, 5, 6, 7.
8-216	**oom, oon:**	(*Top*) Children should circle Boom, boom, Boom, boom, room. (*Bottom*) Children should circle moon, noon, soon.
8-217.	**oop, oot:**	(*Top*) Children should circle Boop, hoop, coop, hoop. (*Bottom*) Children should circle soot, loot, root.
8-218.	**Long *oo* Review:**	Children should draw lines between toot and train, clock and noon, tool and hammer, zoom and jet, food and dinner plate, stool and picture of stool, broom and picture of broom, boot and picture of boot.
8-219.	**Long *oo* Spelling Variations:**	Children should circle pictures of shoe, the number 2, broom, soup, glue.
8-220.	**More Long *oo* Spelling Variations:**	1. who, you; 2. Lou; 3. school; 4. cool, moon; 5. Do, moo; 6. Do, moo, too; 7. to; 8. true

8-221.	The Moon:	3, 6, 1, 5, 4, 2
8-222.	ood, oof:	(*Top*) Children should circle wood, hood, good. (*Bottom*) Children should circle hoof, roof, Woof, woof.
8-223.	ook:	Children should circle wood, hook, cook.
8-224.	Pam Can Read:	1. o͝o, 2. o͞o, 3. o͞o, 4. o͞o, 5. o͝o, 6. o͞o, 7. o͞o, 8. o͞o, 9. o͝o, 10. o͞o, 11. o͝o, 12. o͝o, 13. o͞o, 14. o͞o, 15. o͝o

Section 9: Initial Consonant Blends

9-225.	bl:	1. bloom, 2. blow, 3. blink, 4. black, 5. block, 6. blaze, 7. blue, 8. blouse
9-226.	br:	broom, brush, braids, brick, bridge, bride, broccoli
9-227.	ch:	church, cheap, chess, chain, chick
9-228.	cl:	Children should circle clop, clinks, clap, clock, cluck, clops, clomps, clang, clang, clang, clank, clank, clank.
9-229.	cr:	1. crackers, 2. cream, 3. crib, 4. crown, 5. crayon, 6. cross, 7. crust

9-230. dr:

<table>
<tr><td></td><td></td><td></td><td>D</td><td>R</td><td>A</td><td>G</td><td>O</td><td>N</td></tr>
<tr><td></td><td></td><td>D</td><td>R</td><td>I</td><td>P</td><td></td><td></td><td></td></tr>
<tr><td></td><td>D</td><td>R</td><td>E</td><td>W</td><td></td><td></td><td></td><td></td></tr>
<tr><td></td><td>D</td><td>R</td><td>A</td><td>W</td><td></td><td></td><td></td><td></td></tr>
<tr><td>D</td><td>R</td><td>U</td><td>M</td><td></td><td></td><td></td><td></td><td></td></tr>
<tr><td>D</td><td>R</td><td>E</td><td>S</td><td>S</td><td></td><td></td><td></td><td></td></tr>
</table>

9-231.	fl:	1. flew, 2. flat, 3. flock, 4. flight, 5. flies, 6. flour, 7. flame, 8. flap
9-232.	fr:	fr (frame), dr (dresser), tr (triangle), fr (fry), tr (train), br (bride)
9-233.	gl:	pl, fl, bl, gl, fl, gl

9-234.	gr:	1. grandmother, 2. green, 3. grin, 4. grass grows, 5. grade, 6. grunt, 7. grandfather, 8. Greg
9-235.	pl:	3, 6, 10, 12, 13, 14, 16
9-236.	pr:	prize, prince, pretzel
9-237.	sc, sk:	sk, sk, sl, sl, sc, sk, sk, sk
9-238.	sh:	

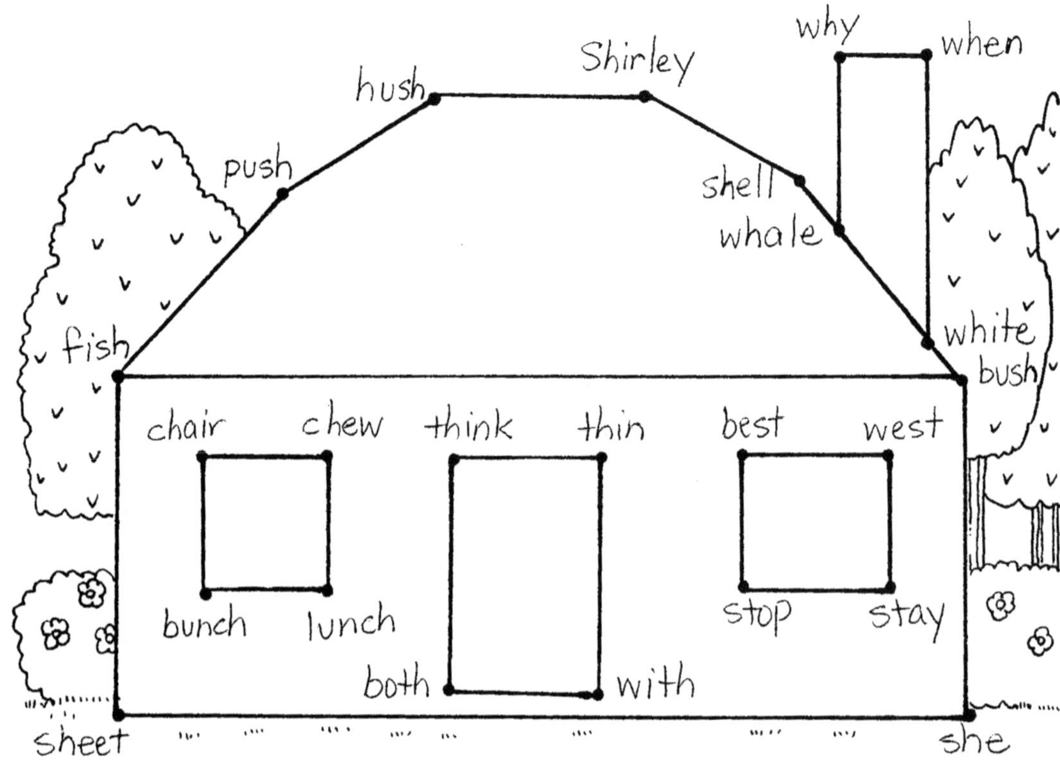

9-239.	sl:	1, 5, 4, 2, 3
9-240.	sm, sn:	snack, small, smoke, snake, smock, smell
9-241.	sn:	Children should draw lines to form snap, sniff, smell, snail, smoke, smock, snout, smile.
9-242.	sp:	coffee spilling, spoon, spot
9-243.	squ:	Children should draw lines between square and picture of square, squash and picture of squash, squat and picture of child squatting, squeak and picture of mouse, squiggle and picture of curly line, squirrel and picture of squirrel, squirt and picture of whale leaping out of the water.
9-244.	st:	1. stairs, 2. slap, 3. smack, 4. stout, 5. speak, 6. slacks, 7. stove, 8. smell

9-245.	sw:	4, 2, 6, 3, 5, 1
9-246.	th:	Children should circle 1, 2, 5, 6, 7, 10.
9-247.	tr:	1. trunk; 2. trash, tray; 3. train, track; 4. tremble; 5. trick, treat; 6. trade
9-248.	tw:	5, 4, 2, 1, 3, 6
9-249.	wh:	1. Where, 2. What, 3. Which, 4. whistle, 5. white, 6. wheels, 7. whack, 8. When, 9. Why, 10. whole

Section 10: Final Consonant Blends

10-250.	atch, itch, utch:	hatch, match, stitch, patch, watch, catch, crutch, ditch
10-251.	each:	

10-252.	unch:	1. bunch, 2. bunch, 3. lunch, 4. inch, 5. punch, 6. crunch, 7. ranch, 8. bench, 9. pinch, 10. clench
10-253.	act:	1. ack, 2. act, 3. ack, 4. ack, 5. act, 6. ack, 7. act, 8. act, 9. ack, 10. ack, 11. act, 12. act
10-254.	ift:	Children should circle raft, gift, left, lift.
10-255.	ild:	kite, mice, nine, rice, wild
10-256.	old:	Answers will vary.
10-257.	elt, olt:	1. melt, knelt, felt; 2. bolt, jolt; 3. spilt, Milt; 4. halt, Walt, fault
10-258.	amp:	1. cramp, 2. camp, 3. ramp, 4. stamp, 5. tramp, 6. lamp, 7. damp, 8. champ
10-259.	ump:	1. pump, 2. jump, 3. rump, 4. bump (or lump), 5. mumps, 6. humps, 7. plump, 8. clump, 9. stump, 10. dump; (*Bottom*) hump, jump, dump
10-260.	and:	1. lend, 2. sand, 3. band, 4. mend, 5. hand, 6. stand, 7. send, 8. end, 9. and, 10. bend
10-261.	end:	ent, end, ants, end, and
10-262.	ind:	YES, YES, NO, NO
10-263.	ound:	Answers will vary. Possibilities are: 1. bound, found, mound, pound, round, sound; 2. mouse, louse; 3. bow, how, now, pow, row, sow, vow; 4. low, mow, know, row, sow, tow; 5. about, shout, snout; 6. dot got, hot, jot, lot, pot, rot, tot
10-264.	ang, ing, ung:	RED—bang, sang, hang; GREEN—sing, ring, wing; BLUE—song, long, bong; PURPLE—hung, lung, rung
10-265.	ank, ink, unk:	junk, sink (or sunk), bank, bunk, ink, Hank
10-266.	ant, ent:	Children should circle wants, went, tent, went, slant, bent, went, spent, lent, plant, can't.
10-267.	ash:	3, 6, 1, 2, 4, 5
10-268.	ish:	1. B, 2. F, 3. H, 4. J, 5. I, 6. D, 7. L, 8. K, 9. A, 10. E, 11. C, 12. G
10-269.	ush:	BUSH: push, book, wood, put, good, hood; HUSH: rush, mush, luck, tub, bug, must, dust, gum
10-270.	ask:	sk, sk, st, st, st, sk
10-271.	ast:	1. ask, 2. est, 3. est, 4. ast, 5. ast, 6. ask, 7. ask, 8. ast, 9. ast, 10. est, 11. ast, 12. est

10-272.	est:	chest, best, test, west, rest, forest, tallest
10-273.	oast:	a. 4, b. 1, c. 5, d. 2, e. 6
10-274.	ost:	Children should circle rope, goat, nose, toe. Children should cross out claw, Paul.
10-275.	ust:	1. crust, 2. dust, 3. just, 4. must, 5. gust, 6. trust, 7. rust
10-276.	th:	Children should draw lines from 1—F, 2—D, 3—G, 4—C, 5—A, 6—E, 7—B.